ROBERT S. ROESCHLAUB

Limited Edition

This is copy **25**
of 160 copies signed by
the authors

Francine Haber

Francine Haber

Kenneth R. Fuller

Kenneth R. Fuller

David N. Wetzel

David N. Wetzel

ROBERT S. ROESCHLAUB

Architect of the Emerging West 1843-1923

Francine Haber
University of Colorado—Denver

Kenneth R. Fuller
Fellow, American Institute of Architects

David N. Wetzel
Colorado Historical Society

The Colorado Historical Society extends its deep gratitude
to the following generous contributors

Trinity United Methodist Church
Colorado Society of Architects, AIA
Ellen C. Micaud Memorial Fund

Colorado Historical Society
1988

Designer
Kevin A. Scott, *Denver*

Cover Photographs
David Diaz Guerrero

Contemporary Photographs
Peter A. Dulan, *Denver*
David Diaz Guerrero, Colorado Historical Society
Bryan E. McCay, *Victoria* Magazine
Greg Tzinberg, *Denver*

Photo Credits
Art Institute of Chicago; Sandra Dallas Atchison, *Denver;* Chicago Historical Society; Denver Public Library, Western History Department; Peter A. Dulan, *Denver;* East High School, *Denver;* Fremont-Custer Historical Society; Kenneth R. Fuller, *Denver;* George Irwin, *Quincy, Illinois;* Carl Landrum, *Quincy, Illinois;* Long Hoeft Architects, *Denver;* Bryan E. McCay, *New York City;* Jeanne Pfeiffer, *Quincy, Illinois;* Pueblo Public Library; Virginia Roberts, *Denver;* Frank von Roeschlaub, *Gloversville, New York;* Trinity United Methodist Church, *Denver;* University of Denver.

Typeset by The Typesetter, Inc., Denver
Printed by Publishers Press, Salt Lake City, Utah

93 92 91 90 89   5 4 3 2

Library of Congress Cataloging-in-Publication Data

Haber, Francine, 1945-
   Robert S. Roeschlaub : architect of the emerging West, 1843-1923/ Francine Haber, Kenneth R. Fuller, David N. Wetzel.
    p. cm.
    Bibliography: p.
    Includes index.
    ISBN 0-942576-01-2. ISBN 0-942576-31-4 (pbk.)
    1. Roeschlaub, Robert Sawers, 1843-1923. 2. Architects—United States—Biography. 3. Architecture—Colorado. 4. Architecture, Modern—19th century—Colorado. 5. Architecture, Modern—20th century—Colorado. 6. Architecture—West (U.S.) 7. Architecture, Modern—19th century—West (U.S.) 8. Architecture, Modern—20th century—West (U.S.) I. Fuller, Kenneth R. (Kenneth Roller), 1913-
. II. Wetzel, David N. (David Nevin), 1942- . III. Title.
NA737.R58H3 1988
720'.92'4—dc19
[B]   88-4315
                                    CIP

This book is the product of a long-held vision and the circumstances of time that affect projects of long deliberation. The original author of the manuscript, architect Kenneth R. Fuller, is a professional heir of Robert S. Roeschlaub and the son of Roeschlaub's successor, Robert K. Fuller. It was he who in the late 1960s, while preparing to move his offices to a new location, examined the long-dormant drawings and plans of the firm's originator and, led by curiosity and a sense of their value, began years of research into the life and work of Robert S. Roeschlaub. In 1981, at the request of Barbara Sudler, president of the Colorado Historical Society, and other state officials, Kenneth Fuller donated to the Society all of the Roeschlaub materials—including plans, renderings, photographs, books, and drawing materials—with the agreement that Roeschlaub's life, career, and works would one day be made available to the general public in the form of a book based on his original research.

In the meantime, the Society began preparing an exhibit of the Roeschlaub collection for its permanent display on Colorado history. In the course of research for the exhibit, new information about Roeschlaub's buildings came to light—information based largely on a typewritten list of plans and projects in the office's files prepared by a member of the firm early in this century, possibly before the architect's retirement. Of some 350 projects listed on this office inventory, almost 50 percent have now been documented as Roeschlaub buildings, and the remainder, while by and large lesser accomplishments, are good candidates for attribution to the list of Roeschlaub works. Naturally with the large number of works remaining to be located and confirmed, the authors welcome any future disclosures of Roeschlaub's buildings.

Coincidentally, architectural historian Ellen Micaud, University of Denver, was at the same time investigating Roeschlaub's buildings, and an agreement was made between Kenneth Fuller, Professor Micaud, and the Colorado Historical Society to cooperate on producing a full-scale biography and critical analysis of Roeschlaub and his architecture that would take into account the most recent findings by all parties. Professor Micaud's untimely death in 1985

delayed the project but opened up, by a most unusual circumstance, a great deal of information about Roeschlaub's personal life and activities through the awareness and interest of his granddaughter, Virginia Roberts. With this information, Kenneth Fuller and David Wetzel, the Society's publications director and research historian for the Roeschlaub exhibit, went in search of an architectural historian who could provide the breadth of analysis and critical judgment that would be necessary for a complete study. In 1987 Francine Haber agreed to join the project as a leading coauthor. She contributed extensive new research material as well as a text. The James M. Hunter Award to study architecture of American heritage, presented to Professor Haber by the Educational Fund, Colorado Society of Architects, AIA, in May 1987, provided important research support.

Finally, through another fortunate circumstance, the trustees of Trinity United Methodist Church, led by James H. Ranniger, agreed to help fund the publication of the book, which would appear on the celebration of the church building's centennial year in the spring of 1988. Perhaps most appropriate about this set of circumstances is that Trinity remains one of Roeschlaub's most significant works, and no better legacy of the architect's could testify to the enlightened self-interest and social concern of historic preservation than the decision of Trinity's trustees and congregation to keep this historic church a landmark of early Denver.

Considering the long evolution of this book, far more people contributed to it than can be acknowledged here, but among those who variously supported the project in its earliest stages are the late Alan B. Fisher; DeVon M. Carlson, dean emeritus, School of Architecture, University of Colorado; and Peter A. Dulan, husband of the late Ellen C. Micaud. During the early 1980s, when further research accompanied the preparation of the Society's exhibit on Roeschlaub and his work, George Irwin, an architectural historian in Quincy, helped to establish the connection between Roeschlaub and Robert Bunce, and Allen M. Oakley, former editor of the *Quincy Herald-Whig*, has been a continuing source of support and information. With his wife Carol and daughters Annie Wright and Susan

Day, Oakley supplied photographs of standing Bunce buildings, provided copies of early documents, and acted as an important liaison between the authors and people in Quincy who had information that helped to give substance to Roeschlaub's early life and practice. Chief among these is Carl Landrum, a historical writer whose articles have appeared in the *Quincy Herald-Whig* and whose research on this project led to correspondence with Robert Handschin, Bunce's great-nephew. In Denver, Virginia Roberts freely gave access to photographs, letters, and other materials that provided rich information on aspects of Roeschlaub's life in Denver, as did Frank S. von Roeschlaub, a grandson from Gloversville, New York.

During the past year of intensive research on additional buildings listed on the architect's inventory of plans, the authors were assisted by a number of volunteers and interns, some of whom found documentary evidence of new buildings and helped to sort out confusions and misattributions. We wish to thank especially Janis Falkenberg, a historical researcher and member of the Society's board of directors; Nancy Lee, a student in the Master of Architecture program at the University of Colorado-Denver; Leslie Ullman, who conducted research for the book at the University of Denver; and Martha Ewald, a member of the Volunteers of the Society. Others who contributed to the project are Caroline Campbell, George Companionett, Greg Tzinberg, and Robert Walker. Stan Oliner, the Society's curator of books and manuscripts, offered welcomed assistance, and Peg Ekstrand, another Society staff member, provided valuable information from her master's research on Denver's Capitol Hill. In addition, several people outside the Society gave of their time and effort to track down various buildings that would add to Roeschlaub's repertoire of works. Among these are Mildred Rabens for her work at the Chicago Art Institute; Colorado historian Duane Smith in Durango; Karlene McKean in Cheyenne Wells, Colorado; Mary Owen in Hugo, Colorado; Dolores Plested in Denver; Howard Hickson, director of the Northeastern Nevada Historical Society in Elko; and John McCormick, historian at the Utah Historical Society.

Research for this book took place in a number of libraries and historical societies across the country but primarily at the Colorado Historical Society and in the Denver Public Library's Western History Department, under the direction, respectively, of Katherine Kane and Eleanor Gehres. We wish to thank all of those in the Society's Stephen H. Hart Library and the Western History Department (DPL) for their expert assistance and support. So many researchers were at work on this project at any one time that it is impossible to acknowledge everyone on the staffs of these two institutions who guided us to the right file card or manuscript holding, but a few guided us many times. They are Mercedes Buckingham, Catherine Engel, Jim Lavender-Teliha, Jim Parker and Alice Sharp at the Society and Lisa Backman, Nancy Chase, Don Dilley, Phil Panum, Lynn Taylor, and Barbara Walton in the Western History Department. For their assistance in photographic selection and processing—an essential component in a book like this—we thank Eric Paddock and Katie McClintock at the Society and Augie Mastrogiuseppe in the Western History Department. In addition, Linda Kirby and Rob Socolofsky at Trinity United Methodist Church were of great support in both respects. Stephen Fisher provided assistance at the University of Denver-Special Collections. Finally, we wish to acknowledge David Diaz Guerrero, whose skill in photographic development is equal to his artistry as a photographer, and the book's designer, Kevin Scott.

As the manuscript developed, several people read and commented upon different sections. Their suggestions to a large degree have been incorporated; where they have not, the authors assume responsibility. Reviewers include Judith L. Gamble, Society editor; Gary Long of Long Hoeft Architects; Barbara Norgren, National Register coordinator for the Colorado Office of Archaeology and Historic Preservation; and Joy Lynn Wetzel of Metropolitan State College in Denver. The authors would also like to thank Kathleen Hoeft, Herbert S. Gaskill, Roberta Greengard, Edward D. White, Gary Crowell, Assistant Minister Dan Mahoney of the Metropolitan Community Church, and Cheryl D. Fisher.

Contents

The Architect

By David N. Wetzel

R O E S C H L A U B

During Robert Roeschlaub's lifetime, the American West was elevated from a geographical territory into a symbol of national empire. By the time he reached Denver in 1873, a trained architect at the age of thirty, Roeschlaub had witnessed first-hand the promise of western enterprise in the gold rush of 1859 and had fought in the Civil War—both of them experiences that underscored the momentum and destiny of American civilization. A firm believer in the idea of western progress—quite in line with his regional contemporaries and friends, like the visionary William Gilpin—Roeschlaub nevertheless held to a broader perspective than that of Manifest Destiny or Gilpin's belief in the eventual geographical predominance of the West. From the evidence of his writings, Roeschlaub adopted a more urbane and tempered view of civilization than that of the typical early westerner—one that rejected regional boosterism and defensiveness in favor of architectural values that were national and even international in scope.

Throughout his career as an architect, Roeschlaub tempered his love for the new and vigorous region of the American West with a respect for what he believed to be the universal lessons of the past. His work reflects a consistent rejection of current styles or fashions for their own sake and a search for the underlying principles that had invigorated Western architecture for centuries. Perhaps the strength and vitality of his architecture lies in the fact that he was neither wholly an idealist nor a pragmatist, a westerner nor a cosmopolite, a traditionalist nor a radical innovator. He was at bottom a working architect whose awareness of his place in the development of his city and region was informed by wide reading and study of architectural forms and whose contribution can be measured as much by its traditional humanism as by its artistic merits.

Life and Career

Sometime in 1845 Michael J. Roeschlaub, a physician and surgeon who had practiced in the city of Munich for almost twenty years, took the final steps necessary to leave his native country of Bavaria for the farthest reaches of settled America. At thirty-nine he was energetic, highly educated, well-to-do, and willing to give up an established career in the face of what he considered insupportable restrictions on his freedom of speech. While his specific grievances are not known, his dissatisfaction with the government mirrored the sentiments of other citizens who chafed under the increasingly autocratic rule of Ludwig I, king of Bavaria.[1]

Given Roeschlaub's social position, he was not a typical dissenter. His father was no less than the king's private physician and the dean of the medical school at the University of Munich. After graduating from the university with a degree in literature in 1825, Michael followed his father into medicine and began practicing three years later, eventually becoming county physician. At some point on his way to comfortable achievement in medical teaching and practice, he married and had a son. However, the death of his first wife brought major changes to his life—a new family, the possible adoption of a new faith, and eventual discontent with the order of things. The most important of these was his marriage in 1843 to Margaret Sawers, the daughter of a Scotsman who had come to Bavaria to teach scientific farming. Margaret, a Presbyterian, could hardly have been comfortable in a country so heavily Catholic. Moreover, the birth of Michael's second son, Robert Sawers Roeschlaub, four months before the couple was married, could have added to the strains that eventually led them to America.[2]

Figure 1-1
Quincy, Illinois, about 1850, as it looked when Robert Roeschlaub was a boy.
Courtesy Carl Landrum

2

1-1

Fluent in several languages, the experienced German doctor could have done well in any of the new nation's larger cities. Yet the family settled in Palmyra, ten miles northwest of Hannibal, Missouri, where eleven-year-old Samuel Clemens was then enjoying the boyhood days that would become a theme of his later fiction. According to Alice Roeschlaub Williams, the doctor's granddaughter, Michael bought a large tract of land on the outskirts of Palmyra, and the family remained there for two years. In 1849 they moved across the river to Quincy, Illinois, a town whose anti-slavery atmosphere may have been more amenable to the doctor's liberal temperament than that in slave-holding Palmyra. In addition, Quincy was then in the grip of a cholera epidemic so severe that it claimed four hundred lives in Adams county. There is little doubt that Roeschlaub was among the vanguard of doctors treating the sick and dying, for the epidemic was in large part responsible for the creation of the county medical society, of which he was a charter member.[3]

With its prosperous river trade, Quincy was the second largest city in Illinois; yet, as Mark Twain recalled in *Life on the Mississippi*, it had "the aspect and ways of a model New England town" (Fig. 1–1). The Roeschlaubs were among a growing population of German immigrants, many of them like-minded liberals, and their influence was immediately felt in politics and social life. "As a frontier town," states one local historian, "Quincy was never prudish. Rivermen, sawmill workers, and factory hands tended to be lusty and wet and not infrequently free-swinging. However, the streams of immigrants, notably Irish and Germans, were composed for the most part of non-flamboyant, solid individuals who created a generally quiet and stable community."[4]

As Robert Roeschlaub grew up, four more children were born into the Roeschlaub family: an elder daughter, Victoria; sons Frank and Henry; and a younger daughter, Jessie.[5] With a university-trained father and a mother who came from an educated family, the children were no doubt taught to respect literature, music, and the arts. Dr. Roeschlaub himself made friends with a monk, the head of Quincy's Franciscan monastery, with whom he had conversations in Latin.[6]

The advantages of the Roeschlaubs' cultured but easy-going family atmosphere is reflected in a story, told by Alice Roeschlaub Williams, about a tenor who traveled with the opera troupe of the internationally famous soprano Adelina Patti. During an engagement in Quincy he became very ill and had to be left behind. "He called for a physician who could speak French," Alice stated, "so Dr. Roeschlaub took the case, and through[out] the convalescence the tenor was [treated as] a member of his family, and became so interested in the doctor's 16-year-old daughter that he gave her singing lessons, resulting in her holding leading choir positions for years."

Aside from such brief family portraits, Robert Roeschlaub's early life is unknown. His childhood adventures and early schooling never found their way into written recollections—and this is unfortunate, because he was a skillful writer who in his mature years captured a few memorable experiences very well. The first of these occurred in 1859, when he was a sixteen-year-old student at the Quincy high school. For months news reports claimed that parties of prospectors had discovered gold throughout the Pikes Peak region of the Rocky Mountains. At that time the country was still suffering from the economic pall following the Panic of 1857, and the restless trading population that made its home along the Mississippi River saw either direct riches from easily extracted gold or great opportunities for business in the enlivened economy that was sure to flourish hundreds of miles to the west. The appeal was strongest for those westerners on the fringes of the plains, who were confident that the territory could be crossed with adequate provisions in a few weeks. A man like Michael Roeschlaub, whose livelihood as a doctor did not follow the trends of supply and demand, would seem to be the last person interested in such a gamble of life and fortune, yet he was (Fig. 1–2). He agreed to travel to the goldfields in a party with the Illinois secretary of state.[7]

During the excitement of the gold rush, Quincy became a gathering center for Fifty-niners because, as

1–2

Figure 1–2
Dr. Michael Roeschlaub, fluent in several languages, enjoyed conversing in Latin with the head of the local Franciscan monastery.

Robert Roeschlaub recalled nearly half a century later, it had a convenient ferry crossing on the Mississippi River. In words that create in concrete detail an atmosphere of both great adventure and immediacy, he describes the exodus that he and his friends watched from the Quincy side.

> With the shouting and cracking of whips the long line of teams became an apparently hopeless tangle at the wharf being packed on the ferry. A blast from the whistle, a snort from fifty steers, and the waters of the great Mississippi widen between us. Soon could be seen on the opposite shore what might have been taken for a huge, endless serpent, in broad stripes of brown and white, wending its sinuous way into the dark forest. We would stand on Sunset Hill, with the deep river flowing at our feet, and look over the Missouri forest till all was lost in sightless haze, and wondered that, though our eyes were young and sharp, we could see so far and yet not discern that vast, unknown and dreaded land which in our geographies was dotted all over with little black spots, and across which trailed the words "The Great American Desert."[8]

Speaking in hindsight—for this was an address given in 1907 to an august pioneer group of the Sons of Colorado—Roeschlaub larded his largely second-hand description of travel to and from the goldfields with stock images of pioneer women ("Prairie Queens"), savage Indians, pioneer men who tested their mettle against the hardships of the high plains, and all the trappings of a heroic adventure that in a few years would become celebrated in the popular culture of the West. Yet there is an element of truth and integrity in what he writes, primarily from his recall of specific discussions he had had with the Fifty-niners themselves. "We listened with bated breath," he states, "to a man who told of his narrow escape from capture by the Indians. He showed us the scarred palm of his hand— the muscles torn and contracted. He had seized and warded off the Indian's spear which was thrust at his heart and, when the savage tore it from his clasp, it left him thus. An arrow had plowed a furrow across his cheek and we took his word for the seven arrows that had been drawn from various parts of his body." As

this description attests, the young Roeschlaub was intimately familiar with the gold rush as a spectator, and he undoubtedly heard his father's stories about Denver and the Clear Creek mining camps when the doctor finally returned from the Rocky Mountains in the spring of 1860.[9]

Romanticized though it is, Roeschlaub's account also contains a sharp-eyed assessment of the ravages that the Fifty-niners suffered. "When early winter came," he states, "there was a back tide which brought to us broken remnents [sic] of the 'desert ship' we saw sail away to the West. 'Twas those who had ventured without proper equipment; some discouraged by the sickness and often death that stalked amidst the little company; and many who lacked the grit found so necessary to carry them through the trials and dangers of their undertaking."[10] Yet for those who *did* make their destination, like his father, he had only the highest admiration:

> Is it not reasonable that the pioneer who "came through" should have grown beyond the ordinary in the stature of manhood and have been peculiarly fitted for the founding and administration of a commonwealth like Colorado? He gained in pluck, recourse in time of need; far-sightedness; indomitable energy; faith in himself and his friends; unselfishness; brotherly love, and all those attributes which made for the building up of a great commonwealth in the midst of the wilderness.[11]

Of course, at sixteen, when he witnessed this great adventure, Roeschlaub could not have foreseen in the as-yet unnamed territory of Colorado the emergence of a great commonwealth, only that his father had gone off on the journey of a lifetime. As he grew older, however, this episode and the appeal of the West that it suggests, became more firmly fixed in his sense of personal destiny, so that by the time he was an established Coloradan, Roeschlaub had identified himself as a pioneer.[12]

The second momentous event in Roeschlaub's early life was the Civil War. By the time hostilities began, in the spring of 1861, he was not yet eighteen, but he likely shared the premonition of war that followed the secession of South Carolina in December

1860. Despite the popularity that Democrat Stephen H. Douglas enjoyed in southern Illinois during the previous election, the course of events show that the Roeschlaubs supported the new president, the maintenance of the union, and, when it finally came to call on Illinois, the war itself.

Still, over a year passed between the Confederate attack on Fort Sumter and Roeschlaub's enlistment in the Eighty-fourth Illinois Volunteer Infantry, which was organized at Quincy in August of 1862.[13] During these months, while the war was slowly developing momentum in the East, Roeschlaub graduated from high school and was beginning his studies at the Quincy Academy, established in 1860. Whatever his prewar career interests might have been—and they have been variously described as either medicine or architecture—they were short-lived, since from the time of his enlistment he had only one occupation, and that was the life of a foot soldier.[14]

Promoted from private to sergeant in the first month of active service, Roeschlaub followed his company to Louisville, Kentucky, and there became a part of the newly formed Army of the Cumberland. He first saw action in the battle of Perryville and joined in a skirmish at Crab Orchard on the army's march to Nashville, where his company remained for a month in preparation for the army's drive to push Bragg out of Tennessee. In that campaign, at the battle of Stone River, Roeschlaub was shot in the left foot but was treated in the field and resumed his duties. Following a six-month interval, after which the young but seasoned sergeant became a second lieutenant, the company joined in the Tullahoma campaign, which drove the Confederate forces out of Tennessee and pursued them to the bloodiest battleground of the western war, Chickamauga, where Roeschlaub sustained a severe gunshot wound in the left thigh. During the next five months, while the Union army regrouped after its defeat, Roeschlaub was hospitalized at the front, sent back to Nashville, and finally sent home to Quincy, where he recuperated under his father's care.

On his return to the front in February of 1864, Roeschlaub became the leading officer of his company and remained so until the end of the war. In the early

1–3

THE 84TH ILL. VOL'S. NEAR COLUMBIA TENN. NOV. 24TH 1864.

1–4

summer, with Sherman, he took part in the siege of Atlanta.[15] Then, when the Union army learned that General J. B. Hood's forces were moving quickly north to counterattack the Union's stronghold in Tennessee, Sherman sent a contingent of his troops, under General George Thomas, to race after Hood (Figs. 1–3 and 1–4). Roeschlaub and his company were among those pursuers, and the urgency of the objective, while it led to the decisive defeat of Hood at Nashville and the demise of the Confederate army in the West, may have been the greatest test of the war for the young officer. "I have been hungry," he stated years later, "and have suffered for the want of water, but never did I undergo

Figure 1–3
Severely wounded at the battle of Chickamauga, Capt. Robert Roeschlaub at twenty-two had received three medals of honor.
CHS F44745

Figure 1–4
Drawn by Roeschlaub years later, this scene of the Civil War depicts the battle of Nashville.
CHS F31204

1-5

Figure 1-5
Robert Bunce, Roeschlaub's mentor,
worked in the offices of Edward
Burling, one of Chicago's pioneer
architects.
Courtesy Carl Landrum

such excruciating suffering as on that march to Nashville, for the want of sleep."[16]

Roeschlaub's reminiscences of that last campaign, like his recollections of the march of the Fifty-niners across the Mississippi River to the gold fields of the Pikes Peak region, say a good deal about his temperament. Although something of an idealist, he had a great respect for unpretentious honesty, displayed an easy sense of humor, and insisted on an uncompromising fidelity to the simple facts of experience. His war reminiscences reflect this even better than his address before the Sons of Colorado, for he had lived through everything he described. In fact, what prompted him to write about the war at all was to counter what he believed to be a popular misconception that the life of a Civil War soldier was filled with either moments of glory or lazy days spent "chasing the Tennessee porcine racer, visiting the hen-roost and smokehouse, prospecting for the yam, and living high generally."[17] On the contrary, he stated, "Such a life must be endured to be comprehended."[18]

Following the battle of Nashville, Roeschlaub was commissioned first lieutenant and then, two days before being mustered out on June 8, 1865, was made a captain. This title he retained for the rest of his life, and in years to come he saved not only his Civil War letters to his family but his three medals of honor and other memorabilia, including an oil painting of his regimental insignia (see back cover).[19]

On his return to Quincy as a young man of twenty-two, Roeschlaub did not return to the academy. For a while he appears to have been somewhat aimless, taking a job in a magazine and stationery store while living with his family.[20] It was here, most likely, that he met Robert Bunce, an architect two years his junior whose offices occupied the same building as the store in which Roeschlaub worked. Had Roeschlaub not been interested in architecture before this time, he unquestionably became so in his conversations with Bunce, who had arrived in Quincy from Chicago to start his own practice in 1867 or early 1868.

Born in Wiltshire, England, Bunce (Fig. 1–5) had come to America in 1850 with his widowed mother and four brothers and sisters. He grew up in Elgin, Illinois, and after graduation from high school took a job in 1863 as a draftsman in the well-established Chicago architectural firm of Edward Burling.[21] Although of enlistment age, he remained with Burling until the close of the war, during which time he had the advantage of working with a successful architect during a time of rapid growth.

Although Roeschlaub worked in Bunce's architectural firm for a number of years, the extent of Bunce's influence on him cannot easily be determined. The earliest known record placing Roeschlaub in Bunce's office is the Quincy city directory for 1869–70. Yet Roeschlaub probably started his training a year or two earlier, for he began subscribing to at least one professional journal, *The Workshop*, in 1868.[22] Furthermore, in September of that year he married Annie Fisher, the eldest daughter of prominent Quincy department store owner James H. Fisher, an event that would have been out of the ordinary without some assurance of the young man's steady employment and prospects for a career.[23]

By the time Roeschlaub and Annie Fisher were married, Bunce had already witnessed the grand opening of his Quincy Opera House (later the A. Doerr Department Store), a four-story Italianate building with a mansard roof broken by arched dormers (Fig. 1–6).[24] The opera house owes its general features to the loose ornamentalism of Burling's Chamber of Commerce Building in Chicago (Fig. 1–7), built in 1865 when Bunce was still on the older architect's staff. Squeezed and crowded though its facade is, the opera house is an attempt to carry out the freshly learned lessons of the master, and in doing so Bunce could hardly have failed to pass on to Roeschlaub, his pupil, a set of principles that were far more significant than the design of a single building. The essence of those principles may be found in a contemporary statement about Edward Burling in an article from the *Chicago Tribune*: "The leading characteristics of the buildings erected under his professional care are solidity and thoroughness of construction, elegance and simplicity of design, the avoidance of frippery and unnecessary or vulgar orna-

1-6

mentation, and above all things, adaptation to the purposes for which they are to be used."[25] Whatever Roeschlaub learned from his work with Bunce, the most lasting education, it appears, came to him through Bunce from Edward Burling, a pioneer architect of Chicago.

Roeschlaub's years with Bunce constituted a period of extensive training in the literature, practice, and mechanics of architecture. From the evidence of his later career he applied himself with vigor in all respects, for he came to Denver with a confidence in his design and business abilities that testifies to a greater responsibility in Bunce's firm than the record would suggest. In any case, his training in architecture, beginning perhaps as early as 1866 and continuing through 1872, consisted wholly of what he derived from Bunce (and Burling), his own reading and study of architectural models, the fine points of drafting, the use of materials, and experience with clients.[26]

The next sizable commission for Bunce's firm came with the building of Temple B'nai Shalom (Fig. 1–8). With its cornerstone dating the start of construction as 1869,[27] the synagogue is flanked by two identical Moorish spires joined by a simple facade which features an arched entrance, a round window, and a curious pediment that seems to rest on two clawlike projections. Bunce's interpretation of the congregation's wishes may have been exotic, and the whole face lacks coherence, but it is a *tour de force* in terms of its creative brickwork.

By this time Roeschlaub is certain to have been assisting Bunce in the execution, if not the design, of the firm's commissions. This is likely the case with the First Union Congregational Church (1870–71), an ambitious project commissioned by two Quincy congregations that had rejoined after splitting up in the

Figure 1-6
The Quincy Opera House (1868) stood across the street from the building, *left*, in which Roeschlaub and Robert Bunce first met.
Courtesy Carl Landrum

7

1840s over the volatile issue of abolition (Fig. 1–9).[28] The church, drawn up in the English Gothic style, features a simple, dignified nave with an equally simple, sharply gabled transcept. The emphasis of the exterior, however, lies altogether in the massive main steeple which rises in four stages marked by vertical corner buttresses capped at the top by four flamelike pinnacles. Between this and an offsetting, modest tower, the

1–7

facade opens to two grand, pointed arches, the upper enclosing a great stained-glass window. Whether or not Roeschlaub ventured to suggest any of the elements that inspired such Victorian-age dignity, he learned enough in this project to overcome any timidity he might have had in designing a substantial church in the future. So ambitious was the task of building this one, in fact, that it was not dedicated until October of 1874, more than a year after Roeschlaub had left Quincy for Denver.

One other project, on a much smaller scale, deserves mention among Bunce's work. This is the house of Dr. J. W. Koch (Fig. 1–10), designed sometime before 1872. Although the engraved rendering, published in the *Atlas of Adams County* for that year,

1–8

emphasizes the grand proportions of the house, it also magnifies its equally bad features. Almost every element of the design conspires to give weighty oppression to the Second Empire facade. The entire first floor is of rusticated stone; the corner quoins are repeated unnecessarily on the second-floor pavilion; the entrance and narrow windows are all crowned with flaring voussoirs; and the dormers are spread out heavily on the rest, nullifying the grace of the mansard roof. Altogether the house is an amalgam of stylistic features brought together by an amateur. In comparison with an exquisite and balanced rendering of a Second Empire house done by Roeschlaub at a later date—perhaps drawn in the mid-1870s (PLATE 2)—this poses a problem: Is the Koch design a faltering

Figure 1–7
Edward Burling
Chamber of Commerce Building
Chicago, 1865
Chicago Historical Society
ICHi 19793

Figure 1–8
Robert Bunce
Temple B'nai Shalom
Quincy, Illinois, 1869
Courtesy Carl Landrum

early attempt by Bunce's assistant, or a reflection of Bunce's own inexperience?

The question is unanswerable, but it does indicate how dependent architecture was, before it became a profession, on the expertise of the self-taught or tutored practitioner, who followed the principles of the art from books and journals, from day-to-day experience with clients, or from the example of a mentor. With such an emphasis on personal judgment, the moment inevitably came when the apprentice or junior employee in an architectural firm, like Roeschlaub, had to determine when the apprenticeship would end— and this decision could not well be made without some comparison of personal skills with those of the master. What was involved was not narrowly a question of salary, the opportunity for more satisfying work, or the matter of advancement—as it might be in many instances today—but a major step to begin one's own architectural firm or leave the business altogether. The apprenticeship system offered few alternatives, since most offices at that time expressed the character and judgment of the founder, and the firm continued to operate only so long as he was around to keep its name alive.[29]

Whatever Roeschlaub thought of Bunce, he made his decision to leave in the early 1870s. The Chicago fire of 1871 might have provided one opportunity to build a practice in that burned-over city not far from his native home and family. Another possible move would have been to set up a practice, in competition with Bunce, in the less populated but still thriving town of Quincy. Instead, however, he chose to follow a more personal instinct, perhaps inspired by his father's pioneering season in the Pikes Peak goldfields in 1859, and settled on Denver as his new home.

On the eve of Roeschlaub's departure, Bunce presented him with a warmly inscribed copy of Gwilt's influential *Encyclopedia of Architecture*,[30] a gift that reflected his continuing role as teacher but without detracting from Roeschlaub's knowledge and experience as a full-fledged architect. With that, as well as his own well-organized architectural library, drawing tools, and a family that had grown to include two children, Roeschlaub boarded a train for the Rocky Mountains.

1–9

1–10

When Roeschlaub arrived in Denver in early 1873, he was anything but the stereotypical young man whom later generations would celebrate as escaping from the East to seek his fortune in the unconfined West. For one thing, his father had done that years before—and in a way that Roeschlaub knew he could not imitate, even if he wanted to. Michael Roeschlaub had gone off on a high adventure to prospect in the side canyons of Clear Creek and to winter in one of the two tent-and-cabin towns, Denver and Auraria City, that had sprung up along the banks of the South Platte River. When his son arrived fourteen years later to start an architectural practice, the city of Denver, having long since taken over Auraria, had a population of some 5,000—approximately half the size of Quincy's.[31]

Figure 1–9
Robert Bunce
First Union Congregational Church
Quincy, Illinois, 1870.
Courtesy Jeanne Pfeiffer

Figure 1–10
Robert Bunce
Dr. J. W. Koch Residence and Office
Quincy, Illinois, c. 1872.
Courtesy George Irwin

For another thing, Roeschlaub had no desire to escape the city and "light out for the territories." As an architect, Roeschlaub would have regarded the city as the only place for opportunity, and the undeveloped West offered him the chance to do well personally and contribute to the building of a potentially important city in the process. Unlike one of his contemporaries, photographer William Henry Jackson, who after the Civil War made his way west to explore the wilderness as a photographer for the Hayden Survey, Roeschlaub spent the formative years of his career learning an art and craft that, if anything, would bring civilization to the territories rather than the territories to civilization. That both of them ended up in Denver, and for opposite reasons, testifies to the variety of strains by which the dominant western theme attracted eastern listeners.

That theme, in the early 1870s, was the development of the West into a diverse empire built on agriculture, ranching, mining, and commerce, its burgeoning cities linked by railroads and its natural beauty and grandeur attracting tourists and settlers by the thousands. In 1870, only a year before Jackson's photographs of Yellowstone helped to convince Congress to set the area aside as a national park, the explorers of the Washburn-Langford-Doane party, aware that incoming speculators would appropriate the scenic beauty and wonder of the Yellowstone for the enjoyment of a few, made a campfire pact to preserve the region for the benefit of all the nation's people.[32] That pact rested on the then-reasonable belief, underscored by the near completion of the transcontinental railroad, that the West would someday be populated as thickly as the East.

Denver's leaders in the early 1870s shared the same belief, but their optimism was tempered by the realization that they had to act quickly to make their city a center of the developing West. Denver, situated a hundred miles from the path of the transcontinental railroad and at the foot of a formidable range of mountains, had little hope of becoming the hub of all western travel, but it could become the hub of regional commerce by capitalizing on its proximity to the silver mines of the interior Rockies and its recently estab-lished railroad linkages to the transcontinental on the north, near Cheyenne, and to St. Louis on the east. Consequently, it sent out organized parties of recruiters to promote immigration, and their efforts—not to mention those of the railroads—were so successful that by the spring of 1873, according to historian Lyle Dorsett, "the city's labor market [had become] glutted."[33] Had Roeschlaub not already been disposed to go west to begin an independent career as an architect, some of the promotional literature advertising the benefits of life in Denver may well have persuaded him.

The architect's first impressions of the city were neither unduly complimentary nor unflattering. A year earlier, world traveler Isabella Bird had stayed in town long enough to look back on Denver as "a great braggart city . . . spread out, brown and treeless, upon the brown and treeless plain."[34] Roeschlaub, while he may have shared Bird's opinion of Denver's barren streets and yards, noted the simplicity and suitability of the buildings that occupied those dusty lots. Without giving any weight to the "braggart" claims of the city's promoters, he foresaw a substantial city arising from the raw efforts of the first builders.[35] Then, too, he came to Denver for a purpose quite different from Bird's, and he could hardly have regarded the barrenness of the city as anything other than a field of opportunity for architectural improvement and civic pride.

What Roeschlaub did find on his arrival in Denver was a city far less developed than Quincy but on the verge of tremendous growth. The business district, which had been rebuilt largely in brick after a disastrous fire ten years earlier, was beginning to spread to the southeast in a broad pattern from Larimer Street along Fourteenth to Eighteenth streets, following Cherry Creek upstream from the bottomlands where it met the South Platte River. In the process, the homes of the earliest citizens, many of whom now owned valuable land, were being replaced by commercial buildings, while residents with money from these sales moved beyond the margin of growth into more elegant homes to the east.[36] Throughout the expanding city, however, private residences often occupied the same blocks as churches, business establishments, and schools in a heterogeneous cluster that reflected the incessant activity that almost daily changed the face of Denver's neighborhoods. On one quiet afternoon, an early Denver photographer, aware of the remarkable expansion of the city and conscious of the need to capture its youthful urban vigor for posterity, took a set of documentary photographs from the rooftop of the newly built Arapahoe High School. One of these shows, in a glance, the prospect for opportunity that met Roeschlaub when he arrived—a few scattered professionally designed buildings amidst a sea of others built by the pattern book or the carpenter's rule-of-thumb (Fig. 1–11).

It took little time, by way of records, for the Roeschlaubs to find a place to live—a sparsely populated neighborhood, southeast of the city center, that looked down a long, sloping grade to Cherry Creek and the South Platte River beyond. They settled into a rental home just off Colfax Avenue on Antelope Street, which in later years had its name changed from Antelope to South Thirteenth to Tremont and, finally, to Delaware.[37] In spite of the additions of land that were being opened regularly to the north and east of the city—and to the west, across the river—the Roeschlaubs preferred the area south of Colfax. They saved enough in three years to buy property there, later to build a house of the architect's design, and eventually to see the entire neighborhood filled with Roeschlaub's homes, cottages, and terraces.[38]

Almost immediately after his arrival in Denver, Roeschlaub seems to have attracted enough clients to open an office in the Clayton Block, a frame building on the south corner of Larimer and Fifteenth.[39] During the Panic of 1873 and its subsequent recession in Denver,[40] his office remained open. However, in a letter written to his mother in the spring of 1874, he reveals something about both the sluggish economy and the nature of clients. Of the architectural projects he has on hand, he states, they are "not much but wanted in a hurry."[41]

In the meantime, Annie Roeschlaub had given birth to their third child, Arthur, an occasion for other members of the family to visit. They included Robert's

younger sister Jessie and one of his aunts, both of whom undoubtedly got a tour of Denver and perhaps a ride on the narrow-gauge Denver and Rio Grande Railroad to Colorado Springs to see the Garden of the Gods, Manitou Springs, or Seven Falls. For, almost immediately after the completion of the transcontinental railroad—true to the anticipations of the Yellowstone party—tourists began arriving to see the wonder and beauty of the West. And although Roeschlaub still

1–11

referred to this new country as the Great American Desert, he rarely wrote home without sketching or describing the vistas of the Front Range or life as he found it in his adopted city at the foot of the Rockies (Figs. 1–12 and 1–13).

In fact, according to his daughter Alice, who was then five years old, her father joined a small party during these years to climb Pikes Peak along with two men who would become Roeschlaub's close friends and professional allies, Aaron Gove and James Baker.[42] Gove, a native of Illinois who also served in the Civil War, was an educator who came to Denver to direct the program of the East Denver schools. Baker, another educator, became the principal of the high school and later president of the University of Colorado. With

Figure 1–11
Denver, about 1874, in a view looking northeast from the top of the city's first high school at Eighteenth and Arapahoe streets.
CHS F13842

them Roeschlaub almost single-handedly gave architectural expression to liberal education in Denver's most prestigious school district, which lay in the area of the core city to the east of the Platte River and to the north of Cherry Creek.

In 1874, however, Roeschlaub was not known as a school architect—or, for that matter, as an architectural specialist of any kind. He is commonly regarded now as Denver's first office-trained architect, as opposed to

Long Peak, from our Kitchen door.   1–12

the more typical superintendent of building construction whose ideas arose more often from pattern books or well-tested practices than from a conception of design that attempted to integrate style, ornament, and the arrangement of a building with the needs of the client. In the early 1870s, only a few years after the first architectural school was established at M.I.T., the distinction between architect and building superintendent in most parts of the country was narrow, based largely on the credentials of experience rather than formal education. As a result, Roeschlaub's earliest commissions in Denver—now all but unknown—might be considered little more than projects in the development of his architectural portfolio.[43]

It was not until 1875 that Roeschlaub established himself firmly as an architect in the rapidly growing city. Not only did he include a large ad in the Denver city directory for that year, but his business had suddenly grown to such proportions that he had to take on

several temporary employees. In September he wrote to his mother (Fig. 1–14), with a mixture of exasperation and pride, about his work and prospects:

> I've been *very* busy this season, being obliged to work day *and night* parts of the time. My being laid up played the mischief with me, in that I have been able to do only a days work in *two* days, until within the last three weeks. This of course cost me *money*. Then everything got tangled up by every one wanting their work *immediately*, so that at one time about two weeks ago I was obliged for a few days to employ four men, viz: a young graduate of a Baltimore architectural school, a german map drawer to make tracings, a "contractor and Builder" to work on drawings of a frame house, and a young lawyer to copy Specifications. So my *profits* have been melting away.[44]

In spite of his alarm over diminishing profits, Roeschlaub later states that he and Annie "have made a prettie good living, and made a first payment on a nice building [site] on the top of the hill opposite Elberts [Ebert's] block. So I don't think we have reason to complain."

This letter, one of the most remarkable documents of early Denver architectural history, is worth quoting extensively because it not only encapsulates the story of Roeschlaub's first successful year but also testifies to the building boom that followed the influx of people whom the railroads brought to Denver in the 1870s. In the context of his work, he lists the projects that he has on hand, along with their costs, which total some $95,000. Subtracting the projects not yet accomplished, he shows a figure of $46,868, of which he earns about 5 percent. "You see," he states, "that if affairs would only 'pan out' right, I would have made quite a snug little sum, but of these, some I can't collect, and not *all* of it brought 5%, but, I have done well, become known, and am much talked about for having any contracts *carried out*, something new for this country." Finally, he concludes with a realistic assessment of the year to come, along with his hopes:

> A great many business houses have been erected this year, but few residences. I don't think, however, that there will be much to do next year, though I *hope* there may be, for while we have been getting money enough

Figure 1–12
View of Longs Peak in a sketch by Robert Roeschlaub, about 1875. *Courtesy Virginia Roberts*

Figure 1–13
Sketch by the architect of Denver City, Golden, and the Front Range, about 1875. *Courtesy Virginia Roberts*

to keep us, it comes in "fits and starts," and *our* bills must be paid right along, so that it would be *real* convenient to have a bank account. Then I *would* like to build, and get rid of paying rent.

The building projects that Roeschlaub enumerates in the letter range from the smallest to the largest kinds of jobs. They include a home, a church, a business block, one or two storefronts, a school, and various kinds of "improvements," a category that defies description and thus rarely finds its way into architectural histories despite the fact that such work often was—and is—the bread and butter of many architects.[45]

Two buildings stand out from this list as noteworthy not only in their cost but also in their significance to Roeschlaub's career. The first is the Central Presbyterian Church, which he estimated at $49,000, and the second is the "Broadway School House" at $21,145. Although the church must be considered the most important commission Roeschlaub had received at the time, the Broadway School, modest though it was, led to a fourteen-year appointment as architect for the East Denver (then Arapahoe County) public schools, a position that offered him not only prestige but an affiliation with one of Denver's most stable and expanding institutions.

For the moment, however, Central Presbyterian—a church he designed for his own congregation—was by far the most glamorous of his 1875 projects. Not as ambitious as Bunce's First Union Congregational Church of Quincy, on which Roeschlaub worked, the Presbyterian church was the hallmark of simplicity—if such could be said of any building done in the currently fashionable Gothic style. Built on Eighteenth and Champa (the cornerstone was laid on January 6, 1876), it consisted of little more than a high-gabled nave and a steeple, although it featured a transept at the rear, flush with the exterior walls, that was perhaps more noticeable on the exterior than in the sanctuary itself (Fig. 2–1). Had the steeple been completed, as conceived in a contemporary engraving, the church would have become a prominent landmark. As it was, the citizens of Denver, who still thought in terms of the city's marginal growth during the 1860s, were dumbfounded that any prominent building could be con-structed so far away from the center of the community.[46]

If Roeschlaub's Central Presbyterian Church is a study in restraint based on principle, the Broadway School (Fig. 1–15), built on the present site of the Colorado History Museum and Judicial Center Complex, typifies restraint based on necessity. The East Denver school board, having just completed the Arapahoe High School in the year that the Roeschlaubs arrived, and the Stout Street School a year later, saw the district falling behind the steady expansion of the city to the east, and its decision to place an elementary school as far away as Broadway and Fourteenth Avenue (then Capitol) suggests that, following some of the more bullish land speculators, it anticipated the direction and rate of urban growth.[47] Still, there was not enough income from the tax rolls or enough students living in the area to justify a large schoolhouse. In February 1875 Superintendent Aaron Gove sought proposals for the design of the Broadway School, and Roeschlaub submitted his plans.[48]

Heavily quoined for its modest size, the Broadway School may have seemed a bit too elegant to the architect four years later, when he designed the Twenty-fourth Street School (Fig. 3–4). The latter building, almost identical in plan but faced with rustic stone instead of brick with heavy stone trim, shows how much Roeschlaub had matured in the intervening years. He even admitted that the Broadway's design was defective in some respects. In three of the seven classrooms, light entering from the windows came from the direction of the right rather than the left, a violation of a popular edict with which Roeschlaub may not have been familiar.[49] Nevertheless, the East Denver school board was happy enough with the classical look of this minimalist Palladian building—its small lamp of learning proclaiming it a home of the liberal arts—and impressed enough with its architect, after it was completed, to offer him a permanent job.

In the meantime Roeschlaub continued to scout for commissions. He was not above submitting the same school plan to two different boards, for while he disliked the practice of copying another architect's work wholesale, he saw nothing wrong in borrowing from

1-14

his own.[50] "I have in prospect," he wrote his mother in the letter mentioned above, "a $20,000 block for Cheaver [Chever], a duplicate of the [Broadway] school House in Pueblo, and some other work." The Centennial School, built in Pueblo in 1876, was the first of several that Roeschlaub would do for school boards in this and other Colorado towns and cities, including Colorado Springs, Greeley, Platteville, Canon City (Fig. 1–16), and Lake City, to mention only those in which

1–15

his schoolhouses have been confirmed. From the outset Roeschlaub, like any good architect in a sparsely populated country, ranged far and wide for business, and his reputation kept clients coming back to him for new projects. His early foothold in Pueblo, with the Centennial School, proved to be particularly beneficial, for it led to the construction of Centennial High School (1881), Hinsdale School (1883), and the elegant Central High School of 1905.

In the mid-1870s, however, the work of *looking* for work in Colorado must have reminded the young architect of the early prospectors who spent days and months in search of "color," only to find in most cases that the gold they discovered only provided enough wealth to grubstake another search. The economy, despite the city's growing population, could not support large-scale construction, and property values were low. Even as architect for the East Denver schools, Roeschlaub had to wait another four years before he was asked to produce another one. The prediction he made to his mother in the flush year of 1875—that there would be little to do the next—proved correct for the following two, since nothing shows up as a part of his work in 1877. Yet if the tone and substance of an 1876 letter is any indication, he and his family, now increased with the arrival of a fourth child, Frank, were doing as well as could be expected. After hailing the imminent inauguration of Colorado as the nation's Centennial State, Roeschlaub writes: "I think we have done exceptionally well all things considered. Besides living comfortably...we have been enabled to pay off old scores here, and have bought some lots [on the corner of what is now Colfax and Delaware]....The next thing to do is to lay up...money enough to build upon it."[51] He closes with an invitation to the entire family to visit in the summer, when they could spend the Fourth of July on the top of Pikes Peak and his father could "look over his old stamping ground."

Two years later, with no major commissions for the architect to report, the Roeschlaubs' Christmas letter home still exudes confidence, a sense of humor, and mention of their latest child, Grace. Along with the letter Roeschlaub sent a family portrait taken by a freelance photographer. The photo session, as he describes it, was a debacle (Fig. 1–17):

When he had got us all to making faces pretty well, in order to attract the baby's attention, and make perfect the bland smile on Annie's face, he commenced jumping about, first on the right foot, with the left foot in the air, and then on his left foot, with his right straight out, and then on both feet. And all this while he was whistling and shouting, and flourishing the hat which he had taken from the glass, and just as we were looking to see him turn a grand double sommersalt, before the attracted crowd got so thick that he wouldn't have room, he clapped the hat on the glass, seized the "plate" and rushed away with it.

In addition to Roeschlaub's skill as pencil artist, he was also by this time interested in photography, which perhaps made matters worse. "I was informed," he writes, "that if I didn't look at the sun I would have a great black spot on my nose, and I told him I *liked* to

1–16

have my picture taken with a black spot on my nose."

In the closing lines of this letter, Roeschlaub mentions the gifts that he and Annie got for the children—a box of animals for Charlie, some "every day dishes" and a doll's head for Alice—and then shows his indomitable pride in saying, "We have the pleasure of thinking that *we made* the money to buy these with, and that we can now paddle our canoe better this Christmas than we did last."[52] How different the tone of this letter, written during the family's most difficult times thus far, from that of ten months later—which consists of nothing more than a paragraph in which he apologizes for its brevity because he has more work than he can handle. "Annie started and wrote about 10 lines of a letter to you," he states, "but the last half she wrote when she was asleep...waiting for me to return from the Office....I am about two thirds asleep myself, so that *my* letter won't amount to much....I am still *very* busy so that I have to work at night."[53]

The cause of such a great turnaround in the Roeschlaubs' daily life and fortunes—which would occur more than once in future years—can be attributed in large part to one of the biggest events of the decade, the discovery of silver at Leadville. The Leadville boom, which hit full stride in early 1878, created a city that quickly grew to become the second largest in Colorado, if only for a time, and its good fortune had an immediate and stimulating effect not only on Denver's economy but also on that of the entire region.[54] From Leadville came some of Denver's first millionaires. This alone, however, did not revive the confidence of the city's businessmen so much as the knowledge that the new-found wealth would invigorate an already sound and experienced industrial and commercial community. Among Denver's leaders were seasoned bankers, railroad magnates, retailers, land speculators, industrialists, and an assortment of entrepreneurs who carefully weighed the risks and benefits of investment—and while over time their homes and estates became more extravagant, their business blocks and storefronts were paragons of good sense and integrity.

One of the commissions that may have taken up Roeschlaub's evening hours in 1878 was the design for the Boston and Colorado Smelter. Under the direction of Nathaniel P. Hill, a professionally trained metallurgical chemist who had found a solution to refining Colorado's recalcitrant gold and silver ores, the smelter had operated successfully in Black Hawk, near Central City, for a decade. Realizing Denver to be a more central location—what with the opportunity of broader markets, the lack of space for expansion in Clear Creek Canyon, and a lawsuit over the decimation of the mountainsides for wood to fire the furnaces—Hill decided to place the smelter directly on the Denver Pacific line, north of the city, at Argo.[55] For Roeschlaub, the commission could not have come at a better time, even though the design of a smelter works and railroad sheds, before the advent of industrial architecture in the early twentieth century, would have been no distinction for a trained architect. Nevertheless, he was able to depart from the purely mechanical aspects of the project to place a central office building, complete with an octagonal tower, at the entrance to the works as

1

1–17

15

a statement that factories could rise above their base functions (Fig. 4–2 and 4–3).

In direct contrast to the Argo smelter, but also arising from the mining roots of Colorado's economy, Roeschlaub received another important commission in 1878, the Central City Opera House (Fig. 1–18). He was not alone in believing that industry and commerce by themselves failed to satisfy human needs, for the citizens of Central City, repairing their town from a

1–18

disastrous fire in 1874, were determined to use their wealth to celebrate opera, one of the highest forms of nineteenth-century culture. Like the Argo smelter, this was a totally new kind of project for the architect, one that he more than likely accepted with a special sense of mission. Recalling, perhaps, the fussy details of the Quincy Opera House designed by his mentor, Robert

Bunce, Roeschlaub conceived of a simple exterior that took into consideration the character of the town, its setting within a narrow valley surrounded by mountains and gold-tinted hills, and the aspirations of its citizens. The result was a building of remarkable visual strength, a paragon of the new West. Although the original plans, now in the possession of the Central City Opera House Association, show a wealth of external niceties, the massing and central components of the opera house testify to Roeschlaub's singular intention to make this building both spare and monumental.[56] It remains one of his most powerful and lasting designs.[57]

The Central City Opera House marks a transition in Roeschlaub's development as an architect. Nothing in his earlier work would seem to have led him to such a pronounced assertion of simplicity and unfettered honesty. Years later his daughter Alice claimed that the opera house signified her father's love and respect for the Rocky Mountains and his need to express these in his architecture. With a remarkable clarity of memory, she said of the opera house that "the moneyed men back of this, in their enthusiasm, wished to make the building a most elaborate affair; but Mr. Roeschlaub stood fast for a different type—one that should be in harmony with the great mountains surrounding it, and an expression of the new and simple West."[58] While this may be true—as it has been true of other architects whose work has been inspired by the geography and landscape around them—Roeschlaub nevertheless came to Denver with a disposition toward restraint and moderation in design that he could well have found conducive to the setting of Colorado's Front Range. Thus, even if the Rocky Mountains did not make Roeschlaub the architect that he was, they offered him a rationale for expressing the principles of architecture that were a part of his earlier training and temperament. So greatly had he influenced his eldest child in this idea—and so well did the Central City Opera House epitomize it—that years after her father's death Alice composed a sonnet in memory of this building as a symbol of his entire work: "And in a little mining town alone," it concluded, "this builder wrought his dream; a structure rose/Against the mountainside, of massive stone,/ To house the tales of love and storied woes—/ The great ones of the earth would tread that stage/And add new glory to our Western page!"[59]

Roeschlaub's attention to the opera house, however, was soon to be replaced by other pressing projects in Denver, one of which was his next East Denver school. Intriguingly, he brought to this design, the Twenty-fourth Street School (1879), a combination of elements similar to those of the French-inspired Central City Opera House—and for about the same cost.[60] The plan was based on the Broadway School but the style suggests a total rethinking of the architect's principles.

Certainly one thought that was uppermost in Roeschlaub's mind at that time, quite as much as the matter of its appearance, was the school's solidity and "conveniences" (that is, light, heat, ventilation, and arrangement of rooms) and safety. Part of his duties as architect for the East Denver district was to monitor repairs and alterations in the three schools that had already been built—only one of them his. Nothing could have convinced him more of the foolishness and danger of cost-cutting in either design or construction than the problems that attended the five-year-old Stout Street School. Constructed in the summer of 1874 from plans submitted by a short-lived firm, the school had begun falling apart almost from its first year. Nearly $4,000 had to be put into repair work, on top of an initial cost of $17,714, before the building was finally condemned in 1881. The major problem, as the *Rocky Mountain News* pointed out in a series of articles at the height of the controversy, was that some of the walls were pulling away from the floors, posing such a danger to the students that parents eventually refused to let their children attend. Roeschlaub took a few temporary measures to allay the parents' fears but recommended extensive repairs "to insure its perfect and permanent safety and security." He also recommended that the building be examined by the city, and a special committee of the city council, hearing what would have to be spent to shore up the walls, decided against its further use as a school. It burned down a short time later, after vandals broke into and set fire to the abandoned building.[61]

Coincidentally, the problems attending the Stout Street School came at a time when public confidence in building safety had been shaken by the partial collapse of the Tabor Grand Opera House during its construction and, to make matters worse, the death of a worker in the collapse of the Straus Building on Larimer Street.[62] These disasters had "placed the entire community on the *qui vive* for unsubstantial buildings," stated the school board's annual report, "and no where more than in the fifth ward, where resided the parents of nearly five hundred children, who were daily placed under the roof of the Stout-street school." Roeschlaub, who had designed the new Twenty-fourth Street School shortly before this crisis, must have realized, if he had not done so before, the tremendous responsibility he had undertaken as architect for the school district, and his concern for sound construction in every type of building project only deepened as time went on. It was quite possibly the foundation of his efforts ten years later to professionalize the practice of architecture.[63]

The Tabor Grand and Straus Building episodes may also have weighed heavily on Roeschlaub as he designed two new business blocks for downtown Denver—the Barth Block, housing the City National Bank on the corner of Sixteenth and Lawrence (not to be confused with the second Barth Block, built in 1887 at Sixteenth and Stout), and the King Block a few paces to the northeast on Lawrence (Figs. 4–15 and 4–11). One of the earliest of Roeschlaub's larger commercial structures, the Barth building (c. 1879–80) drew from the architect's new vocabulary of design, balancing the vigor of rusticated stone with the cultured expressions of a mansard roof and other Second Empire detailing. For the King Block, which did not have the advantage of a corner site and thus a unifying focus, he broke the long facade into several bays and set off the second floor with a scheme of tripartite Gothic windows. The three-story King Block, into which Roeschlaub moved his office in 1880, may have been built with the intention of adding a few more stories, for eventually he gave life to the central bays by extending them two

1–20

1–19

Figure 1–19
Roeschlaub's own home, depicted here in a rendering, was amply designed for a family of nine. It was built near the corner of Colfax and Delaware.

Figure 1–20
A family portrait, taken in the late 1880s, includes, *from left to right*, Ralph, Alice, Robert, Francis (Frank), Grace, Charles, Arthur, Walter, and Annie.
Courtesy Frank von Roeschlaub

stories and adding a mansard roof.[64] This effectively wrote a conclusion to the earlier facade treatment.

The phenomenal growth of Denver and the prosperity that accompanied the beginning of the 1880s could be detailed in countless ways, but a mere glance at Roeschlaub's commissions for the first two years of the decade speak eloquently of its impact on his success. In twenty-four months he constructed at least forty-four buildings. Among these were ten business blocks, five schools, twenty-four residences, one warehouse, a smelter (this one in the passing boom town of Gothic City), and additions to Wolfe Hall and Denver General Hospital.[65] Moreover, Roeschlaub was not even the most successful of Denver's architects: in 1880, based on the value of construction (which, of course, determined the architect's fees), his firm ranked only fourth among the city's top five.[66]

Nevertheless, by 1880 Roeschlaub's prospects had undergone a sea change in barely two years. Now he could finally build upon his long-nourished property at Colfax and Delaware, and the home he designed (Fig. 1–19), while not as grand as the mansions he built for some of his clients, was substantial and well-to-do. The family's prosperity, in fact, came just in time, for in 1879 and 1880 Robert and Annie had two sons in quick succession—Walter and Ralph respectively. The home would suffice to raise the Roeschlaub children for the next twenty-four years (Fig. 1–20), from the eldest, Alice (who was ten years old when Walter was born) to the youngest, Ralph.[67]

In his business, Roeschlaub took on a young graduate of the Cornell School of Architecture, Frederic Hale, who had shown distinction in his education by winning a competition sponsored by *Carpentry and Building* magazine. Hale came to work for Roeschlaub in 1880 and was his chief draftsman for the next three years.[68] His experience with Roeschlaub during this hectic time of the office's growth proved beneficial for both men. Hale's influence on the appearance of Roeschlaub's buildings during the early 1880s—or Roeschlaub's influence on Hale's later architecture—is impossible to determine from the available records, but it is clear that the work of the firm in all respects was taking a new and exciting turn.

The most important project that Roeschlaub's new chief draftsman encountered was the design of the East Denver High School, a massive structure that would replace the old Arapahoe High School several blocks to the northwest. Although it was not completed for almost a decade, East Denver High was undoubtedly conceived in its entirety in the months of 1880 and 1881. When the first wing finally rose on a portion of the block that had been dedicated for the school (Fig. 1–21), it served as a self-contained institution with enough room to house Denver's new public library, but the building was obviously a truncated portion of Roeschlaub's final conception (Fig. 1–22). Denverites would not see the completed structure until 1889, and by then its stripped-down classicism gave a hint of Roeschlaub's rejection of the wild experimentation that marked High Victorian architecture.

Nevertheless, the high school received high public approval (as did every new building in the self-conscious West) and fulfilled Aaron Gove's aspirations for an institution that would be the roof and crown of liberal learning. As if the building itself, with its observatory, chemical laboratories, and statued alcoves did not reflect this imperative well enough, he looked for a symbol to express the heritage of Western learning. Roeschlaub, along with sculptor Preston Powers and two other members of a specially appointed committee, came up with the idea of an angel or cherub, a stone sculpture that would stand as the keystone of the school's central arch (Fig. 1–23). The committee went in search not only of a suitable artist to do the job but also a young model among the school district's thousands of children. In both cases they could not have had better luck, for the sculptor was Daniel Chester French, who later modeled the statue of Abraham Lincoln that has become one of the nation's greatest memorial

shrines, and the subject for the cherub was six-year-old Ella Catherine Matty, the last and most appealing of some five thousand girls whose classrooms were certainly thrown into excitement by the sweeping gaze of a dignified group of judges.[69]

While plans for the East Denver High School were being prepared, Roeschlaub was already designing the elementary or grammar schools that would comprise the minions of the educational system. With Fred Hale

1-21

and a new assistant, Ezra M. Cornell, in supervisory charge of the high school,[70] he embarked on a plan to meet the needs of the rapidly expanding district by making each new school a variant of one basic design—at least this was what he stated in a lengthy report to the school board in 1885.[71] In fact, having gained the confidence of the board members with the spare beauty and solidity of the Twenty-fourth Street School, he launched into a period of intense experimentation not only with interior plans but also outside appearances, building upon the merits of each design in the one to follow while improving upon past mistakes. Common to all of these schools, as Richard Brettell points out in his valuable and incisive study, *Historic Denver*, is a "compactness and simplicity" that make them "paradigms of good, economical, tight architecture."[72]

Figure 1–21
A W. H. Jackson view of Denver, including the first wing of Roeschlaub's East Denver High School, *center left*, also shows St. John's Cathedral, *right*, and parts of newly developed Capitol Hill.
Denver Public Library, Western History Department
F30733

These schools—Ebert (1880), Gilpin (1881), and Longfellow (1881-82)—are reductive versions of easily recognizable current styles (Figs. 3–7, 3–8, and 3–5). The cornice of each is clean and sharp, characterized by uniform brick corbeling that joins the mass of the roof effortlessly to the body of the structure, while light or dark banding accentuates the floor divisions and window transoms. Except for Ebert (Fig. 1–24), they have no heavy bell towers or other elements of ostentation

1-22

so common to Victorian schools, and Ebert's tower is little more than a peaked roof. One can only speculate on the source of rigorous discipline that marks the design of these buildings—budgetary restrictions, new trends in school architecture, or personal temperament. Whatever the reason, Roeschlaub set a tone for the East Denver schools that was one of both dignity and enlightenment, and his earliest schools show how much that tone derived from the mutual respect and educational thinking that he and Aaron Gove shared.

Nothing could better illustrate the confidence that Gove had in Roeschlaub than an exchange of letters

between the superintendent and G. P. Randall, a Chicago architect who had designed the Arapahoe High School, which after only a decade of use was to be replaced by the first wing of Roeschlaub's new building. Learning that the board was planning to construct a new grammar school (Ebert), Randall wrote to Gove in March 1880 offering his services and noting that he had already designed the district's present high school. Gove wrote back extolling the virtues of the

Twenty-fourth Street School and informing Randall that he was quite happy with his own architect. In response, chagrined and with sardonic humor, Randall wrote:

Dear Sir: Yours of the 2nd inst. is [received] and contents noted in which you make this rather startling assertion "we can show you the model Eight room [schoolhouse] of the world." Now, I am glad to know you are making such [an] advance in school architecture, but I will bet you a *big apple* that I will send you a better model of an Eight room house than you have there. I refer now to the floor plans or interior arrange-

Figure 1–22
Another W. H. Jackson view of East Denver High School taken from the northeast in about 1889.
CHS J2051

ments which is substantially all there is of a school house building. Now if you want to take this *bet*, I will exchange tracings with you, and...if the excellence of either is not so far in advance of the other as to make it clear who is entitled to the apple we will each eat our own.[73]

So far as is known, Gove never took up the challenge—or, if he did, Roeschlaub's Ebert School design, commissioned only a month later, satisfied him enough to send Randall's back.[74]

During his first highly successful years in Denver, from 1879 to 1882, Roeschlaub established himself as a versatile and pragmatic architect. In addition to the number of commissions he received, there were few types of projects that he could not (or would not) assume, and the names of his clients were drawn from the top echelon of Denver's rapidly developing business and professional communities.[75] From his work with Nathaniel Hill on the Boston and Colorado Smelter, Roeschlaub was commissioned in 1880 to design the interior of the Hill Mansion, and from his acquaintance with Dr. F. J. Bancroft, who was president of the East Denver school board from 1873 to 1875, he was asked to design the first Bancroft Block (1881) on the corner of Sixteenth and Stout, which had been the site of Bancroft's home.[76] Other clients included John R. Hanna, president of the City National Bank; William D. Todd, cashier at the Union Bank and later treasurer of the Chamber of Commerce; Charles G. Chever, a noted pioneer land speculator and city developer; Joseph A. Thatcher, president of the Denver National Bank; William Barth, businessman and banker; and lawyer Thomas M. Patterson, one of Colorado's congressional representatives. For Joshua S. Raynolds, who was on the first board of directors for the Colorado National Bank, Roeschlaub in 1882 designed a Stick Style house in Las Vegas, New Mexico (Fig. 1–25), which he later used as a selling point in his advertisements.[77] Outside of Denver, in addition to the William A. Hamill complex and the John B. Church Home in Georgetown (all of which can be ascribed to Roeschlaub on the basis of his office inventory of building plans), his clients

included Col. William Moore in Idaho Springs, Maj. J. W. Stanton in Pueblo, and Benjamin H. Eaton, who became governor of Colorado in 1885.

Besides Roeschlaub's schools, two outstanding business blocks emerge from this period of bustling activity, and they are noteworthy not only in themselves but because they mark the last major commercial buildings that the architect attempted in Denver for the next twenty years. These are the Times Block of 1881

1–24

and the Union Bank Block, built a year later (Figs. 4–18 and 4–16). The first, designed for the offices of the *Denver Times*, received widespread approbation for its sophistication and beauty. Quite unlike anything that Roeschlaub had done before, the Times Block was finished in dressed stone—the first time that he had been allowed such luxury—and its facade presented three and a half stories of academic splendor inspired mostly by the architecture of the Italian Renaissance.[78]

Until 1882 Roeschlaub actively sought and obtained commissions for downtown buildings, whether they happened to be whole blocks, storefronts, or merely warehouses. Indeed, with the Chever, Bancroft, Brandenburg, Nesmith, Barth, King, Times, and Union blocks he seemed to be widening the scope of his reputation as a commercial architect. The

1–23

Figure 1–23
Ella Catherine Matty, the "angel" of East High School, was an early model for Daniel Chester French, who later sculpted the figure of Abraham Lincoln for the Lincoln Memorial. *Courtesy East High School*

Figure 1–24
Ebert School
Denver, 1880
CHS F44847

absence of his hand in the business development of the city from that time forward is something of a mystery, especially since the few commercial blocks that he did in later years show not only structural competence but mastery of style. Yet, whatever his personal reasons for abandoning this avenue of architectural possibilities, they were informed by two social factors. First, the number of architects in Denver was growing to such an extent that competition was extraordinary, even for

1–25

someone as well established as Roeschlaub. Second, this competition was heightened by a downturn in construction that halted expansion and building for the next three years. The causes of this recession in building activity, according to historian Frank Hall, were so numerous as to be undefinable. "In 1883," he states,

> the tide began to recede, when the shrinkage of values, though not sudden nor great, was distinctly visible in the gradual dismissal of thousands of carpenters, builders, brickmakers and layers, plumbers, indeed of all classes of mechanics and laborers, who were obliged to seek employment elsewhere. While at no time did the course of development entirely cease, thereafter, until the beginning of 1886, it was sluggish. Real estate dealers, agents and owners suffered from loss of business. . . . It was one of the periods which invariably succeed epochs of excessive activity in iron manufacture, railway building, and speculation.[79]

On the heels of his former success, Roeschlaub was able to hold on to his practice, but he lost Fred Hale to another firm and his commissions dropped to a fraction of what they had been before 1882. Of these, only two are noteworthy—and both of them were products of his role as school architect. Departing from the pattern it had established for small elementary school buildings on the model of Twenty-fourth Street, the board asked Roeschlaub to draw up plans for larger structures, one of them far to the northeast of the city center and the other in the newly developing area of Capitol Hill. With the expanded resources of the board open to him, the architect began to design the contours of a different type of school than he had so far contemplated. His plan for the high school, which had been conceptualized before 1882, allowed for an ample central hall that rose more than two stories and provided for an overlook from the second floor, bisected by a crosswalk. This kind of monumental interior, in combination with a set of grand staircases, he tried to adapt to his newest district schools.

The first, Whittier (1883), broke from anything Roeschlaub had so far done in school design (Fig. 1–26). Although the exterior was basically an expression of his earlier schools on a massive scale, the interior plan did away with a central corridor and replaced it with an enormous hall—wider than the schoolrooms themselves—built around a double staircase. More radical still, he set the entrances to the building on the four corners rather than on the long axis, emphasizing the sense of the hall as a public space and deriving from the corner entrances an imposing and satisfying complexity on the outside (Fig. 3–11). The plan allowed for such unity and so many variations and surprises that Roeschlaub returned to it more than once in later years.

The second, Emerson (1884), was even more of a departure than Whittier, for it broke the pattern of symmetry that Roeschlaub had followed in his earlier schools and introduced a bold, massive, high-pitched roof that was a model for all of his later school designs (Fig. 1–27). Although it was too small for a central staircase, Emerson carried forward Roeschlaub's notion of the hall as a public court with angled classroom

Figure 1–25
Joshua S. Raynolds Residence
Las Vegas, New Mexico, 1882
CHS F44827

doors that allowed teachers to observe the progress of students from class to class and for the principal to observe the activity of any classroom at a glance (Fig. 3–13). The most impressive feature of Emerson, however, was its daring facade, including a windowless wall that consisted of nothing more than band courses and a large, white, Indiana limestone sundial within an ornamental arch.[80] The balance and unity of the building is both striking and calming, and the interplay of

large-plate photographs of the buildings, and the exhibit brought more than local or regional attention to Roeschlaub's work.[81] This honor could hardly have come at a better time, for aside from the two schools, Roeschlaub's only confirmed commissions during the mid-decade were a home for merchant William R. Owen (later general manager of the Denver Dry Goods Company) and a clubhouse in Laramie, Wyoming (Fig. 1–28). And although this paucity of projects does not

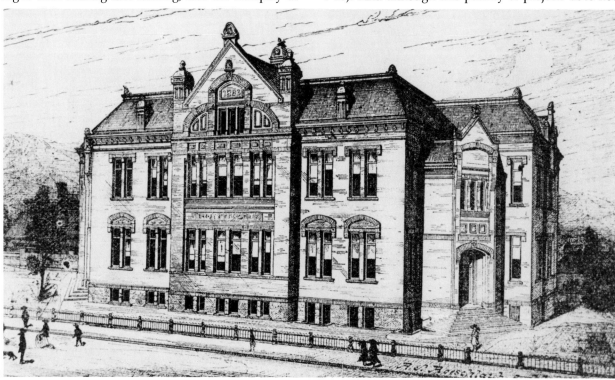

1-26

vertical and horizontal elements is masterful.

That is, at least, what a visiting commission of educators thought about these two schools—in general effect, if not in substance. Although the precise circumstances are not entirely clear, Roeschlaub was invited by the Department of Education in Washington to prepare an exhibit of plans and photographs of Whittier and Emerson for the upcoming World's Industrial and Cotton Centennial Exhibition to be held in New Orleans in late 1884. William Henry Jackson took

reflect the actual work of the firm—only the difficulty of attributing buildings to the architect that are above question—his business was undoubtedly slower than usual and the commissions small.[82]

Roeschlaub could hardly have kept his pride and accomplishment over the New Orleans exhibit from his parents in Quincy. Thus the news of his father's death six months later was an event not only for sadness but also reflection. The distance between the scruffy supply town that Michael Roeschlaub had visited in 1859 and

Figure 1–26
Whittier School, rendering
Denver, 1883
CHS F49935

the cosmopolitan city of some 50,000 people (by now far outstripping Quincy) that celebrated his son's architecture was not only vast but too quickly bridged to allow for reasonable comprehension. The city had changed so rapidly in barely over a generation that its pioneer past was in danger of being lost. Already, in 1881, Roeschlaub had become concerned enough about this threatened legacy to become one of the "curators" of the State Historical and Natural History Society of

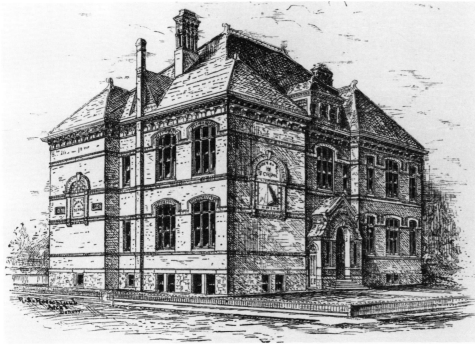

1–27

Colorado, a three-year-old institution just then struggling to assemble the material history of the state from its origins in the gold rush of 1859. Possibly influencing him in the decision to accept this appointment were his friends Dr. Frederick J. Bancroft, who was the society's first president, and Aaron Gove, who served as another curator.[83]

In 1885 there were thirteen architectural firms in Denver, down from a high of twenty-one in the peak year of 1883. In 1886 there were three fewer, and then the

number began to climb—to seventeen in 1888, twenty-four in 1889, and an astounding forty-one in 1890—only to be excelled in the next year by the arrival of six more firms.[84] The building slump of the mid-1880s preceded a boom that far surpassed the infusion of wealth which the Leadville strike of 1879 brought to Denver. For a time the growth exceeded the ability of established firms to keep up—Roeschlaub's among them—and suddenly the city was deluged with architects who stood ready to cater to any whim of a wealthy client. Not only did competition among architects increase dramatically, but the opportunity for success bore a direct relationship to the freedom offered by the legitimacy of eclecticism in architecture and the client's often uninformed notions of modern taste. In this milieu Roeschlaub was a conservative—but an enlightened one, for he kept abreast of every newly introduced style and variation as quickly as he received issues of the *American Architect and Building News*, published in Boston, and the *Inland Architect*, published in Chicago.

For the western architect like Roeschlaub, these professional journals effectively destroyed the lag of months or years that had formerly accompanied the introduction of an idea in the East and its appearance in the West. During the early 1860s, when Denver was a pioneer town, a Greek Revival facade imposed on a house of log construction was not unusual,[85] while in the East the gothic country houses of Andrew Jackson Downing represented the cutting edge of modernity.[86] Some twenty years later, architects could look at engravings of buildings designed only months before, and by the late 1880s the newest designs coming out of Boston, New York, Philadelphia, and Chicago were available in a matter of days. Thus, although western architects struggled constantly against the entrenched notion of regional backwardness, they were among the first to realize the advantage of belonging to a nation-wide profession in which individual merit could be honored over the mere privilege of being at the center of architectural creativity.

Although he never wrote at length about his architectural principles, Roeschlaub's few published statements manifest an awareness of this transforma-

Figure 1–27
Emerson School
Denver, 1884
CHS F49936

tion and a confident acceptance of his place within a national community of architects. Not neglecting his role as a western architect in a city that owed its livelihood to gold and silver mines, cattle, and health-seekers, he showed a surprising lack of regional defensiveness and displayed a canny judgment of the nation's architectural tastes during the late 1880s and into the 1890s. From this broad perspective, he was free to criticize or praise the accomplishments and pretensions of his own city just as he might any other. Speaking of Denver's middle-class homes, for example, he stated:

> It is in this class of buildings that we see too much of the overstrained and fantastic in their architecture. A reaching out, in some cases, after what is impossible for want of means. A large proportion of these buildings indicate a following after "fads"—to use a slang expression. "Narrow dogmas are the watchword of cliques, and the cause of most of the art absurdities of the day." It is to be deplored that this state of feeling exists in all parts of the country at the present time, and is rather prominent in Denver, but it is gratifying to see these "fads" gradually disappearing and good taste prevailing, on the whole.[87]

During his career Roeschlaub rarely departed from his own principles of good taste and held up the same test for architecture in Denver as in New York, Chicago, or Minneapolis. His personally well-defined standards of good architecture, in concert with his urbane and tempered judgment, made him an excellent candidate to promote the idea of a profession that would extend across regional boundaries and soften individual rivalries.

In 1886, however, Roeschlaub's office practice and commissions took second place to little else. Following the building slump of the mid-decade, Denver was entering a period of enormous growth, replicating on a large, metropolitan scale the kind of boom that affected so many earlier mining camps. Perhaps because there was suddenly so much work to be done, Fred Hale returned to the Roeschlaub firm, now as a full partner, and the two men sought and kept their own commissions.[88] Shortly thereafter Aaron M. Gove, the son of Roeschlaub's friend and educational colleague Aaron

Gove, joined the firm as an assistant to fill the void of Ezra Cornell, who had left in 1885. In the years to follow, Roeschlaub had five known assistants besides the younger Gove: they were Rudolf Liden, who remained only a year; Robert Willison, whose tenure was also short-lived; Thomas F. Walsh, who supervised the construction of Trinity Methodist Church; and John Rainbow, who stayed with Roeschlaub from 1888 to 1892—a long apprenticeship during that highly active

PROPOSED CLUB-HOUSE, LARIMER-CITY. W.T
R. S. ROESCHLAUB, Architect

1-28

period and one that did not apparently bear the same fruit as Gove's work. Gove enrolled in the architectural school of the University of Illinois and returned in the 1890s to become an accomplished local architect in his own right—perhaps with the blessings of his mentor, Robert Roeschlaub, whose concern for the profession would have undoubtedly favored the kind of training that he did not enjoy in his own day.[89]

As all of this activity suggests, Roeschlaub was a very busy architect from the mid-1880s forward. This was certainly true from 1887 until 1892, a five-year

Figure 1-28
Project for a clubhouse
Laramie, Wyoming

period that would mark his highest level of productivity and embrace the very best of his work. It was also a period in which he expanded his network of clients, from the businessmen and bankers of central Denver, some of whom had school board connections, to the institution-builders of Colorado, primarily those who wanted to establish colleges up and down the Front Range. Roeschlaub never shed his early reputation as a school architect, a mixed blessing that offered steady work and opportunity but did not allow his wide-ranging capacities to attract the attention of downtown commercial developers, who had begun to favor high buildings with impressive Chicago-style facades. More and more they turned locally to Frank Edbrooke, who

1-29

Figure 1-29
E. B. Light Terrace
("Tuxedo Place")
Denver, 1890
CHS F44738

was easily as versatile and accomplished as Roeschlaub and who eventually established a reputation for commercial architecture that dominated the downtown skyline. Although both architects ventured into each other's domain, they seem to have drawn broad lines of personal expertise and preference that increasingly identified one as commercial and the other as institutional.[90]

Roeschlaub's decided step towards institutional architecture occurred over a two-year period, from 1887 to 1889, in designs for two churches, two new East

Denver schools, college buildings for the University of Denver and the Colorado School of Mines, and a new kind of venture—terraces and apartment complexes (Fig. 1–29). In fact, of his known works during the half decade from 1887 to 1891, Roeschlaub had over four times as many commissions for schools, churches, and campus buildings as for commercial structures, and with a few notable exceptions he practically divided his work between public and religious architecture on the one hand and private residences, duplexes, and terraces on the other.

With the completion of the A. Z. Salomon Block ("Salomon's Bazaar") in 1891—one of Denver's first buildings to feature terra-cotta ornament—Roeschlaub turned once again, after a long absence, to religious architecture in the design of the First Presbyterian Church of Colorado Springs (1887). In spite of the years he had spent in the service of secular public architecture, he clearly had not forgotten how to bring dignity, sanctity, and inspiration to a sacred building (Fig. 2-28). His collection of architectural engravings from contemporary journals, bound eventually into a series of volumes on different building types, shows that he never failed to stay informed of developments in church styles and motifs. Nevertheless, the First Presbyterian Church so well blends the current themes of Romanesque architecture with those of the Renaissance that it can be classed as little else than the architect's own highly individual statement.

Yet, if the First Presbyterian Church marks Roeschlaub's return to religious architecture, Trinity Methodist Church, begun in the same year, epitomizes not only his complete mastery of the form but also the highest point of his career. No other building has secured his reputation so assuredly as this, and Roeschlaub's subsequent use of advertisements depicting the construction of its unique stone tower testifies to his own recognition of its importance. Taking maximum advantage of an excellent site—the intersection of Broadway, Eighteenth Avenue, and Tremont Street—the architect placed the church's massive tower dramatically in the foreground and half-enclosed it with two high-gabled faces flanked by smaller towers at each end (Fig. 1–30). All the elements of Trinity's

1-30

1-31

Figure 1-30
View of Trinity Methodist Episcopal
Church (now Trinity United Methodist
Church), 1888, looking northeast from
Eighteenth Street.
CHS F31126

Figure 1-31
Roeschlaub's rendering of a
courthouse, date unknown, is similar
in many respects to H. H.
Richardson's Allegheny County
Courthouse and Jail, 1884-87, in
Pittsburgh.

exterior contribute to the commanding presence of the corner tower. Yet in the design of the sanctuary inside, Roeschlaub departed from the pointed arch and vaulted ceiling of traditional Gothic architecture to emphasize instead the beauty of its central feature—a thirty-six-foot-high Roosevelt organ whose pipes were monumentally arrayed within a simple but dignified proscenium frame.

Like much of Roeschlaub's architecture of this period, Trinity reflects his indebtedness to Henry Hobson Richardson, one of the most influential innovators of the time. Yet in his other work, as in Trinity, Roeschlaub carefully selected only those elements of Richardson's successful buildings that fit within a composite all his own, often mixed with other eclectic features that accent a wholly personal insistence on simplicity, honesty, and integrity. His familiarity with Richardson's work came only after years spent in defining his own style, and this he did by addressing in each design the relevance of ornament or other stylistic elaboration to the unity of the whole (Fig. 1–31).

The sheer number of buildings that Roeschlaub designed in the era of Trinity Methodist Church prohibits an adequate discussion of any one (Fig. 1–32). A few, however, may represent his achievement as an architect who took pains to concentrate on each one

principles of rationalism just as it indicates, in its setting, how many of Denver's wealthy citizens were building their homes on the brow of Capitol Hill (Fig. 1–33). Farther down in the city, Roeschlaub in the same year completed the Haish Manual Training School for the University of Denver (Fig. 1–34), an utterly utilitarian building that in the process of design opened up opportunities for the architect with the trustees of the university just as had the Broadway School thirteen

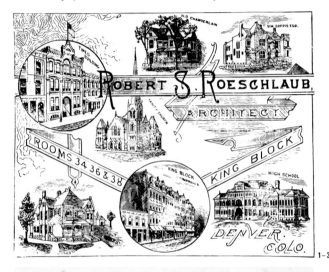

1–32

1–33

Figure 1–32
By the late 1880s and early 1890s, Roeschlaub's success allowed him to place large, full-page ads in the Denver City Directory.

Figure 1–33
This W. H. Jackson panorama of Denver, taken about 1890, captures Trinity Church, East Denver High School, and the Gottesleben Mansion—all Roeschlaub buildings. Streets have been misnamed on the original photograph: Lincoln, unmarked, appears to be little more than an alleyway from the angle of the photograph; the street identified as Lincoln should be Sherman; and Sherman should be Grant. The Gottesleben Mansion stood at 1901 Sherman.
CHS F31123/F31124

even as he was enlarging the body of his work. In his residential architecture at this time, few known houses stand out more than the Peter Gottesleben Mansion (1888), which architecturally expresses Roeschlaub's

years before. Finally, on the campus of the Colorado School of Mines, Roeschlaub in 1889 built an extension, known as the Executive Building, on to an evolving Old Main complex. This addition, openly derivative of

Richardson and handsomely integrated with the older buildings, led to another commission on the Mines campus—the Engineering Hall (1894), which still stands (Figs. 5–10 and 5–11).

Given the overwhelming design work of Roeschlaub's firm after 1887 and the nearly exhausting petty details that were involved in his duties as architect of the East Denver schools, he resigned his post with the school district in December of 1889, and his resignation was accepted in the spring of the following year.[92] Nevertheless, he completed two of the district's finest schools before his departure. They represent his most mature work in school design up to and perhaps beyond that point. The first was the Hyde Park School (Fig. 1–35), a complete departure from his earlier conceptions, including the celebrated Emerson School of 1884. Hyde Park was freer and bolder than anything Roeschlaub had attempted before in a school, a tower-centered, asymmetrical building that incorporated the informality of Queen Anne exuberance. The second was Corona School (now Dora Moore), the crowning achievement of Roeschlaub's school architecture, a highly symmetrical design expressing the complete integration of his notions of interior atrium and exterior corner towers and featuring some of the best use of terra cotta to be found in Denver (Fig. 1–36).

In terms of both quantity of commissions and quality of design, Roeschlaub's work during the highly expansive period following Trinity Methodist Church speaks of an architect at the top of his form. Despite the sharp increase in the number of architects practicing in Denver from 1886 to 1892, Roeschlaub's own office activity rose to its highest level during this time—a clear indication that he was meeting his competition step by step as a consequence of his well-established reputation and business acumen (Fig. 1–37). It is equally clear, however, that a new spirit had descended upon Denver's architectural community—the drive to gain commissions at any cost, which led to intense rivalries and cutthroat practices, not to mention inferior designs. A caustic letter to the editor of the *Western Architect and Building News*, written by a Glenwood

Springs architect in 1890, captures some of the flavor of both. "You have a set of tramps, hoosiers and humbugs in your city," the writer states, "who style themselves architects."

> There are some professionals in Denver, like Humphries & Kidder, Varian & Sterner, Schweinfurth, Eberly, Roberts, Stuckert, Roeschlaub and Andrews, Jaques & Rantoul, but the majority of the rest could not fill a place in my office as tracers. Believe me, *I know* them! Not that I have the doubtful pleasure of their personal acquaintance, but "by their works ye shall know them."[93]

Such harsh words, favorable to Roeschlaub or not, constituted a challenge that reflected the public insecurity of the architectural profession as much as it did the

1–34

confident opinions of the writer. In fact, it may be taken as direct testimony that no profession, as we know it today, existed at all.[94]

The discomfort that some members of Denver's

Figure 1–34
Haish Manual Training School
Denver, 1888
W. H. Jackson photograph
CHS J3815

architectural community felt over the divisiveness in its ranks emerged in an appeal printed several months earlier in the same journal over the signature of "Stone." While acknowledging that every architect's work "should be a subject of legitimate criticism," the writer states that

> more often an architect is judged, condemned and executed by careless, fault-finding men, whose motives are directed from an innate littleness of spirit

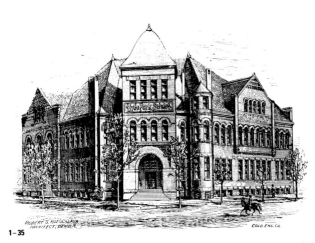

1–35

> or jealousy of a more fortunate rival. ... A report is circulated by an expert against the stability of a building. The work goes on, and does not fall as predicted; but then, with an ominous shake of the head, the public is notified that this proves nothing. The building will certainly fall sometime because of organic defects, and the public mind is left in a state of insecurity and uncertainty.[95]

These words could almost have been written by Roeschlaub himself, for at the height of his success, only three years after the supreme accomplishment of Trinity, an episode occurred that was hauntingly like the scandal of the Stout Street School—only worse. On a Friday afternoon in February 1891, a few minutes after students at Ebert School left their classrooms, one of its chimneys collapsed, bringing tons of brick and debris into the upper hallway. Reporters immediately got onto the story, and the *Rocky Mountain News* set out to show that the building's architect, Robert

Roeschlaub, was incompetent at best and a hazardous designer at worst.[96]

One of the most unusual twists of this near-tragedy is that Roeschlaub was a master of mechanical systems and of their integration into a building's structure. The architect, sure of his position, brought his plans to the newspaper's office to vindicate his original design. Nevertheless, the *News* took the position that he was responsible for the "faulty construction of the

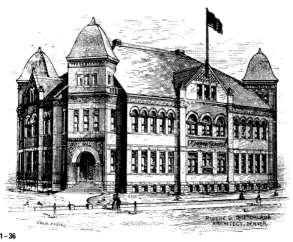

1–36

chimney" and plainly suggested that its collapse bordered on criminal negligence. In presenting its argument—a perfectly acceptable fusion, for that time, of direct reporting and editorial commentary—the paper assumed a knowledge of construction techniques that could only have come from some unknown person who was also an architect or builder.[97] The next day's issue, even more damning of Roeschlaub, cited faulty construction in the arch of the high school building and in the Haish Manual Training School.[98] Clearly, someone was feeding the *News* information explicitly to damage the architect's reputation.

Although Roeschlaub put up a calm and reasoned defense—stating persuasively that the chimney of Ebert School had stood free of problems for over a decade until a maintenance crew began tampering with its base—the words of the anonymous "Stone" turned out to be a prophetic statement of Roeschlaub's predicament: "It is so easy," the writer stated, "for an expert to implant a sense of insecurity in the public mind, through its very ignorance of technique, that unjust suspicion does incalculable injury to the reputation and business of the accused, [one] that not even the complete success of his work will eradicate."[99]

Aware of the seriousness of the newspaper's charge, Roeschlaub sought redress through official channels. The March 1891 issue of the *American Architect and Building News* included a letter by F. H. Jackson, the city inspector of buildings, stating that an investigation of the chimneys at Ebert and other East Denver schools found no "weakness in the original construction of these stacks or any crushing at the base."[100] Such vindication, announced in a professional journal, was important, but nothing appeared in the *News* during the following months to recant or modify the initial charges. So far as the wider community of Roeschlaub's clients knew, his reputation suffered from a fatal flaw—a neglectful inattention to sound construction, the most basic premise of architecture.

The effect of this episode on Roeschlaub's later work can only be guessed. Certainly it did not alter the trust that the school board, privy to the details of the event, placed in him. Immediately the board, perhaps at the suggestion of its current architect, John J. Huddart, asked Roeschlaub not only to repair the damage but to enlarge the school—a request that went far beyond a simple face-saving gesture. Nor did they fail to call upon him to design other schools in later years, despite the proven competence of Huddart, who gave them at least one distinctive new building in Swansea School (1891). Perhaps the sorriest consequence of the Ebert imbroglio was that it came at a time when the great boom had peaked, unbeknownst to any who did not realize (as few then could) that construction is one of the basic indexes of economic trends. Roeschlaub's business plummeted in the year of the Ebert chimney collapse—so much so that his known commissions fell to a quarter of the previous year's total. This, in addition to the pressures of competition and the intense personal rivalries that plagued the profession during the boom years of the late 1880s and early 1890s, made him wary and perhaps defensive, though by

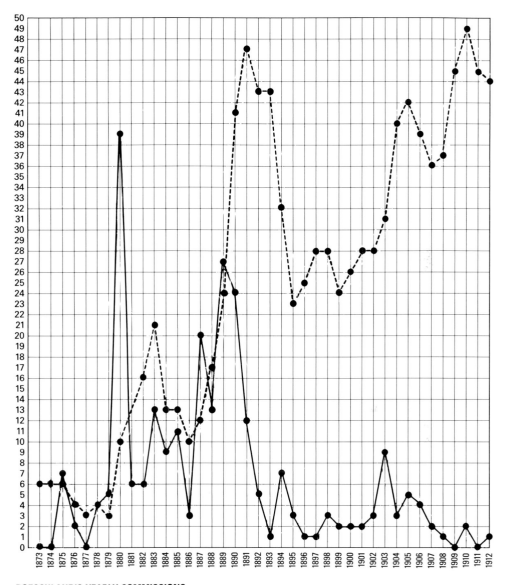

ROESCHLAUB'S YEARLY COMMISSIONS COMPARED WITH THE NUMBER OF ARCHITECTURAL FIRMS PRACTICING IN DENVER, 1873-1912

LEGEND:

-‑-‑- Number of Architects
——— RSR's Commissions

Figure 1-37
Comparison of Roeschlaub's yearly commissions with the number of architects practicing in Denver, 1873–1912 (data taken from Roeschlaub office inventory and Denver City Directory)

now he and Annie (Figs. 1–38 and 1–39) were accustomed to the conditions of an architect's life.

Fortunately this set of attitudes, which appears in some of his later correspondence, did not characterize his architecture or drive him into embittered isolation. On the contrary, Roeschlaub seems to have confronted the sorry state of architecture directly, just at a time when his own practice—for whatever reason—was in decline. This new commitment actually began two

1–38 1–39

years earlier with the establishment of a remarkable new professional journal, the *Western Architect and Building News*, under the able and inspiring leadership of Jesse B. Dorman.[101] The earliest issues are replete with references to Roeschlaub's building projects, and the support Dorman received from local architects incontestably included Roeschlaub's good will if not his active mentoring. Over its three-year history of publication, the *Western Architect* sponsored the formation

of several profession-related groups, including the Society of Civil Engineers and Architects, the Denver Architectural Sketch Club (consisting largely of draftsmen in the employ of the city's architectural firms), various trades organizations, and finally, in December 1890, the Rocky Mountain Association of Architects. Each new addition solidified the journal's respectability, and by nurturing such groups Dorman introduced one aspect of Progressive reform into Denver's complex urban life—that of professional self-esteem and the affiliation of local organizations into a national network of their counterparts.

Roeschlaub, who at the age of forty-eight was now the longest practicing architect in Denver, assumed the vice-presidency of the Rocky Mountain Association. The aims of the association addressed three of the most pressing problems facing the profession locally, all of them having in one way or another surfaced in the pages of the *Western Architect* over the previous months. The benefits of organization, it stated, were:

> *First*—To the members of the profession in establishing a more friendly relation, one with the other, and do away with those petty jealousies which, no doubt, exist to a greater or less extent. *Second*—To the public in the discussion and consideration of subjects pertaining to better building and the modification of our own building laws, that there need be no question as to their [e.g., the buildings'] proper construction. *Third*— For mutual protection from those persons who have established themselves as Architects, but who have not the slightest claim to that title other than they can draw a reasonably straight line with a two-foot rule, and present a plan which a student in an office would be ashamed to own.[102]

While these concerns of the newly formed association had a decidedly local character, they also reflected well-established assumptions that had guided the formation and development of the architectural profession nationally—namely, the elevation of architects over others less qualified by imposing standards for architectural training and practice, by more clearly defining the architect from other members of the building trades, and by encouraging mutual respect and good will among practitioners in a competitive profession.

This movement towards the identification and protection of professional interests had begun nationally at least as early as 1857 with the formation of the American Institute of Architects.[103] Denver's infant organization, which changed its name to the Colorado Association of Architects shortly before its first annual meeting in May 1891, realized early on that it had little chance of survival without affiliating itself with the prestigious national association.[104] Although it ambitiously claimed to represent architects in the "States of Colorado and Wyoming and the territories of Utah and New Mexico," the organization's first annual meeting banquet made painfully but humorously clear how disunited even Denver's own architects were. "The banquet developed one remarkable fact," stated the *Western Architect*: "That the majority of Denver architects are strangers to each other. It devolved upon each one present of introducing his right hand neighbor. A look of consternation immediately fell upon the faces of the majority of those present, and many introductions followed."[105] Within a year's time, however, the organization had applied for and received a charter as a chapter of the American Institute of Architects, and Robert S. Roeschlaub became the chapter's president. He held that position for the next twenty years, until shortly before his retirement, and actively worked to build a strong professional identity among local, regional, and national architects (Fig. 1–40).

It is ironic that just as Roeschlaub rose to prominence as head of Denver's architectural profession, his own practice fell to a scant proportion of the consistent success he had achieved in the late 1880s. In 1892, when the Colorado Chapter of the American Institute of Architects was formed, Roeschlaub received only seven known commissions, his lowest number since the depressed year of 1886. Nor was this a matter of private misfortune. Like a bellwether of what was to come, the building trades industry felt a severe downturn in 1892, months before the general economic crash of 1893, which came with the announcement that the government would no longer support the Sherman Silver Purchase Act. While jobless miners gathered in the streets and Denver's banks tottered, the city's architects left in droves. In the space of three years, half of the architectural firms that had competed so energetically for prosperous clients and boom-inspired commissions were gone. So, too, was the *Western Architect and Building News*, whose existence relied upon the subscriptions of well-to-do readers in the profession.

Equally coincidental is the fact that over the whole

1–40

span of Roeschlaub's career, the year 1893 marks only the mid-point. In retrospect, his ability thereafter to endure almost twenty years of lean commissions and a level of work that had dropped to less than half of his earlier output testifies not only to his tenacity but also the reputation he had achieved by the 1890s. This reputation—which he protected as fiercely as his Civil War record—rested on a series of important buildings that in quick succession followed the achievement of Trinity Methodist Church. Two of them, in fact, undoubtedly came from his privileged position as Trinity's architect, for they were both designed for the Methodist campus of the University of Denver.

Figure 1–40
Meeting of the Colorado Chapter of the American Institute of Architects, held at the Roeschlaub home in 1901. Seated, *left to right*, are John W. Roberts, Ernest P. Varian, Franklin E. Kidder, [?] MacLaren, Harold W. or Viggio E. Baerresen, Harlan Thomas, Eugene R. or Walter E. Rice, Albert J. Norton, and James Murdock. Standing, *left to right*, are Thomas F. Walsh, Frederick J. Sterner, William Cowe, Aaron M. Gove, and Robert S. Roeschlaub.
CHS F31205

The first was University Hall (Old Main), the initial administrative and classroom building for the university, which was erected on a desolate, sloping plain southeast of the city (Fig. 1–41) in the farsighted confidence of the trustees that the land on which it stood would eventually be filled with suburban homes and other campus buildings.[106] More derivative of Richardson and less visually complex than Roeschlaub's East Denver schools of the period, Uni-

1–41

versity Hall nevertheless exhibits his superb combination of simplicity of design with a variety of planes and surfaces (Fig. 1–42). The second building—in some respects more interesting than University Hall because it is so unusual—is the Chamberlin Observatory (Fig. 1–43), a gift to the university of Humphrey B. Chamberlin, who was one of the benefactors of Trinity Methodist Church.[107] Originally featuring a balcony that encircled the tower portion of the two-story structure and integrated the arched entranceway with the rest, the observatory took better than three years to complete (1888–92) and was perhaps one of the most challenging of Roeschlaub's projects. As it evolved, he may have adapted ideas from published plans of the Goodsell Observatory, completed in 1887 for Carleton College in Minnesota,[108] and he consulted with DU's noted professor of astronomy, Herbert A. Howe,

whose University Park home he designed at the edge of the observatory's park in 1891.

These buildings Roeschlaub looked upon as among the best examples of his work when in the depressed mid-1890s he was invited to contribute a biographical article to Frank Hall's *History of the State of Colorado*.[109] Besides these—and, of course, Trinity Methodist Church—two others also ranked high in his estimation: the State School for the Deaf and Blind in

1–42

Colorado Springs (Fig. 1–44) and the State Normal School (Cranford Hall) at what is now the University of Northern Colorado (Fig. 1–45). Both buildings were designed in the highly productive period of the late 1880s, and a comparison of the two reveals that Roeschlaub was turning away from Victorian Gothic, Richardsonian, and Queen Anne styles to a more formal classicism. The School for the Deaf and Blind, though still essentially Gothic, is sedate and regular, its two entrance bays marked quite as much by formal staircases, balconies, and shallow arches as by peaked gables. Cranford Hall carries a direct interest in classicism much further. This, according to one scholar, "was

Figure 1–41
An artist's rendering of Denver, looking north, captures the isolation of University Park. Roeschlaub's University Hall and Chamberlin Observatory are visible at middle right.
CHS F1402

Figure 1–42
From the north, University Hall, 1890, bears a close resemblance to H. H. Richardson's Sever Hall at Harvard, 1880.
Courtesy Peter A. Dulan

a key document in a portfolio of Roeschlaub designs that rejected the brash 'Frenchified' post–Civil War General Grant mode of architecture and replaced it with a classicism that was neither timidly old-fashioned...nor rigidly academic."[110]

If these were the highest achievements of Roeschlaub's mid-career, however, there were many other buildings—schools, terraces, churches, and houses—that illustrate the same restless pursuit of new ideas while expressing in their final form a simple dignity and independence from any stylistic creed or fashion. His freedom to experiment seems most visible in his schools, which he continued to produce for the East Denver district as a contract architect, and resulted in plans that were strikingly different variations on the underlying theme that he first conceptualized in the Whittier School of 1883. Some, like the Wyman School of 1890 (Fig. 1–46), blended Romanesque strength with Renaissance austerity. In fact, the preliminary plans for this school, which were later changed, featured a number of motifs later found in the Classic Revival buildings of McKim, Mead and White. Others built throughout the 1890s—Columbine in 1891, Lafayette (Maria Mitchell) in 1898, and Clayton (Stevens) in 1899—individualized certain aspects of Roeschlaub's repertoire, from the treatment of main bays and windows to the balanced distribution of parts and the emphasis given to the location and character of entrances (Figs. 3–38, 3–43, and 3–48).

Perhaps the most surprising architectural experiment of all, given Aaron Gove's conviction that education should teach the liberal arts and avoid the narrowness of vocational training,[111] is Roeschlaub's design for the Manual Training High School (1893), a highly rationalized set of planes and flat surfaces that epitomized industrial work. Clearly, for Roeschlaub an industrial arts school needed little or nothing but its clean, rational shape to announce its purpose (Fig. 3–47).

The same thing could be said of Roeschlaub's last school—or, at least, the last in which he took a personal hand. This was Pueblo's Central High School (1905), a large, exceptionally clean design that was unified by a wide, horizontal facade capped with a low

dome (never built) and superbly terminated with graceful, rounded ends (PLATE 19). This building, like the less ambitious libraries at the University of Denver and the University of Northern Colorado, both built during the following two years, represents Roeschlaub's smooth transition from the Victorian eclecticism to the flowering of Classic Revival architecture at the turn of the century—almost as if his own more generally classical principles of restraint, balance,

1–43

and cleanliness of line had simply waited for architectural tastes and styles to catch up with him. Most impressive is his consistency as a designer and his almost total absorption in the details of architecture—from the look of a building and the logic of its plan to matters of heating, ventilation, and the movement of people.[112] If Roeschlaub was not an innovator like his

Figure 1–43
Chamberlin Observatory
University of Denver, 1889
W. H. Jackson photograph
CHS J3825

well-known contemporary, H. H. Richardson, he was definitely a stylist who impressed his own personality on almost every building he created.

By now almost sixty, Roeschlaub designed his final buildings with the energy of an architect half his age—and perhaps double the wisdom. If taken alone, his stylistic development seems to have been confident, aware, and principled—unaffected by the vagaries of fashion or the understandable self-consciousness of a

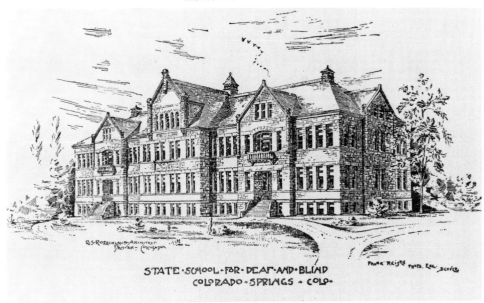

1-44

STATE·SCHOOL·FOR·DEAF·AND·BLIND
COLORADO·SPRINGS·COLO

1-45

Figure 1-44
State School for the Deaf and Blind
Colorado Springs, 1890
CHS F31249

Figure 1-45
Cranford Hall (Old Main)
University of Northern Colorado, 1889
CHS F14304

regional architect who lived far from the sources of architectural thought. At the very least, his architecture was urbane and knowledgeable, and his professional contacts across the nation increased as he continued to represent the Colorado Chapter of the American Institute of Architects. In 1900, in fact, he was made a Fellow of the Institute, the first in Colorado.

Yet the extraordinary sluggish economy of the 1890s had slowed his practice almost to a standstill, and though far more secure than he had been in the late 1870s, the prospect of few yearly commissions carried the suggestion of a practice in decline. This may have been in the back of his mind when he composed his autobiographical account for Hall's *History* in 1895. Speaking of his past school designs, he states that

"some of these edifices have been pronounced by competent critics the finest models in the world."

If this fact had not been widely recognized in the educational literature of the United States, Germany and England, the statement would appear extravagant. It is undoubtedly true that no other American architect has been so largely commended for the excellence of his designs, and the uniform superiority of construction.... Copies of [my school plans] have been sent to England and Germany, at the request of the educational authorities of those governments, and several buildings were erected from them. Other copies have been furnished nearly every state of our Union [Vol. 4, p. 551].

Doubtful as are the inflated claims of nineteenth-century entrepreneurs and professionals, who often embellished their accomplishments for just such publications, Roeschlaub's words once again carry a ring of truth. Despite the large number and variety of buildings that he designed during the expansive years of the late 1880s and early 1890s, his schools had been the backbone of his reputation, and now he sought refuge in their worthiness when few other clients made demands upon his skills (Fig. 1–47).

The vulnerability of Roeschlaub's pride in his schools manifested itself more acutely several years later, when a member of the East Denver school board, or perhaps the current architect, criticized the work that he had done. Only Aaron Gove's letter to Roeschlaub remains to suggest the actual incident, but it reveals how deeply the accusation—real or imagined—had cut the architect, who had so deftly responded to the newspaper's charges in the Ebert chimney incident more than ten years before. "My Dear Roeschlaub," Gove wrote,

> No man is more pleased than I to know of the work of the summer for you; no hour of my life has ever passed in which I have not confidence, admiration and respect for you in every way, who taught me all about architecture that I know. In my judgment no better architect of schoolhouses lives than yourself. I have heard no comment detrimental to you or your reputation. . . .
>
> You will never find the time when you cannot call upon me for anything that one friend can do for another, and you may depend that if any opportunity occurs where an attack is made or defense required with regard to integrity, ability, or truth I shall rush into the conflict with all my might to defend and protect. A man's life devoted as yours has been, to one client, cannot be smirched by the vapors of transient, new and strange comers.[113]

In spite of his confidence in his work, Roeschlaub as he grew older became more sensitive to slights and less capable of diffusing criticism, implied or expressed. In 1907 he sent an indignant letter to his old friend Henry A. Buchtel, chancellor of the University of Denver and governor of the state, complaining that certain buildings had been taken out of his hands and that the development of the campus should be under the

direction of one architect—namely, himself.[114] Yet for all his proud and defiant gestures of this sort, his attachment to the profession and to its practitioners grew steadily, and his colleagues elected him, two years later, to the rank of first licensed architect in Colorado.

By the early 1900s the tempo of construction in Denver had begun to increase, and Roeschlaub's commissions, which had so far conformed to the low level of economic activity, did likewise. Now, however, the ratio between Denver's population of architects and Roeschlaub's number of commissions—a comparative indication of his business performance in the face of

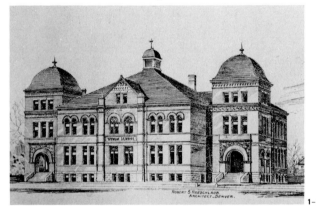

1–46

increasing competition—rose abruptly around 1903 and then returned to the pattern of three or four a year. For some time his third son, Frank, had worked as a draftsman for the firm, and in 1902, with business increasing, Roeschlaub made him a full partner.

In the meantime, he continued to pursue work throughout Colorado, whether large or small. For every Central High School or Carnegie Library, he designed several smaller buildings and worked on improvements for others. Plans for three Greeley schools, the Weld County Hospital, and the president's home at the University of Northern Colorado became a part of his office's files, as did the Eaton Bank (1907) and the Salida Ward School (1903). Two unusual residences also eventually showed up on the office's inventory, one for John

Figure 1–46
Wyman (Wyatt) School, rendering
Denver, 1890
CHS F49440

37

Henderson in Elko, Nevada, and another for William Byrd Page in Green Spring Valley, Maryland. Of his confirmed designs, most were residences and small office blocks, such as one for Dr. F. Gengenbach (1903), the I. F. Williams Store in the location of the old Elephant Corral on Wazee Street, and a duplex for Mary C. Michael (1901), his neighbor directly to the south on Delaware.

Among his best buildings of the later period, however, three stand out—the First Congregational Church in Denver (1907), the new Greeley High School (1911), and the last project before his retirement, the Isis Theater (1912). Once again in search of new forms, Roeschlaub looked to the Italian Lombard style for the church, constructing its graceful arches and decorative corbels with light-colored, smooth-faced brick thinly mortared (Fig. 2–29).[115] The Greeley High School returned to a sedate classicism (Fig. 3–49), and for its rendering Roeschlaub had the assistance of a new member of the firm, Robert K. Fuller, who came to the office in the spring of 1910 with the expressed purpose of working for a man of his reputation. The son of Montezuma W. Fuller of Fort Collins, also an architect of longstanding in Colorado, Robert Fuller brought with him a sound knowledge of engineering and an architectural temperament similar to Roeschlaub's. As a result, the last two buildings in which Roeschlaub had a significant hand also bore the stamp of his eventual successor, Robert Fuller (Fig. 1–48).[116]

The Isis Theater, on which Roeschlaub, his son Frank, and Robert Fuller all worked (Fig. 1–49), is as uncharacteristic of the architect's lifetime restraint and sobriety of design as Shakespeare's last play, *The Tempest*, is of the playwright's monumental dramas. Both, however, seem appropriate masques expressing a closing statement of the evanescence of life. The Isis gave Roeschlaub an opportunity that was quite unlike anything he had done before, and its exuberant shell-like facade and glittering acceptance of the new era of the motion picture bear an uncanny reminder of Prospero's statement:

> Our revels are now ended. These our actors,
> As I foretold you, were all spirits, and

Figure 1–47
Roeschlaub, *right*, and his good friends and colleagues Aaron Gove *left*, and James K. Baker, *center*, stand before the entrance to East Denver High School.
CHS F49605

> Are melted into air, into thin air.
> And, like the baseless fabric of this vision,
> The cloud-capped towers, the gorgeous palaces,
> The solemn temples, the great globe itself—
> Yea, all which it inherit—shall dissolve
> And, like this insubstantial pageant faded,
> Leave not a rack behind. We are such stuff
> As dreams are made on, and our little life
> Is rounded with a sleep [Act 4, Sc. 1, 148]

Roeschlaub must also have been aware that Isis represented a wholly new kind of city—one that looked forward to the automobile, the motion picture, and the skyscraper—than the one he had lived in for forty years. Even though he had consistently accepted change and new technology—his was one of the first offices in Denver to install a telephone in 1879—he did not have the energy or strength to sustain another ten years of creative architectural design.

This was apparent, when, after moving to a smaller house at 439 Lafayette Street, Robert and Annie had to face leaving their beloved city on the advice of Roeschlaub's doctor. The architect's physical problems are unknown, but they were serious enough to force the couple to move to San Diego soon after the Isis was completed. Roeschlaub gave up his presidency of the Colorado Chapter of the American Institute of Architects, left his home in the custody of his children, and retired with Annie to the West Coast (Fig. 1–50).

Roeschlaub's years of retirement are wholly personal. Very little of his thought, let alone his activities, comes down through the historical record. Of a certainty he gave up the practice of architecture completely, although his professional ties remained strong. One of his companions from the most active of his Denver years was William Quayle, another retired architect who had been Roeschlaub's counterpart in Denver's School District 2, which encompassed the north part of the city and included the Ashland (North) High School. A second vital contact with Denver was Roeschlaub's son Frank, who visited his father often, leaving the care of the firm in the hands of Robert Fuller, now Frank's partner and the man who gradually assumed the role of the firm's senior member. Most of all, however, were the older architects of Denver, many of whom could still identify Roeschlaub's buildings throughout the city and who remembered the contribution he had made to their profession. On the night of January 24, 1920, they honored him at a dinner of the former members of the Triangle Club.

When Roeschlaub received a letter from his colleagues containing the sentiments that were expressed that night, his response showed how long he had been away and how much his life had changed. "My dear old Friends," it began,

I wonder if you ever had your hearts stirred by memories of pleasure, evidences of Friendships leal and true after many years, a newborn joy, as my heart was stirred, when there came out of the darkness of my days, your words of kind remembrance. . . . I speak of —you may not know that I have [lost] my sight and sit in total darkness. It is a great affliction. . . . To see and now to sit in darkness, is indeed a trial which can only be borne with the help of Him who shares our burdens for the asking.

1–49

1–48

Of all these pictures which memory paints before me in all their brilliant hues, upon my dark canvass, none [is] more brilliant or dearer to my inward vision [than] the genuine, true-hearted Friendship that has always been shown me by every one of you gentlemen. And now, though nearly a decade has passed since my exile, out over the years comes to me your words of commendation, condolence, and well wishes.[117]

Almost lost in this poignant revelation of his blindness is Roeschlaub's matter-of-fact reference to living in exile—a state of mind that suggests how much he loved and missed the city of Denver and regarded it still as his home. In fact, had he been able to see the city in 1920, his unflagging confidence in its potential, coupled with his unique, humanistic view of architecture, would have undoubtedly led him to approve of its new directions.

One of these had to do with his own firm and the other with a recent form of architectural eclecticism that Roeschlaub had himself anticipated in the late 1890s. After almost twenty years in the service of the

Figure 1–48
Grand opening of the Isis Theater Denver, 1912
CHS F15489

Figure 1–49
Drafting studio of Roeschlaub and Son in the Foster Building, 1911. From left to right are Robert K. Fuller, Sidney G. Frazier, and William F. Hollings.
CHS F31210

firm, Frank Roeschlaub made it clear to his father that he was leaving the profession. Given his son's extended visits to San Diego, this news perhaps came as no shock to the retired architect, and he may have recalled that his own father had left a successful practice in Bavaria at about the same age—or that, while a much younger man, he himself departed from the family tradition to announce that architecture, not medicine, was to be his life's career. In any case, Frank Roeschlaub left the firm to Robert Fuller, who wisely kept the Roeschlaub name—as Roeschlaub and Fuller—until 1917, when his own success had gathered enough momentum to effect a transition from the reputation of Robert Roeschlaub's name to that of his own.

As for Denver's architectural development, Roeschlaub would have had to go against his own principles to find fault with the results of the City Beautiful movement that began under the administration of Mayor Robert Speer, who entered office long before the architect had retired and whose accomplishments by 1920 had laid the groundwork for a core of civic buildings, an extensive park system, and a host of other improvements.[118] Meanwhile, the austerity imposed on Denver during the 1890s had resulted in the development of the American Foursquare (or "Denver Square")—a middle-class home of imposing size but little ornamental pretension—and finer houses that borrowed their character from a variety of sources—Spanish Colonial, Mediterranian, American Colonial, and English Tudor. Nothing, really, had changed in American preferences from the period of the late 1880s, when Roeschlaub chastised his fellow architects for catering to temporary styles; yet he would have approved of the restraint and traditional adaptations of such firms as Fisher and Fisher, who replaced Edbrooke as the trend-setters in downtown architecture, or a host of other architects who continued to refine the language of period architecture up to the 1930s.

Yet, gradually losing his eyesight during the years of his retirement, and totally blind by 1920, Roeschlaub could not have attempted to keep up with developments in the nation's architecture after World War I, even if he had wanted to. By the time of his death in

1–50

1923,[119] the spirit of eclecticism was very much alive in Denver, as it was in the rest of the country. The years of prosperity which marked urban life during the 1920s produced a new generation of homes and public buildings that in one way or another drew upon historical antecedents that became finer and more exact in direct proportion to the wealth, knowledge, and taste of the client.

All this Roeschlaub would have understood as an evolution of architecture, based on references to the past, that by degrees raised Denver from its lowly beginnings into a metropolis that could stand on an equal footing with any other in the United States. What he may not have known, at the time of his death, was that the forces of technology would so revolutionize daily life throughout the nation that no city would stand apart, except for the character of its geography, and the once-vital business called "pioneering" would be regarded as a quaint or romantic vestige of the nation's past.

The transformation was so complete that by the mid-1920s Robert Roeschlaub and the work he had done for Denver during the previous half century were almost completely forgotten, even though his major buildings stood throughout the city and state. Remarkably, a historical account of Colorado's architecture, edited in 1927 by his one-time friend and colleague, James Baker, totally ignored the contributions of Roeschlaub, Edbrooke, and many of the other architects of the previous generation, concentrating instead on the work of more contemporary designers. Ten years later, a history of the state, funded by the WPA, made only the briefest mention of Denver's pioneer architects.[120] It would be thirty years, in fact, before Roeschlaub's name would again appear in the newspapers—at a time when the extremes of modernism for its own sake raised unprecedented concerns about the destruction of Denver's architectural heritage. Yet, even as the Gottesleben Mansion, one of Roeschlaub's most impressive homes, was being razed in the late 1960s, the architect's plans and drawings lay intact in the files of the firm that he had established in 1873, a remarkable legacy of architecture in the emerging West of the nineteenth century.

Color Plates

PLATE 1
Hamill Residence
Georgetown, Colorado
Expanded, 1879
Bryan E. McCay

PLATE 2
Second Empire House
Project, date unknown

41

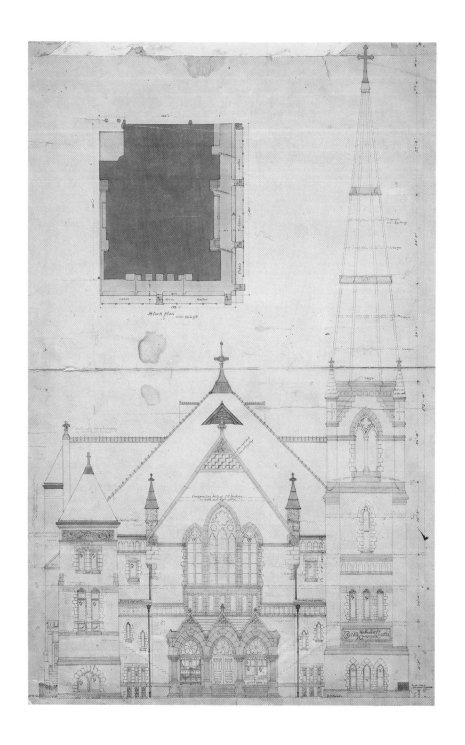

PLATE 4
Trinity Methodist Church
Interior: half elevation of screen and
detail of proscenium arch

43

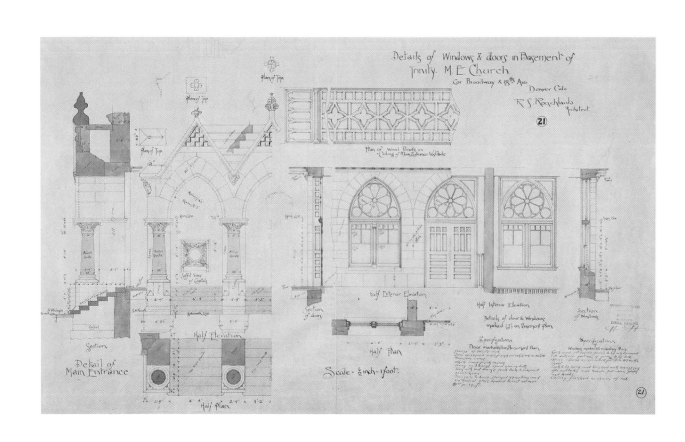

PLATE 5
Trinity Methodist Church
Details of main entrance

PLATE 6
Trinity Methodist Church
Main entrance, Broadway
Peter A. Dulan

45

A

B

C

PLATE 7
Trinity Methodist Church
Detail of stained-glass windows
By Healy and Millet, Chicago
David Diaz Guerrero

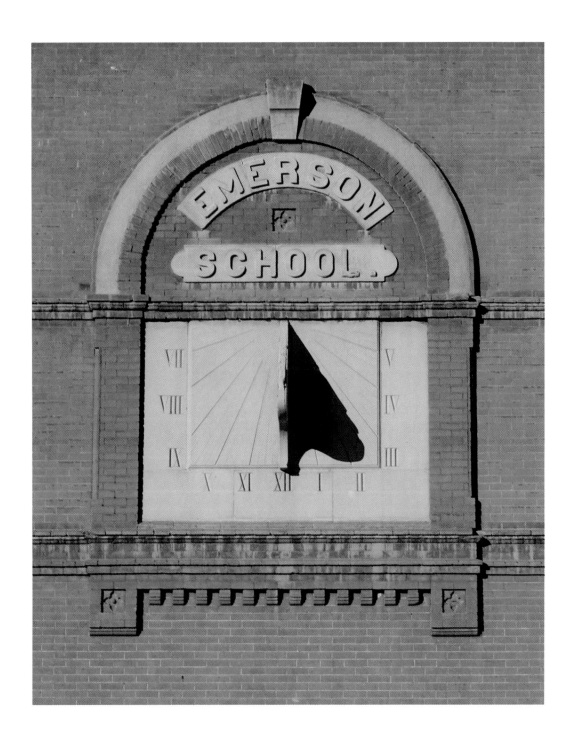

PLATE 8
Emerson School
Denver, 1884
Detail of sundial
Peter A. Dulan

47

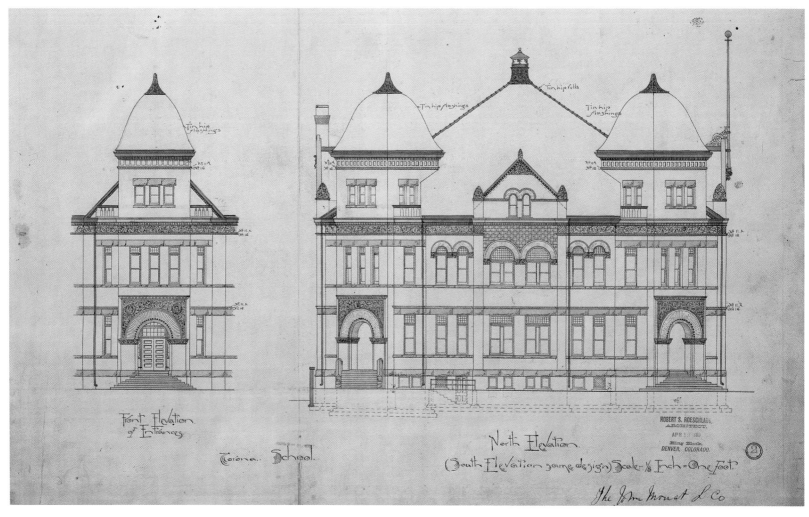

Front Elevation
of Entrances

Corona School.

North Elevation
(South Elevation same design) Scale-⅛ Inch=One Foot.

ROBERT S. ROESCHLAUB,
ARCHITECT.
APR 17 89
King Block,
DENVER, COLORADO.

The John Mouat L Co

PLATE 9
Corona (Dora Moore) School
Denver, 1889
North and east elevations

PLATE 10
Corona School, 1889
West elevation

Toronto School.   Front or West Elevation.   Scale ⅛ Inch = One Foot.

PLATE 11
Corona School, 1889
Detail of upper elevation
Peter A. Dulan

PLATE 12
University Hall
University of Denver
Denver, 1890
Greg Tzinberg

PLATE 13
University Hall, 1890
Front elevation
Peter A. Dulan

Scale ⅛" = One foot.

=Union·Ave·Elevation=   SEP 8 1889

CENTRAL BLOCK,
PUEBLO
for Thurlow

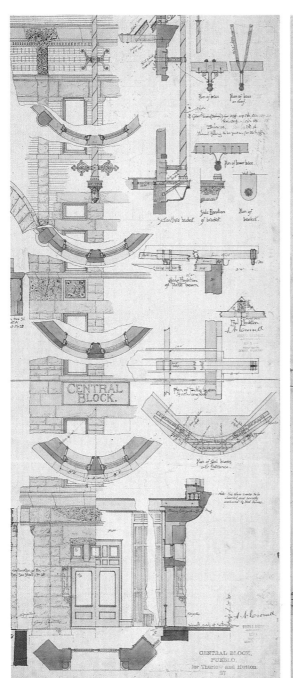

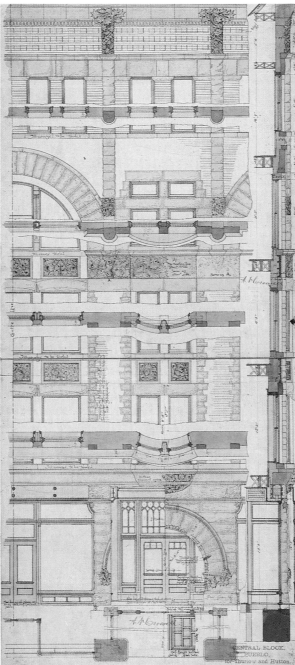

PLATE 14
Central Block
(Thurlow and Hutton Building)
Pueblo, 1889
Elevation

PLATE 15
Central Block, 1889
Details of elevation

53

PLATE 16
Clayton (Stevens) School
Denver, 1889–1900
Entrance
Greg Tzinberg

54

PLATE 17
Carnegie Library
University of Denver
Denver, 1906
Detail
Francine Haber

PLATE 18
Carnegie Library, 1906
Peter A. Dulan

55

PLATE 19
Central High School
Pueblo, 1905

The Architecture

By Francine Haber

R O E S C H L A U B

Robert Sawers Roeschlaub was the consummate urban architect. From the time he arrived in Denver in 1873, he imposed his vision of the city on the newly developing Front Range. This vision was one of an architecture of institutions which carried the inherited cultural association of civilization to the neutral grids of young western cities. As a coherent body of work, his school designs were his most significant contribution to the development of an architectural building type. Yet he also created urban monuments in designs for the Central Presbyterian Church (1875), Trinity Methodist Episcopal Church (1887-88), and theaters such as the prominent opera house in Central City (1878) and the Isis cinema (1911). As a backdrop to these special places of civic and social ritual, he designed commercial buildings that reinforced the human scale and urban setting of the street. With two exceptions—the Central Block of Pueblo (1889) and the W. A. Hover Wholesale Drug Warehouse in Denver (1901)—these were less individualized works. His enormous output in the design of residences mostly follows national and local vernacular models in contrast to the original stamp of his institutional work.

As to the question of Roeschlaub's national stature, he gained a reputation, first and foremost, for his school architecture. Furthermore, as a contributor to the Sullivanesque in the West, Roeschlaub employed Healy and Millet, the Chicago firm of interior decorators which often worked with Louis Sullivan. Roeschlaub was a worthy practitioner in the American Arts and Crafts movement. Trinity Methodist Church and the Central Block demonstrate stylistic evidence of this Colorado-Chicago connection, both erected while Dankmar Adler and Louis Sullivan attended to their opera house in Pueblo.

To the extent that Roeschlaub effected a regional architecture from the eclecticism of the 1870s and early 1880s, he used indigenous materials, such as Castle Rock lava, based on local geology and landscape—a practice not exclusive to this architect. This regional Colorado identity began in fact in 1879 with the construction of the Twenty-fourth Street School, the first stone schoolhouse in Denver. His later work, from about 1887 to 1891, influenced by H. H. Richardson, emphasized the rugged grandeur and intrinsic beauty of this native stone.

In contrast to this theme of a regional architectural identity, Roeschlaub was well known for his mastery of up-to-date technology—a progressive and cosmopolitan point of view. For approximately twenty years after his arrival in Colorado, his architectural hallmark was the integration of heating, ventilation, and lighting systems into the aesthetics of his buildings. In the heyday of his largest commissions in the late 1880s, Roeschlaub's architecture was distinguished by the care, profusion, and exquisite design of details overlaid in public buildings by a unique and insistent symmetry and spatial complexity.

In the end, however, Roeschlaub was influenced—as was the entire American architectural community—by the idealism and dignified coherence of the planning and architecture of the classical White City presented at the World's Columbian Exposition of 1893 in Chicago. Lastly, Roeschlaub was a talented draftsman. His drawings survive as prized documents of the building arts of the late nineteenth century. As founder of the sixth oldest architectural firm in continuous practice in the United States, Roeschlaub was a significant figure in the ranks of American architectural history.

Churches

Society must have its sacred spaces. So integral to the symbolic image of the city is the physical presence of churches that, prior to the twentieth century, they may be considered primary monuments or essential urban forms. Church architecture for Roeschlaub was exclusively medieval, made up of lancet and rose windows, or turrets and lattice-topped pinnacles. As the nineteenth-century Gothic Revival in America took over a cultural memory of a European past that it had

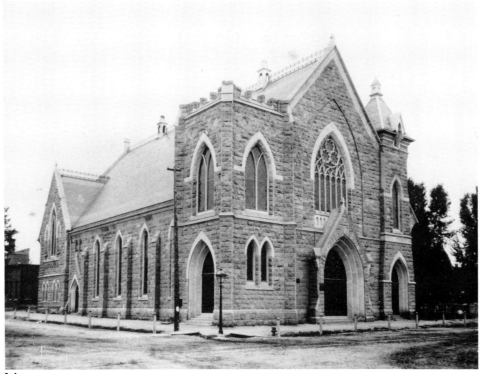

2–1

not shared in fact,[1] Roeschlaub extended this set of received meanings to help define the city of the emerging West. From 1875 to 1907 in Colorado Springs, Denver, and Pueblo, he designed and built major structures for the Congregationalists, Episcopalians, Presbyterians, and Methodists.

Roeschlaub's parish churches loomed over the towns of their day. His stylistic evolution progressed from High Victorian Gothic to an eclectic "scissors-and-paste" fascination with neo-Romanesque (later to

mature into an original adaptation of the clarity of forms inherent in the Romanesque as practiced by H. H. Richardson), to the "modern Gothic" and Arts and Crafts, and, finally, to an eccentric postscript in a Lombard Gothic mode. Of greater significance, true for all his building types, is a change from crude but effective architectural signs or images at the beginning of his career to mastery of a complex architectural vocabulary. A brief perusal reveals a series of connections between the different churches. Repetition, parallelism, and typology are understood as key devices for communicating meaning. For example, all of Roeschlaub's churches are on corner sites; their organization is longitudinal or cruciform, static or dynamic; and all integrate the spire-tower element within the body of the church. Above all, Roeschlaub was interested in the relationship between town and church. These themes elucidate his work, regardless of style.

Central Presbyterian Church, built in 1876 at Eighteenth and Champa (Fig. 2–1), had a curious history. As its membership grew beyond the confines of its first church building, and with the arrival of a new religious leader, the Reverend Willis Lord, in February 1875, the congregation made plans for a new building.[2] The commission went to Robert Roeschlaub, a member of the congregation, later that same year. Although the new church was originally estimated to cost $32,000, it turned out to be an expensive enterprise, closer to $50,000.[3]

The congregation remained in the church at Eighteenth and Champa for sixteen years, but by the early 1890s, with a sizable increase in its numbers and the expansion of the commercial district into the neighborhood, it was ready for a new and larger home.[4] Central Presbyterian moved to a new church at 1660 Sherman Street, and the old church building and its furnishings were sold to the Twenty-third Avenue congregation for a nominal sum. On December 28, 1890, farewell services were held in the old building, which soon thereafter "was carefully taken down and removed to the new location [at Twenty-third and Ogden], there being rebuilt in the same form and . . . rededicated to the same uses and purposes" (Fig. 2–2).[5] Until destroyed by fire

Figure 2–1
Central Presbyterian Church
Denver, 1875
CHS F30976

in 1906, "the mellow old building," now renamed the Twenty-third Avenue Presbyterian Church, continued to be used as a place of worship.[6]

Central Presbyterian Church was "clearly a young man's building," a provincial variation on a style that "shows considerable influence from English High Victorian Gothic churches."[7] With its pointed arches consistently shaping the windows and doorway, it is the only instance of the Middle Pointed Style uniformly

2-2

applied by Roeschlaub to his churches. It is the most singularly Gothic, too, in its attempt at verticality—a somewhat failed attempt in the work as built—conveyed by a central nave which appears high and narrow, squeezed between the square corner tower and

a secondary flanking vestigial tower with hipped roof and dormer window.

This is a plain building. The walls are buttressed but there are no clerestory windows. Each high style flourish stands out in isolation, the charm and definition of the provincial. One can see this in the intricacy of the west window with its six delicate, slender lancets intertwined with triple circles within a circle, a typical Gothic sense of interdependency of parts found nowhere else on this church. So, too, the roof lozenges or diamond shapes and striations are conventional elements in the High Victorian Gothic repertoire that exhibit a taste for multicolored patterning.

The tower, truncated and stubby, terminates in a crenelated parapet, a Norman detail favored by Roeschlaub in his first churches. In the earliest church architecture of the American Gothic Revival in the 1840s and 1850s, Norman appeared side by side with detailing from later centuries of the middle ages. Authentic historical models for the battlemented parapet were available—mostly English sources but also some German and Italian Gothic, which were incorporated into the earliest phase of the ecclesiastical nineteenth-century Gothic Revival.[8]

Central Presbyterian is the first example of what was to be Roeschlaub's formula for a town church. A square tower base is firmly planted on the street and building corner. This organization occurs in all five of his known churches. In this early model of the type, the simple nave provides a strong longitudinal orientation. On the principal west facade there is a struggle for dominance between entry and tower as the main focal point. The relationship to street and city is not yet resolved, although this awkwardness has the charm of youth.

There is greater pretension in the architect's proposed design, which had a spire (Fig. 2–3). A third story with triple window openings added to the tower's base, plus the very height of the spire itself, would have resolved the problems of dominance. The form of the spire was modeled on familiar sources that go back to A. W. Pugin's St. Oswald's (Liverpool, England, 1839–42) and in the United States to Richard Upjohn's St. Mary's Church (Burlington, New Jersey, 1846–48),

Figure 2–2
Twenty-third Avenue Church
(Reconstructed from Central
Presbyterian Church)
Denver, c. 1890

59

and was common architectural currency by 1875. The earlier ecclesiastics preferred the regularity of a spire over the central crossing, or in the middle of the west front, but its placement at the front corner of the church was typical of Roeschlaub's time.

The intellectual background of the High Victorian Gothic, on the evidence of this work, hardly preoccupied the architect. He was not reforming the Victorian city but creating one. The building is conserva-

tive in a basic sense, carrying with it the importance of civilized life in a town still new and building.

Colorado's prosperity in the late 1880s accounts for the nearly simultaneous appearance of three Roeschlaub

churches between 1887 and 1890: St. Peter's in Pueblo, Trinity Methodist Episcopal Church in Denver, and the First Presbyterian Church in Colorado Springs. The elements of a square-based tower and parapet Roeschlaub used again in two proposals for the ultimately unexecuted project for St. Peter's Church of the late 1880s (Figs. 2–4 and 2–5). In the ambitious first scheme, known only as St. Peter's alternate design (1887), Roeschlaub tried once more for a spire. The relationship between tower and spire in the rendering—in particular how the tapered spire sits well within the borders of the four-sided base with a crenelated parapet—can be traced back to 1850 in Frank Wills's proposed Trinity Church of San Francisco (although Wills's example was polygonal). Also at Wills's church, and new in Roeschlaub's repertoire, is the buttressing of the tower. The spire's general form is modeled indirectly on another quintessential early American Gothic Revival precedent, John Notman's Philadelphia town church, St. Mark's (1847).[9] The type of spire—a broach spire, an octagon rising directly from a tower without any intervening feature—had been in continuous use ever since.

But it is the variation and development possible within a church typology rather than precedent which occupies Roeschlaub's interest. St. Peter's first alternate design is an extravaganza. The project looks as if Roeschlaub thought he had more money than he knew what to do with—and, indeed, a "real estate boom in 1887," states a recent writer, "is credited with splitting St. Peter's congregation. Because of wild speculation with church property, many members left the group.... Shortly after the split, St. Peter's Church asked the groups [to] unite, but because of the debts and shaky financial arrangements at St. Peter's the new group said no."[10] Roeschlaub's clients, it turns out, were the dreamers and spendthrifts.

In the first scheme there are three Norman towers as well as full transepts, a substantial rectory behind the church, and a parish house on the opposite side flanking the composition like book ends. Roeschlaub starts with a design that is fundamentally the same building as the earlier Central Presbyterian—exterior buttressing along a long nave, a high roof, fancy Late

2-3

Figure 2-3
Central Presbyterian Church
Original conception with spire
Denver, 1875
Courtesy Sandra Dallas Atchison

Gothic tracery in a pronounced pointed arch with vertical emphasis on the main facade, and a tower pulled out to mark the front corner. This is Roeschlaub's most randomly eclectic church in attitude and style. It is an agglomeration of Gothic and Romanesque motifs. The semicircular half-apse, jammed against the west facade, hints of experimentation with the new neo-Romanesque of pure mass, but the whole looks old-fashioned.

2–4

The second and final design for St. Peter's, as published in 1890,[11] is unencumbered by subsidiary towers; some Gothic detailing appears, but there is a new feeling to it, definitely one of the solidity of the neo-Romanesque. More importantly, Roeschlaub closed up the main facade. Substituting five stepped lancet windows for open Gothic tracery leaves a sheer rough wall surface, a stronger foil for the semicircular

form below. Now the nave is long and low; the whole strong composition has a breadth which steps up to the tower. Although there is no spire, the tower is complete in itself. There is greater resolution of hierarchical elements—the tower takes precedence as both entrance and mediator to the town. There are also two doorways in the tower porch; the corner now easily draws people in, a neat solution to the problem of a corner site. The seductive quality of the drawing

2–5

emphasizes the intended shadowed surface of ashlar coursing. This is the most interesting and concluding work of Roeschlaub's tower church types that include long naves.

Trinity Methodist Episcopal Church (1887–88)—now Trinity United Methodist Church—is Robert Roeschlaub's masterpiece (Fig. 2–6, PLATE 3) of church design. It represents one of those felicitous circumstances in the history of architecture in which an enlightened client insisted on the most perfect work

Figure 2–4
St. Peter's Church (Pueblo)
Project, 1887
CHS F44838

Figure 2–5
St. Peter's Church (Pueblo)
Project, c. 1887
CHS F44747

2–6

possible from the architect. Dedication to quality inspired both the architect and his patrons—Denver's oldest Methodist congregation.[12] In fact, the congregation had already enjoyed a tradition of fine church architecture. In 1886 the members of the Lawrence Street Methodist Episcopal Church, as it was then known, worshipped in a 450-seat brick church building on the corner of Fourteenth and Lawrence streets. Built in 1864, it was one of the most sophisticated structures in Denver, typical of the earlier, more literal phase of the Gothic Revival in America.[13]

About October 1886, in response to a demographic shift in its membership, the congregation decided to build a new church in the growing, prosperous area of Capitol Hill, to which many members of the congregation had moved. Its capable and exuberant pastor, Dr. Henry Augustus Buchtel, newly appointed, was the catalyst and sustainer of the project. Early minutes of the board of trustees and building committee show that he had a committed group of parishioners around him who consistently donated time, money, property, and especially intelligent supervision to every aspect of the building process.[14] Costly options, including the spire were to be included: "It was decided then to erect a first class building, substantial in construction, artistic in design, and above all, to make it complete in every detail, even to the hitching posts on the street."[15]

Roeschlaub was chosen as the building's architect—without, it seems, any competition. He is first mentioned at a board of trustees' meeting on November 16, 1886, when the board instructed the building committee "to make definite arrangements" with the architect "for plans for a new church Building." Beginning in December 1886 and throughout the initial stages of construction, the trustees met often in Roeschlaub's office at the King Block. Of the several sketches that depicted the very first intentions for the building in late 1886 and early 1887, none survive. However, the original scheme was reported to have been a rather plain stone building providing for a parsonage and 700 seats. In March 1887 the firm of Geddis and Seerie was awarded the subcontract for the foundations and stonework. Roeschlaub's foundation plans also date from March, which means that by then

Trinity's definitive structure had already been conceived. At one point, independently of Roeschlaub, the trustees made construction decisions with Geddis and Seerie, and in a March 21 letter the architect took issue with their action; thereafter the specifications were renegotiated along the lines of his suggestions. From this point on, Roeschlaub exerted the normal prerogatives of an architect, signing off at every stage of construction. Relations with his strong-willed and

2–7

ever-vigilant clients proved to be felicitous.

According to the tradition of this Methodist congregation, fine music was to complement the building's architectural excellence, and their wish for a magnificent organ and choir eventually necessitated a larger building. Accordingly, on April 25 Roeschlaub was instructed to change the plans of the new church. The trustees also decided to build the parsonage on another site, which added more seating capacity to the church and accommodated the organ.[16] A perspective drawing of an intermediary scheme survives (see cover illustration). Modifications between this and the church as it was built—a change from gable to hip roof over the northwest stairwell and the omission of a picturesque turret and secondary spire on the southeast elevation—increase the overall impression that Roeschlaub did not wish for frills in decorating an overtly Gothic style. His drawings for all final plans, elevations, cross-sections, and detailing are dated August 3, 1887,[17] and the cornerstone was laid on September 5,[18] the first Labor Day officially celebrated in the state of Colorado.

Trinity Methodist Church is a work in which contradictory demands were made on the architect to achieve the requirements of the building's program and its symbolic message. In its execution, a series of dualities are happily accommodated: symmetry and asymmetry; obligations of the design to church and town; and an exterior and overall stylistic scheme of late neo-medieval guise and an interior conceived in circulation pattern and plan as a late Rococo theater. The church is an auditorium clothed in a Gothic shell of public expectation. Trinity is full of surprises (Figs. 2–7, 2–8, and 2–9).

The plan is basically symmetrical, although it does not appear so on the exterior because of the different wall treatment accorded each elevation in response to the site and to Roeschlaub's chosen ecclesiastical iconography. The clarity of the circulation pattern, based on the orderliness of the plan, is intellectually and aesthetically satisfying. The heating and ventilation systems, too, recognize the basic symmetry of the building. Indeed, it is *integration*—of the myriad exquisite details, of the dual functions of sanctuary and concert hall, and of technology—that makes Trinity one of the finest "modern Gothic" Arts and Crafts churches in the United States (Figs. 2–10, 2–11, 2–12, and 2–13).[19]

Trinity was the great achievement of Roeschlaub's parish churches, the elegant solution to a corner site. Visually almost free standing, the spire is the key to the

Figure 2–6
Trinity Methodist Church
Denver, 1887
W. H. Jackson photograph
CHS J2062

Figure 2–7
Trinity Methodist Church
Eighteenth Avenue elevation
Kenneth R. Fuller

asymmetrical reading of the building in elevation. The spire, the magnificent goal of Roeschlaub's career as a church designer, rises like a lightning rod at the junction of Broadway, Tremont, and Eighteenth Street—the abrupt edge of Denver's two colliding grids, drawing in energy like a force field. It serves as a linchpin in the city plan, a public monument in addition to its role as a symbol of Methodism.

Just as the spire stands as a beacon in downtown Denver, its ingenious construction, interwoven with an ornamental scheme, highlights the essential character of the church. The idea of religious aspiration parallels the technical feat of its construction (Figs. 2–14, 2–15, and 2–16). The top of the spire is 183 feet from the ground, one of the tallest stone towers in the United States when built.[20] Since it was too high for wood scaffolding or cranes, the stone subcontractors, Geddis and Seerie (Roeschlaub designed the private residences

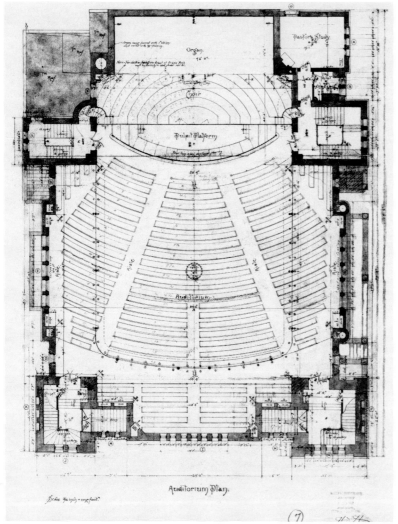

Auditorium Plan.

2–8

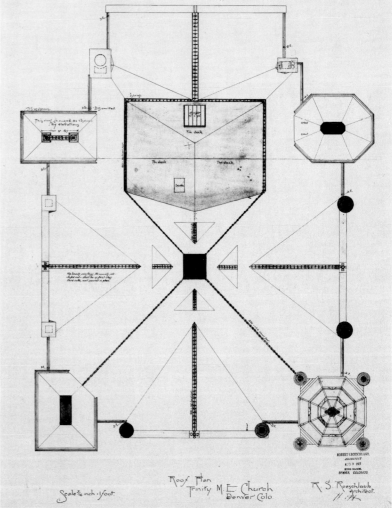

Roof Plan
Trinity M. E. Church
Denver Colo.

2–9

of both), put up large, mastlike "jim poles" anchored by guy wires, while pulleys were used to raise and lower men and materials. The mobility of the system was its advantage: the top of this apparatus was movable and could swing totally around the spire. The result was ingenious, allowing the spire to be built as a hollow, free-standing stone shaft held in place with tie rods and trussed with diagonal bracing.

The foundation of the massive stone tower is

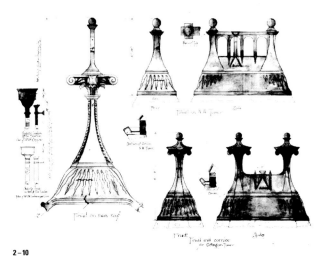

2–10

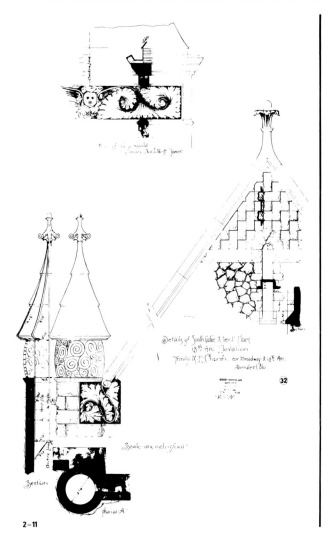

2–11

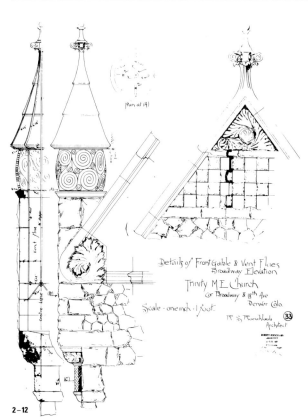

2–12

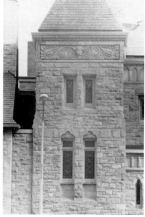

2–13

Figure 2–8
Trinity Methodist Church
Auditorium plan
Kenneth R. Fuller

Figure 2–9
Trinity Methodist Church
Roof plan
Kenneth R. Fuller

Figure 2–10
Trinity Methodist Church
Details of copper and galvanized iron
finials and cornices of roof and tower
Kenneth R. Fuller

Figure 2–11
Trinity Methodist Church
Details of south gable and vent flues
Eighteenth Avenue elevation
Kenneth R. Fuller

Figure 2–12
Trinity Methodist Church
Detail of front gable and vent flues
Broadway elevation
Kenneth R. Fuller

Figure 2–13
Trinity Methodist Church
Side turret
Kenneth R. Fuller

precisely figured, typical of Roeschlaub's mastery of calculation and engineering.[21] While the church as a whole is a structural shell of masonry walls of tremendous strength, the tower base is the most heavily reinforced and features the finest imported English Portland cement. Its rectangular foundation walls are about eleven feet thick, built up in risers or steps, like a hollow, stepped pyramid. The dovetailing of spire into base is a demonstration of what the Victorians called "realism," practiced, for example, by William Butterfield at All Saints (Margaret Street, London, 1850–59). A general attitude among the best of late nineteenth-century American church builders, it characterizes Trinity in every artistic aspect.

Roeschlaub bevels into the base to begin the octagon of the steeple, a device that creates the effect of a needle-thin soaring structure, both abrupt in transition and smooth-flowing in finale compared to his more traditional earlier churches. Unity of material—in this case, Castle Rock volcanic lava—is maintained, but a finer finish for the spire adds to the tapering.[22] The spire's lofty copper cross, lit up by electricity from wires winding up the core of the structure, was an up-to-date expression of the symbolism of light.[23]

The originality and strength of the tower lends an appreciation for the formidable stylistic achievements throughout Trinity Church. This is the "modern Gothic,"[24] a style in which quality and truth were more

2–14

2–15

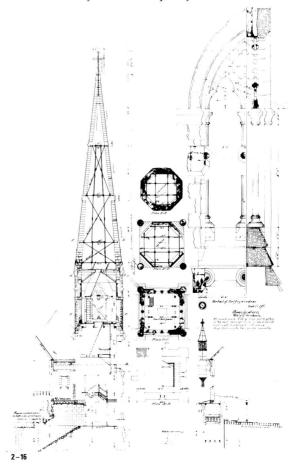

2–16

Figure 2–14
Trinity Methodist Church
Detail of steeple
Kenneth R. Fuller

Figure 2–15
Trinity Methodist Church
Steeple construction
CHS F44840

Figure 2–16
Trinity Methodist Church
Steeple cross-section
Kenneth R. Fuller

66

important than historical precedent and material was to be appreciated for its inherent character. As John Ruskin, father of the English Arts and Crafts movement and an earnest admirer of the Middle Ages, declared, "God is in the details."[25] Indeed, Trinity's numerous details testify to the wealth of artisans in Denver capable of producing this caliber of work, in addition to the national and international network of manufacturers and industrial artists responsible for its realization.

The three sweeping curves of the wrought-iron gates at the main entrance to Trinity Roeschlaub designed in a tight, intricate, filigree pattern reminis-

2–17

cent but not imitative of medieval prototypes (Figs. 2–17, 2–18, and 2–19)[26] The hinges, as well as hardware throughout the interior of the church, have a plain beauty that comes from the care that the architect bestowed on such small items. Details of the south gable on Eighteenth Avenue and the front gable on Broadway show Roeschlaub's freely drawn interpretation of herbaceous ornaments which unfold as though revealing the rhythms of nature. Like his frieze mold under the cornice of the northwest tower, composed of a cherubic head centered amidst undulating pods (much like a motif from his Dora Moore School),

Roeschlaub took as a stylistic starting point late Gothic ornament, but the result is a new, modern design.

The carved oak newel posts which stud the interior, drawn by Roeschlaub down to precise incisions and to interfolded surfaces of leaflike form, are the closest he comes to naturalistic representations (Figs. 2–20 and 2–21) At the other end of his ornamental spectrum is the vertical design that frames the proscenium arch of the auditorium. A long, spindly, wooden

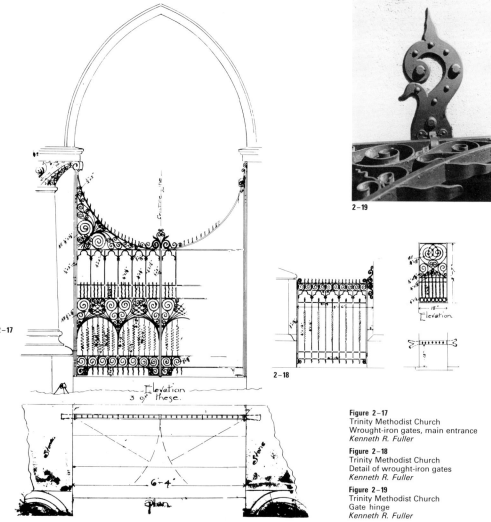

Figure 2–17
Trinity Methodist Church
Wrought-iron gates, main entrance
Kenneth R. Fuller

Figure 2–18
Trinity Methodist Church
Detail of wrought-iron gates
Kenneth R. Fuller

Figure 2–19
Trinity Methodist Church
Gate hinge
Kenneth R. Fuller

central element, it terminates in papier maché work, the origins of which may lie in Celtic arabesques, Byzantine filigree, and Gothic foliage in high relief, but the result, free of all sources except the work of his fellow contemporary architects, is an abstract assemblage of stem, foliage, and blossom (PLATE 4). Just as architects of the past, according to Arts and Crafts precepts, looked to nature for inspiration, so also the designer of the late nineteenth century was expected to follow nature's forms rather than settle for imitation of one or another historic period. Repeatedly, according to these precepts, art sought the principles of nature. Shoddy imitations of one material for another were considered against these laws, even sinful or in error.[27]

Roeschlaub was deservedly proud of his expertise in mechanical systems, but the real merit of his work at Trinity Church is the integration of heating, ventilation, and electric lighting with the aesthetics of the building. Although not one of radical innovation, the church demonstrates Roeschlaub's thorough understanding of heating, ventilation, and long-span truss work (Fig. 2–22). By the end of the Civil War, central heating systems had become the expectation for public buildings and important residences. Trinity was fitted with state-of-the-art direct and indirect steam heating and gravity ventilation. The 1890 Thatcher Mansion in Pueblo, designed by Henry Hudson Holly, the leading eastern architect of fine mansions, had a combination of indirect and direct heating similar to Trinity's, and Denver's Byers-Evans Mansion of 1883 had an identical gravity-flow system. But there was an elegant difference from the systems of other buildings of the time. The decorated elements of Trinity are in seamless harmony with this advanced technology. One detail of many which unequivocally shows Roeschlaub's interest in integration of the emblematic and functional requirements is the pyramidal apex of the roof, the crowning piece of the work. It is the symbolic terminus of the body of the church, decorated with the trefoil that reiterated the theme of the Trinity throughout the building, and it is as well the final element of the air exhaust system. The pinnacles at either side of the rose

window are also gravity exhaust stacks. Thus Roeschlaub merits his reputation for systems' synthesis, but even more so as an artist.

Unity and coherence of the entire work is due to exterior masonry walls, which are faced predominantly with one material, rhyolite (called Castle Rock lava), a highly acidic, granitelike, variously colored volcanic rock. It dominates and subsumes the sensuous details. Except on the spire, the stone is roughly finished "in rusticated blocks of varying heights";[28] these are set in courses on the body of the church and randomly in parts of the gables. Ornamentation is provided from the polychrome of the broken ashlar stone itself, which is pink-beige "with hints of red and blue and the subtle glitter of mica."[29] The drawing of the Eighteenth Avenue elevation indicates that Roeschlaub selected the stone and ordered it cut and quarried for its color variations. For the ornamental checkerboard pattern in the upper portion of the gable end, a note reads: "Blue and pink lava alternating." The trimmings are of tooled purple Utah sandstone.[30] Freer of grain than rhyolite, it was more adapted to delicate carving for intricate exterior details at salient points, such as the lush keystones and terminals of the ogive arch carved by J. A. Byrne around the rose windows. The essence of the material is more important than style. Artistic exploitation of native Colorado stone contributed substantially to a special sense of place; such individuality was universally sought by architects of the Arts and Crafts movement. Roeschlaub has created a native adaptation of the principles of "modern Gothic."

This grand simplification of vigorous masses animated by ornament was the real lesson of the late work of H. H. Richardson on American architecture in the 1880s. Although specific motifs, such as the window groupings of Denver's Trinity, are like Richardson's Trinity Church in Boston (1876), Roeschlaub preferred the example of the country churches of Richardson, such as his Grace Church (Medford, Mass., 1867–68), not in specifics but in breathtaking abstraction of masses, of cube against cone. Roeschlaub had illustrations of all these works.[31]

A key to the double reading of Trinity as a church and as a temple of music—as both a sanctuary and a

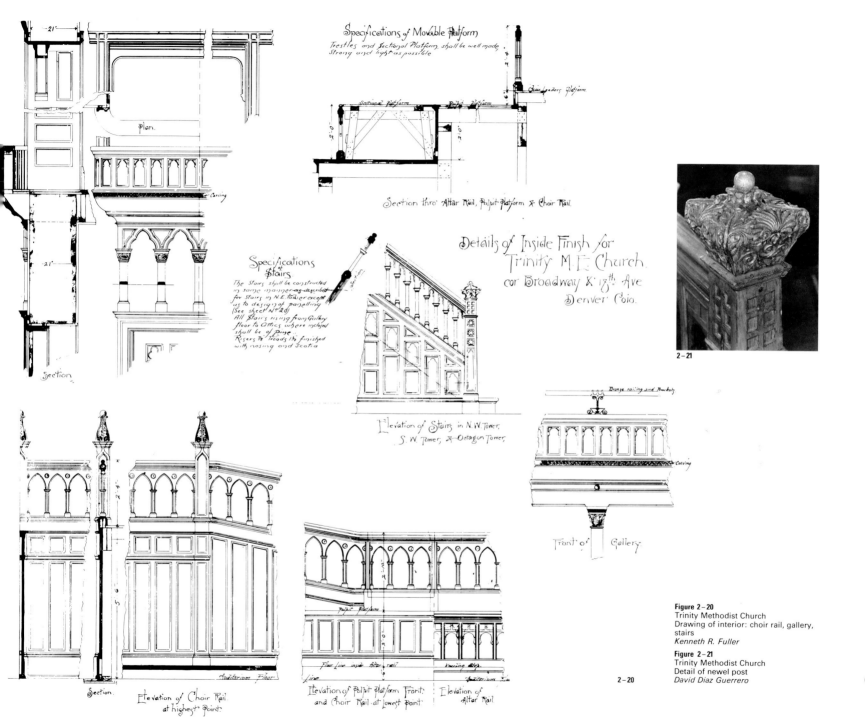

Plan.

Carving

Section

Specifications of Movable Platform

Trestles and Sectional Platform, shall be well made strong and light as possible

Choir Leaders Platform

Sectional Platform   Pulpit Platform

Section thro' Altar Rail, Pulpit Platform & Choir Rail.

Specifications of Stairs

The Stairs shall be constructed in same manner as described for stairs in N.E. tower except as to design of panelling (See sheet N° 20)
All Stairs rising from Gallery floor to Attics where inclosed shall be of pine
Risers ⅞ treads 1⅛ finished with nosing and scotia

Details of Inside Finish for Trinity M.E. Church cor Broadway & 19th Ave Denver Colo.

Elevation of Stairs in N.W. Tower, S.W. Tower, & Octagon Tower.

Bronze railing and Brackets

Carving

Front of Gallery

Section

Elevation of Choir Rail at highest Point.

Auditorium Floor

Pulpit Platform

Floor Line inside Altar rail
Line   Kneeling step.
                        Auditorium Floor

Elevation of Pulpit Platform Front and Choir Rail at lowest Point.

Elevation of Altar Rail.

Figure 2–20
Trinity Methodist Church
Drawing of interior: choir rail, gallery, stairs
Kenneth R. Fuller

Figure 2–21
Trinity Methodist Church
Detail of newel post
David Diaz Guerrero

2–20   2–21

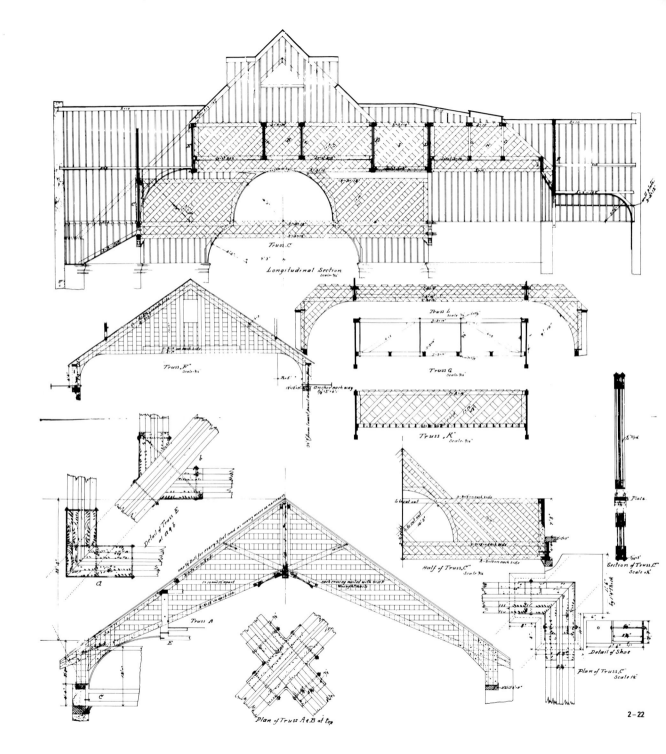

Figure 2–22
Trinity Methodist Church
Roof plan
Kenneth R. Fuller

Figure 2–23
Robert Bunce
First Presbyterian Church
Quincy, Illinois, 1875
Courtesy George Irwin

2-22

concert hall—lies in the circulation of the building. Here the symmetry asserts itself. The main entrance on Broadway sets the experience of Trinity as a series of separate spatial pieces linked by a tight, disciplined axial plan. Three Gothic arches open into a deep, marble-floored recess or vestibule faced with rubbed stonework of a beautiful purple tint. The coffered ceiling of paneled oak is carved in quatrefoil recesses (PLATES 5 and 6). These deep tones and gorgeous materials provide a direct tactile experience of intrinsic beauty and truth from within that establishes the artistic and spiritual theme of this Arts and Crafts church. The three-in-one portal symbolizes the Trinity; the main meaning of the edifice is immediately apparent.

The entrance vestibule is a study in transitions and choice. Although not yet within the building, early worshipers were sheltered and guided by the rules set by its symmetrical composition. The general aspect of Trinity, especially the portal, is close to Robert Bunce's First Presbyterian Church (1875) in Quincy (Fig. 2–23), but the Trinity entrance is meshed into a rigorous architectural organization. Here one perceives that Trinity is not what it seems from the exterior, yet the discovery of this duality is one of delight and lucidity, not tension. Straight ahead is not the main sanctuary; instead, passing through the large oak fly doors, churchgoers descended to the lower level, which housed the communal activities of the congregation.[32]

Turning to the right or left, on the other hand, they ascended to worship. At either end of the open vestibule is a flight of wide slate steps which lead to the main entrance doors and then landings in the two towers. From there one passes through double oak doors into the southwest and northwest angles of the auditorium. As we have seen, the stylistic motifs of Trinity are resolutely ecclesiastical, which in 1888 meant a free Arts and Crafts interpretation of the middle ages, but the spatial organization is borrowed from the prototype of small eighteenth-century opera houses.

In the main sanctuary worshipers entered "one of the grandest assembly rooms in the city" (Figs. 2–24, 2–25, and 2–26).[33] The floor is slightly bowled, as in a theater, yet the religious significance of the space is ever

2–23

Figure 2-24
Trinity Methodist Church
Interior
W. H. Jackson photograph
*Courtesy Trinity United
Methodist Church*

present. The seating plan, for example, was originally splayed out in three sections with no continuous center aisle, as a three-dimensional embodiment of the Trinity. There was a tendency in Protestant churches of the time to use open meeting hall plans for the main sanctuary, and Roeschlaub collected various solutions of this type in his clippings file from architectural periodicals.[34] "Owing to rare good judgement on the part of the architect," quoted Peter Winne, an early church chronicler,

> . . . we have a room here that is designed with a view of obtaining practical results. There are no unnecessary nooks or corners, pillars or bays merely because "it is the style" or is "ecclesiastical." The main thought was to secure a room to accommodate as much of a throng of people as the ground space would permit; to give each hearer a comfortable seat, and secure for each one every facility for seeing and hearing. It is a great audience room, with the faults too often found in churches eliminated, and some of the excellent, well studied features of the theatre and concert room utilized, and yet it is churchly in every detail.[35]

The majestic open effect of this room was achieved by construction of stone walls without and iron posts within. The auditorium floor is supported on cast-iron columns (at the lower level), set on massive stone piers (indicated on the foundation plan). A light and graceful gallery is carried around three sides of the room and supported on iron columns that line up with those on the floor below. So-called invalids' boxes, placed over the northeast and southeast vestibule entrances at gallery level, were originally intended for expectant mothers. They were fitted with upholstered chairs in contrast to fixed chairs with folding seats in the gallery proper. The effect of the hall is one of rich ornamentation, yet it is airy and expansive.

Roeschlaub designed all the oak woodwork, including the intricately carved details for the galleries (which he specified should have an inside finish made of "choice kiln-dried chestnut"), the choir and altar rail, and the pulpit platform. The repetitive blind arches of these features are good but standard work; they provide linking features and background for his special occasions of elaborate ornament. "Perfect harmony has

been observed in the coloring and designs of the glass and decorations, both blending well with the design and finish of the wood work and furnishing."[36] The altar, pulpit, and pulpit chairs were not Roeschlaub's but made under Buchtel's supervision by the well-known firm of J. and R. Lamb of New York.[37] Even the pews of the auditorium floor, solid, mass-produced items, are carved with a trefoil to represent the ubiquitous theme of the Trinity. Unity of artistic attitude draws together these fine, highly individualistic elements.

The perfect integration of lighting with aesthetic and symbolic form is demonstrated in the sanctuary. As to the church's interior decorative scheme, the superior craft and concept of its stained-glass windows also enhance Trinity's reputation as an example of the "modern Gothic." The stained glass, executed by the Chicago firm of Healy and Millet, influential figures in the Arts and Crafts movement in America, is analogous not only to jewels but also to plants and flowers. A complementary series of stained-glass windows on each side of the sanctuary ends the balanced composition of the cross-shaped space above the heads of the worshipers; the magnificent rose windows, each with five lights underneath, grace the north and south galleries; and the crowning glory of the building, the complex ensemble of the west Resurrection window, is flanked by double lancets with seven lights below.

Roeschlaub's attitudes toward art and decor are clearly one with Healy and Millet's. The firm executed the frescoing, stenciling, and the double row of plaster work (papier maché) friezes above the gallery and in the proscenium arch of the sanctuary. Roeschlaub himself designed at least part of the extensive plastic or raised ornamentation in papier maché as indicated on his drawing for the inside finish of the elevation of the proscenium arch, just as he did the exterior capstones, with curled, fan-shaped leafy forms—in which nature reinvented in turn revitalizes art. Thus he most likely provided Healy and Millet with sketches for the three-dimensional work while they had more independence for the stenciling and windows. Roeschlaub probably only supervised the window design, but his overall decorative scheme instructed his collaborators.

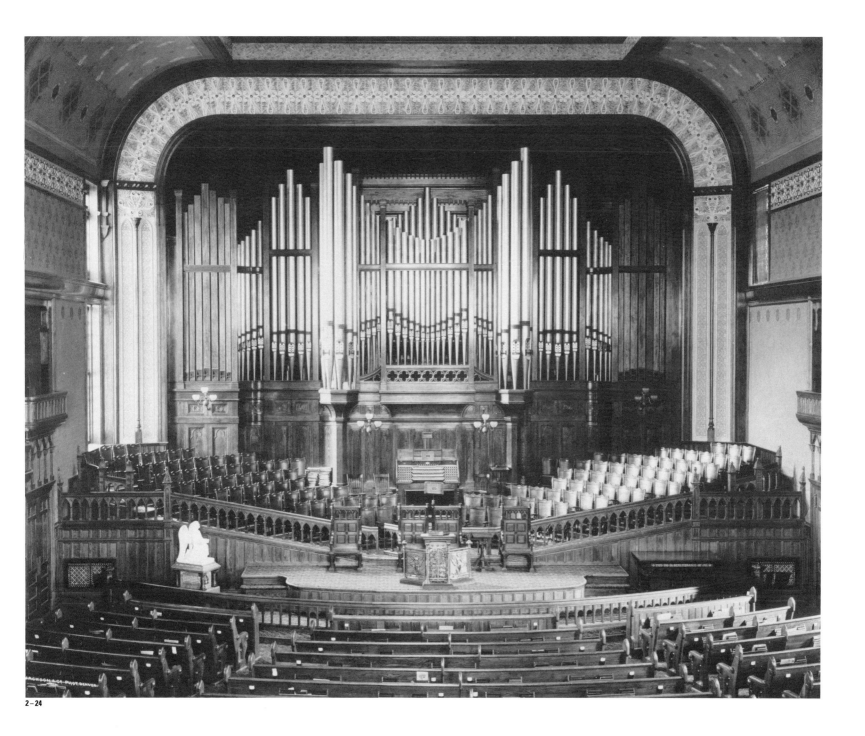

In partnership from 1880 to 1899, Healy and Millet, one of Chicago's most distinguished decorating firms, was recognized in this country and abroad. George Louis Healy and Louis J. Millet were close personal friends of Louis Sullivan, whom they knew as students in Paris. They helped to design, and were entrusted to execute, interiors for several Sullivan buildings, among them the Auditorium Building in Chicago (Fig. 4–22), the Pueblo Opera House, the Chicago Stock Exchange,

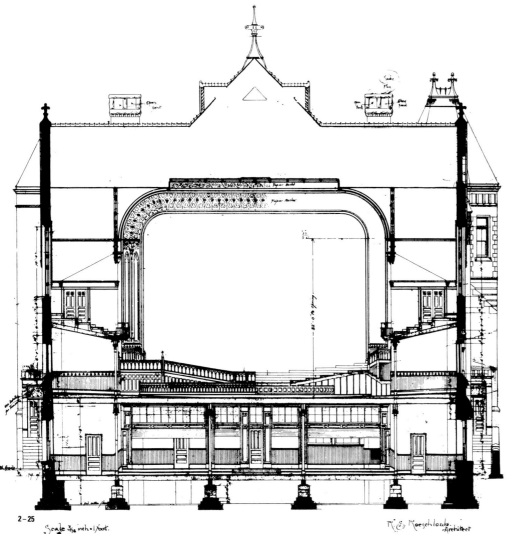

2-25

Scale 3/16 inch=1/foot.

R. G. Roeschlaub, Architect

and Sullivan's midwestern banks.[38] Particularly celebrated for its stained glass, the firm exhibited five windows at the Paris Exposition of 1889 that are very close in style to those of Trinity. These were purchased for the permanent collection of the Museum of Decorative Arts in Paris. The French saw their significance as "windows in striated glass referred to as American Glass."[39] As formal compositions, Healy and Millet's windows were either vinelike, or dense, flat patterns of seminaturalistic foliage, or nearly geometric abstractions of nature (PLATE 7a, b, and c respectively).

Healy and Millet's innovative attitude and method for windows was to assemble colored and textured opalescent glass rather than painted glass.[40] This method represented a return to that of the early medieval stained-glass windows. Thus the painted figurative composition at the center of Trinity's great Resurrection window, poignant as it is, was more conservative in technique than all the rest of the church's luminous windows of innovative "American glass," the latter considered an important contribution to the art.[41]

Millet was an articulate communicator of the theories of the Arts and Crafts movement, which are so in harmony with Roeschlaub's that they may be used to further our understanding of the character of Trinity as a whole. In a series of articles on interior decoration and its development in America, Millet advocated the importance of decoration, which unites "the two sister arts, painting and sculpture, ... under the guidance of their parent Architecture." The excellence of a work of art depends on "its adaptability to the spot it was to occupy and its harmony to the surroundings; for ... 'fitness is the soul of art.'" There should be, according to Millet, a self-conscious pursuit of an art appropriate to modern times:

> Decoration of our day is not, and cannot be, on account of the complicated lives we lead, an art of perfect quiet and harmony, such as the ancients practiced. But it may become an art of strong effects, and although it is still slightly barbaric in its modes of execution and wild in its tendencies toward unlimited originality, it has the great redeeming feature of being a new effort, with no guide beyond the artist's taste and

reason....It may for these reasons be productive of a new chapter of art, and may some day, without copying the forms preferred by the ancients, recognize the excellency of their laws, without which no art can flourish.[42]

Thus Millet accepted a certain differentiation of ornamentation within a work as long as laws of art, deduced from laws of nature, were observed. These principles were defined as a sense of equilibrium and,

of course, honest use of materials.[43]

The 1890s was a time of ferment and renewal in architecture and design. The execution of the Trinity windows in American glass is often of astonishing delicacy. The forms of the lily and iris windows on the west gallery have something of the soft sway associated with the plant life of Art Nouveau or its immediate predecessors, the stylized naturalism of the pre-Raphaelites or Grasset. Indeed, Trinity's stained-glass

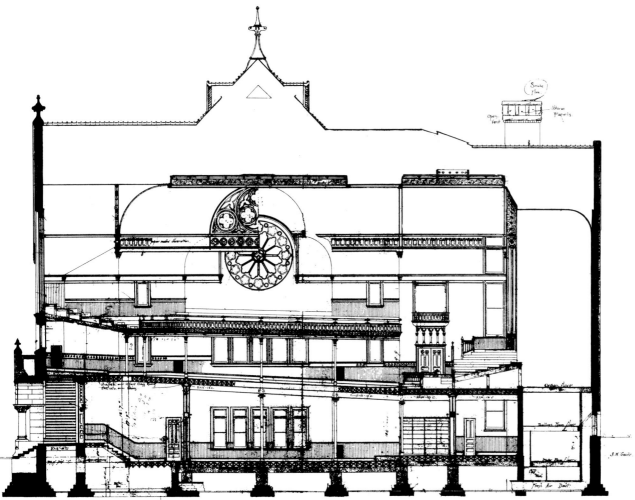

2-26

Figure 2–25
Trinity Methodist Church
Transverse section
Kenneth R. Fuller

Figure 2–26
Trinity Methodist Church
Longitudinal section
Kenneth R. Fuller

windows by Healy and Millet are startlingly close to those designed by the Belgian masters of Art Nouveau, Victor Horta and Henry van de Velde in the 1890s, and it is thought that American windows shown in Paris in 1889 had a formative influence on the Europeans.[44]

Roeschlaub carefully organized artificial light, in addition to the filtered natural light from the stained glass, into his artistic scenario. From the beginning, the entire building was lit by electricity, although some fixtures were a combination of gas and electric. The trustees of Trinity were aware that their decision in favor of electric light was progressive, even audacious. "There are no cumbersome chandeliers pendent from the ceiling," stated *The Trail*. "To a certain extent the source of light is invisible. In the paneled ceiling and frieze some 400 16-candlepower lamps are set in the decorations and [form] a part thereof, [shedding] an evenly diffused light over the room."[45] There was a skylight directly over the pulpit, as shown in the ceiling plan (Fig 2–27). In a period view of the interior taken by one of the West's leading photographers, William Henry Jackson, the skylight reiterates the central axis of the church, focused on the pulpit at the east. The main Broadway portal, the beginning of one's journey through the church on a straight line to the east, may be remembered here. Roeschlaub's message is the pleasure of revelation to one who observes, a building that is not simple but which revels in clarity.

The great proscenium arch, too, frames and reconciles the choir and the organ with the altar and the pulpit. Musical performance at Trinity was understood as one with the celebration of religious observance. This arch was studded with bare electric bulbs, each held in a gilt setting on a bed of repeated, intricate, linear forms of papier maché like so many elements of a jeweled tiara. It is strikingly like a miniaturization of Louis Sullivan's proscenium arch at the Chicago Auditorium in its combination of electric lights and ornament.[46]

The Trinity organ, state of the art both technically and architecturally, was at the time the largest west of the Mississippi and the fourth largest in the United States.[47] As announced in July 1887, "the organ will have a rich case, of dignified and tasteful design, which

will measure about 46 ft. wide by 36 ft. high. The instrument will occupy a floor space of 46 ft. by 16 ft. in front of the congregation, with every acoustic condition designed to secure the most perfect results, and, together with a chorus of 150 and an orchestra of 20 pieces, will undoubtedly insure a musical service that will eclipse all that has ever yet been attempted."[48]

The organ was a feature that gave Trinity an international reputation. Although Roeschlaub did not

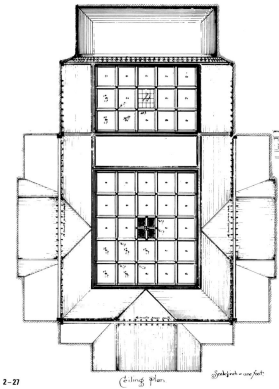

2-27   Ceiling Plan.   Scale ½ inch - one foot?

design the case, there was complete accord between his artistic point of view and that of Sir George Ashdown Audsley of London, who did, as well as integration with the architectural setting that Roeschlaub provided. Audsley, a respected church architect and the foremost organ designer of his period, wrote extensively on Trinity's organ in his important book *The Art of Organ Building*, which compared the most significant examples in America and Europe. Originally

Figure 2–27
Trinity Methodist Church
Ceiling plan
Kenneth R. Fuller

published in 1905, it has become the leading standard work on organ building.[49] Audsley's design, and his commitment to high-quality materials arranged in polychromatic effects of silver, gilt, red, and black, were totally in harmony with Roeschlaub's greater scheme. Contemporaries, in fact, saw this coalescence between organ and architecture: "The organ, like the room, is designed to harmonize with its surroundings and has 'truth' stamped on every detail. There is no excess of

tation of many themes. The progress of its construction received constant attention in the press. The first service in the new building, held in the Sunday School room on Easter Sunday, 1888, evoked congratulations for the city's Methodists from the *Denver Republican*:

> Already the city is adorned with many beautiful edifices, and it is a token of promise for the future that most of the remarkable structures here are intended either for religious or educational purposes.... To the

2–28

casing to fill out a void; no dumb pipes ornamentation...but in all is to be seen and felt, that 'repose' so desirable in a room of this character."[50]

A commitment to a work of distinction united the architect and his client. Trinity Methodist Episcopal Church is a tribute to the period of its construction— architecturally, decoratively, mechanically, and musically. In Trinity Roeschlaub achieved a sonorous adap-

> congregation of [Trinity] church, as Denver citizens, we tender our congratulations and express our thanks, whilst we wish a speedy completion to the building they are raising. The edifice, which is to be the physical expression of their liberal efforts, will remain for future ages a center of moral and spiritual enlightenment [*sic*]; it will also ensure to their denomination and to Denver the possession of one of the most beautiful and stately buildings in the whole continent of America.[51]

Figure 2–28
First Presbyterian Church
Colorado Springs, 1887–89
CHS F49803

The official opening of the church, with the first service in the main sanctuary Christmas week, 1888, was an important civic event. The denominational journal the *Christian Advocate* stated categorically: "To her already long list of superior attractions Colorado now adds that of the finest Methodist church in the world."[52] For once, perhaps, Denver's high estimation of itself and its architecture was justified. The survival of Trinity in her centennial year is due as much to the

2–29

preservationist efforts of her present trustees, led by James H. Ranniger, and to her inspirational pastor, the Reverend James E. Barnes, as to the original uncompromising congregation.[53]

The First Presbyterian Church, a stone building on the southeast corner of Nevada and Bijou streets in Colorado Springs, had its cornerstone laid on April 12, 1888 (Fig. 2–28).[54] At its dedication on March 12, 1889, Roeschlaub "made a brief statement regarding the

dimensions of the building, and its heating and ventilating arrangements."[55] It is apparent that this church was being designed while Trinity was under construction. It has a similar external organization and massing: a square corner tower and an exaggerated cruciform with deep transepts—in origin the broad, square transepts of the prototype of English medieval cathedrals, now so pronounced that they are equilateral to the nave. There is also the same large scale and separate definition of masses, but the Colorado Springs church has even more of a Richardsonian geometric purity and a horizontal emphasis than Trinity due to the broad gabled roofs of nave and transept, and a self-sufficient tower without a spire.

First Presbyterian is also a radical departure from Trinity. The main entrance is emphatically placed within the tower; a new diagonal axis splits the cruciform. Trinity is a balance of tensions and accommodated dualities. In First Presbyterian symmetrical composition unfolds clearly from the corner angle of the belfry tower. This west- and north-facing double entrance is a variation of the motifs Roeschlaub used on the longitudinal church type at St. Peter's, but here steps sweep around to unite both outlooks toward the town. Secondary entrances are low, minor portals. Singularly, too, there are no Gothic elements whatsoever. Present is still the sensuous surface and grandeur of Colorado lava cut by areas of lush ornament, most visible in a band of Queen Anne vines and shields around the tower. The fenestration on the west is grouped in a Palladian motif of central arch and two flanking rectangles that recalls Georgian churches more than Romanesque. Yet this is not just motif mongering. The building has a new feeling for a true sense of classical poise and repose: the balustrade atop the tower is correct, dignified Renaissance. It is disappointing that there is no plan or description of the interior. After Trinity, this is one of the best of Roeschlaub's ecclesiastical works. It is the building of a mature architect who offers a fecund variation on a familiar typology.

In 1907 Roeschlaub and Son designed the First Congregational Church (now the Metropolitan Community Church of the Rockies) at Tenth and Clarkson

Figure 2–29
First Congregational Church
(Metropolitan Community Church
of the Rockies)
Denver, 1907
David Diaz Guerrero

in Denver (Figs. 2–29 and 2–30). In this church Roeschlaub has produced the most outrageous split in style between the medieval outside and the Academic Revival inside. The exterior treatment reveals that, in a way, the architect has returned to the abbreviated vocabulary of his early work. A single refrain of a blind arcade below cornices and gables repeats with obsessional intensity. Associated stylistically with neo-Lombard architecture of the Middle Ages because of the

of means.[56] Yet a young Roeschlaub could not have handled the complicated changes in roof levels (there was originally a peaked pyramid hipped roof with wide eaves over the tower)[57] or organized the system of engaged and folded pilasters which modulate the many shifts in planes of the facade. While the elements of this edifice easily identify it as a public institution, it is domestic in scale and general impression, a friendly one-story structure made of humble brick with stone

2–30

corbeling, this embellishment is childlike appliqué work rather than high style. With a restricted budget, the firm managed to endow the work with all the associations the church type merited with a minimum

trim and pressed metal cornices.

The aedicule of the tower entrance hints of the mixed Renaissance–Georgian Revival vocabulary within. Great pilasters on high pedestals, typical of

Figure 2–30
First Congregational Church
(Metropolitan Community Church
of the Rockies)
Interior view
David Diaz Guerrero

Georgian churches, with molded plaster capitals decorated with shields dot the sanctuary. A full entablature extends around the room, breaking repeatedly at the junction of pilaster and the beams of the low-coved ceiling. In keeping with the Academic repertoire, a Colonial Revival staircase complete with delicately turned balusters gives access to a balcony which extends straight across the west end. The balcony is supported on two cast-iron colonettes with simple Tuscan Doric capitals.[58]

Yet it is not correct classical language but its anomalies that gives this interior its charm. Details are overscaled. The thick-set shields are not contained within the line of their entablature but tilt over the sanctuary. Roeschlaub is still inventive in his attempt to combine modern conveniences and inherited architectural culture. Isolated rosettes are spaced about 2½ feet apart on a blank frieze in the entablature. With molded plaster in a proper Georgian style, Roeschlaub uses a variant of a device found at Trinity but less revolutionary twenty years later: the rosettes of this frieze contain electric lights that also enframe various windows. The effect today leads to affectionate associations with fast-food restaurants rather than with the sobriety usually integral to the Academic Revival. Clear glazing would be historically correct in a Georgian church, not the fine Arts and Crafts stained glass of the First Congregational that local tradition attributes to the Denver firm of Watkins and Company. This glass and its simple tracery in roundheaded windows on the west and north is a medieval refrain which here works successfully both on the facade and interior. Huge pendants, an element of late medieval rather than classical vocabulary, hang from the ceiling. Bare heating pipes at the rear of the pews and the original radiators add to the cumulative impression that, although a late work, there is an ingenuous quality to the interior: perhaps Frank Roeschlaub, the architect's son and partner, is its main author.

The sophisticated plan, however, is the logical finale of Roeschlaub's lifelong investigation of corner sites. Spatially, this church is a distillation of the type developed at the First Presbyterian Church of Colorado Springs: a cubical sanctuary with a rectangular bell tower which serves as a main entrance (with only one portal here which faces onto Clarkson), and a strong diagonal axis. The body of the church reads as a cross from the exterior because of two slightly projecting central pavilions on the north and west. But this reading changes the moment one passes inside from the tower to the sanctuary: the interior maintains the symmetry of the facade but an elliptical apse at the angle opposite the entrance tower rivets the mind and

2–31

eye and actively draws in the worshiper. The fan-shaped pew arrangement of four sections in three aisles, steeply bowled and oriented from northwest to southeast, reinforces a dominant diagonal: Trinity turned forty-five degrees. Still observable, but without its original stained glass, is the oculus in the ceiling over the apse above the original placement of the pulpit, a Baroque device Roeschlaub used at Trinity.[59] The sanctuary of this strange little church is both uncluttered and intimate.

But Roeschlaub's period of elaborate church building was long past. Indeed, his final church is designed in accordance with the recommendation of Franklin Kidder, the great codifier of Denver church design in the 1890s: "to obtain the greatest capacity, convenience, and architectural expression for the least amount of money."[60]

Figure 2–31
"Some Denver Doorways": Trinity Church and East High School (from *Western Architect and Building News*, October 1889)
CHS F31243/F31244

Roeschlaub was an architect *par excellence* of the late nineteenth-century urban school. Although in many ways Denver was still a small town in 1876, even his early schools were a far cry architecturally from the one-room country schoolhouses that flourished in rural America well into the twentieth century.[1] Roeschlaub's architectural practice is credited with about fifty school commissions over a forty-year period—an incredible number—not counting the many additions he made to

these same schools. Based on the expertise he developed and the renown he gained in Denver, Roeschlaub designed schools for cities and towns throughout the region. At the end of his tenure as architect for the East Denver (Arapahoe) School District, a position he held from 1876 to 1889, a contemporary historian wrote: "There is no institution in our community that is more earnestly and effectively fostered, or with which the people are more completely satisfied, than the excellent system of public schools."[2]

Not only symbols of city and civilization in the new, burgeoning West, first-rate schools, like churches, were also pragmatic ventures that attracted easterners. A journalist's reaction to the condition of the Denver public schools in 1880 probably summed up the feelings of his fellow citizens: "Men came to Colorado with but one idea—to get rich with all possible dispatch and

'go back to America'—to quote a common phrase of the time. But about ten years ago the idea began to prevail that homes could be made here. People took root, as it were. In the American mind home is inseparably associated with school and church, hence no sooner did men begin to look upon Colorado as home, than they determined to have schools here which should rival in excellence those of the older states."[3]

School building of this period, whether the Board Schools of London in the 1870s or the public schools of Boston, captured the imagination of the public as impressive and immediately recognizable symbols of enlightenment.[4] Yet Denver's pride in, and identification with, its schools had a special intensity, as demonstrated by an 1879 appreciation of Roeschlaub's recently completed Twenty-fourth Street School:

> Is it not a comment upon the city of Denver, and the character of its population, that the first and only public buildings of note in the city are the school houses and further, does it not forecast a future, certain and reliable, of the high standing in the commonwealth and in the country that Denver reaches, when of all public enterprises, public education is nearest to the hearts of the people? Standing on the west bank of the Platte, at night-fall, when the rays of the setting sun are falling full and bright upon our beautiful city, one looks upon the busy, teeming town, its warehouses, churches, mills, and homes, and towering high, standing like monuments above all other buildings, rise the school houses. The picture is one rarely equalled in nature or in art.[5]

Even the simplest of Roeschlaub's schools, then, were monuments in the landscape above the homes of east Denver. They were building blocks, too, in the definition of a city rich in idealism. The metaphor of youth and hope linked the education of children with the image of a fledgling city in the West.

Not only did Roeschlaub's schools help to raise the image of Denver as a developing metropolis, they also attracted the attention of school boards and educators in other American cities and abroad. "F. W. Bicknell, editor of the *New England Journal of Education*," reported the *Rocky Mountain News* in 1883, "has been spending a week in visiting the Denver schools" and "Mrs. Otis, a very intelligent New England lady who...has been greatly interested in educational and philanthropic movements for a long series of years, has written her impressions of Denver schools to the Boston *Commonwealth*."[6] A year after this announcement was made, the Department of Education requested that plans and photographs of two of Roeschlaub's schools be placed on exhibit in New Orleans, and from this national exposure the architect received requests for plans of his East Denver schools from Canada, England, and Germany.[7]

Indeed, Roeschlaub's schools were models which helped to validate the very concept of free public education in Denver. By the mid-nineteenth century, educational reformers such as Horace Mann, John Pierce, and Henry Barnard had come to view education as a public enterprise. The fight for tax-supported free schools had been a bitter one, yet by 1860 "the question of free public education had been largely settled, and

3–1

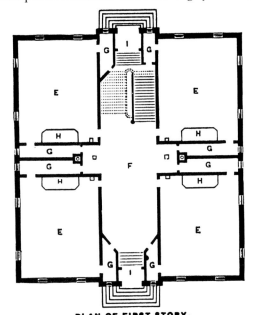

PLAN OF FIRST STORY.

E.—School Rooms, 28x33 ft.
F.—Hall, 18½ ft. wide.
G.—Wardrobes (two to each room).
H.—Platforms.
I.—Arched Entrances.

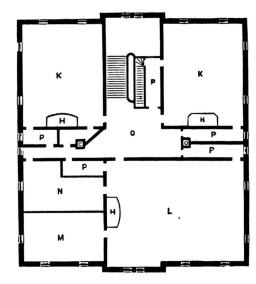

PLAN OF SECOND STORY.

K.—School Rooms, 28x33 ft.
L.—School Room, 47x33 ft.
M.—Recitation Room.
N.—Principal's Room.
O.—Hall.
P.—Wardrobes.

Figure 3–1
Broadway School, rendering
Denver, 1875
CHS F31251

Figure 3–2
Broadway School, 1875
Floor plans

3–2

the concept became firmly established as an American ideal."[8] In Denver, however, it seems to have remained a controversial issue into the 1870s: "Amongst a people made up of men and women from all parts of the country," stated one observer, "it can not be expected that all should unite in approval of public schools. Only those whose antecedents and breeding were where free schools were effective, pure and good, can look with hearty approval upon a free school system. Time

3-3

and results must work a change in the opinion of the few."[9]

Given this continuing debate over public education and the high visibility of the school board, health and hygiene were conscious concerns of those responsible for the children of the community. Commentaries in his own time about Roeschlaub's schools are almost devoid of detailed discussion about style, although the artistry of his buildings is greatly praised in a general way. Instead, the progress of ventilation, heating, sanitation, and lighting took precedence. In 1877 H. K. Steele, a member of Denver's board of education and of the standing committee on buildings and grounds, reflected these concerns in the board's annual report:

> The matter of ventilation has given us the most trouble. Impure air is not always perceptible to the sense of smell, and air that seems unwholesome to that sense, may not be so loaded down with impurities, so injurious to organic life as others of which we take no cognizance. Foul-smelling air, the result of bad breath and uncleanliness of person or clothing, may exist with an abundance of ventilation. I despair of ever

obtaining in our public schools, air that will always seem sweet to the senses.

Roeschlaub had built only one school for the board, the Broadway, at the time of Steele's lugubrious report. Seven years later, however, the city was able to boast proudly of its East Denver school buildings, reserving admiration in particular for their environmental systems. The headline of one 1884 article, which cited East Denver as having "the most magnificent

3-4

schools and finest system in America," stated that "for air, light, and general comfort and convenience they are unequaled in the whole country...a monument to western taste, culture and liberality, placing us in the front rank of progress."[10] Roeschlaub and the board of education partook of the science and pseudo-science which characterized this Victorian preoccupation with dirt and foul air. "A reading of the literature of the nineteenth century concerning ventilation reveals a deep-seated fear of vitiated air, that which is loaded with [so-called] effluvia and carbonic acid (carbon

Figure 3-3
Centennial School
Pueblo, 1875-76
CHS F1021

Figure 3-4
Twenty-fourth Street School
Denver, 1879
CHS F44849

dioxide). . . . The microscope revealed new learning that was disquieting, and, absent other reasonable causes of illness, foul air was assumed a vicious killer."[11] Whatever their basis in science, the psychological and social values reflected were powerful determinants of Roeschlaub's school designs. The moral education of young people, as implied by Steele, could be enhanced by good design.

By their sheer numbers, Roeschlaub's school com-

3-5

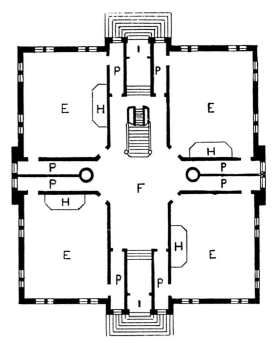

PLAN OF FIRST STORY.

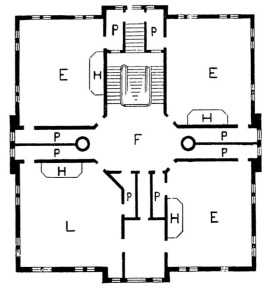

PLAN OF SECOND STORY.

E.—School Rooms, 27x33 feet.
L.—School Room, 32x33 feet.
H.—Teacher's Platforms.
I.—Vestibules, 7.6 wide.
P.—Cloak Halls, 4.2x20.00.

3-6

missions provided him with a kind of laboratory in which to test his ideas. In part this was a response to the accelerated pace of American architectural technology. Journals to which he subscribed, such as the *American Architect and Building News* of Boston and the *Inland Architect* of Chicago, carried detailed technical articles, some illustrated, which provided information on new inventions pertinent to early environmental control systems. Roeschlaub kept up with this fast-

Figure 3–5
Longfellow School
Denver, 1882
CHS F44846

Figure 3–6
Longfellow School, 1882
Floor plans

changing technology and applied it to subsequent phases of his school building designs. A recent study of his use of engineering technology, for example, states: "The means of ventilation and exhaust varied somewhat from school to school...in an experimental search for efficiency [and a] direct expression of [his] quest for performance. Roeschlaub claimed for his schools an evolutionary development of excellence...not unlike the expectations of engineers in product development, but rare for architects then or now. Artist-architects do not generally refine or repeat a single model."[12] As with Trinity Methodist Episcopal Church, Roeschlaub successfully integrated new technology into the total design and arrangement of his school buildings. The concept of a laboratory is important not only in the development of his engineering technology but as a key to understanding the evolution of Roeschlaub's plans and artistry.

Roeschlaub's schools, then, group themselves as developmental prototypes. Indeed, of his first commission in 1875, the Broadway School (Figs. 1–15 and 3–1, 3–2), the board wrote, "We believe it will be the model school house of the territory."[13] Designs related to Broadway include the 1876 Centennial School in Pueblo (Fig. 3–3),[14] the 1879 Twenty-fourth Street School in Denver (Fig. 3–4), the Washington School of 1879–80 in Canon City (Fig. 1–16), and, with a slight modification of the type, the 1882 Longfellow School in Denver (Figs. 3–5 and 3–6).[15] Like the Broadway School, "a well built house, two stories in height,"[16] they are all compact blocks with four corner rooms on each story. Any opportunity for irregularity, such as the small principal's room and recitation room next to the single outsized schoolroom on the second story of the Broadway School, are suppressed.

These are corridor schools, carefully ordered, with a cross-axis beginning and ending squarely in the center of each facade. The placement of the entrances and stairways was of special interest to Roeschlaub. In these models, a short flight of stairs appears on the exterior. Two entrances are placed directly opposite each other, a device thought useful for good ventila-

tion. Girls and boys—for these schools were coeducational from the start—were usually assigned separate entrances; the wardrobes in the halls, too, were divided by gender. In the Broadway School internal stairs are purely a functional item, demonstrated by their unremarkable location at one end of the main corridor and single directional route.

A hint of the wonderful effects Roeschlaub was to create with staircases occurs at Longfellow School. Still

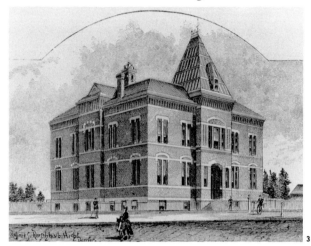

3–7

placed in the unassuming position of the Broadway plan, one flight of stairs at Longfellow is put in the middle of the hall and then, at the landing, continues as two flights, set at either side of the hall. It is a small gesture that begins to create a more complex space at the building's center. Towards this end, Roeschlaub for the first time sets the classroom doors at a diagonal to the hall[17] and begins to push out his buildings from this midpoint, as can be seen in the slight projection of wings on the lateral facades of the Twenty-fourth Street and Longfellow schools. The center is thus marked as the heart of the school, no longer just a passageway.

While their plans are similar, these early schools vary in style. The neo-Palladianism of Broadway and Centennial was old-fashioned by the 1870s if judged by national trends, but it was well suited to cubelike buildings with symmetrical plans and inflected centers. The Broadway School, constructed of stock brick with stone trim,[18] exhibits prominent stone quoining in the

Figure 3–7
Ebert School
Denver, 1880
CHS F49939

manner of English architect James Gibbs, whose works of this type were popular in colonial America. In addition, a string course, classical entablature, wood cornice, and a pediment with an urn at the axis of the main entrance transforms this box into a building of some dignity. At Centennial School a pediment extends across each of the four facades, and a colossal order of pilasters divides the elevations into sections—the entrance into three and the side into five—with no

3–8

apparent rationale. Roeschlaub was irresolute in his treatment of the lateral facades of these two works.

Although less decorated, the Twenty-fourth Street School is more accomplished. The school board commissioned plans from Roeschlaub with instructions that it should be "a duplicate of the Broadway school," but several important changes were nevertheless made.[19] For one thing, it was the first stone schoolhouse in Denver.[20] Commenting on the school in 1879, the *Denver Times* equated stone with permanence: "The stranger arriving at Denver from the East, gazing from the car window for the appearance of the city, first is attracted by the 24th-street building, beautiful in

proportions, constructed of stone, and apparently built to stand for centuries. On inquiring he is informed that it is a school-house, and his first impressions are fortunate."[21] Its native Castle Rock lava masonry, laid in regular courses with rustic facing, gives substance to the work, and Roeschlaub's use of this indigenous material makes this school the first of his that could be considered truly Colorado architecture.

Paradoxically, the school's perfect balance and reticence, rather than the stylistic borrowings of Broadway and Centennial, are a demonstration of the essence of Palladian classicism. The robust organization of a true gable on each of the four facades—which marks the repeated yet slightly modified treatment of a projection in the center of the basic square—and the way the eaves break forward over these projections and under the gable is straightforward, rational work. Decoration is restricted to eave brackets,[22] voussoirs, and smokestacks: Roeschlaub rarely presents an unadorned chimney but finishes it off in an ornamented casing.

The change in style at Longfellow relates it to the next group of Roeschlaub's Denver schools: Ebert of 1880 (Fig. 3–7), Gilpin of 1881 (Figs. 3–8 and 3–9),[23] Whittier of 1883 (Figs. 3–10 and 3–11), and Delgany of 1885. All were given later additions by the architect. They are still sober rectangles but larger and higher with simple, imposing outlines. Roeschlaub's penchant for disciplined massing without monotony and symmetrical ordering relieved by the arrangement and variety of many openings contained within the surface plane produces a rich effect with little aid from decoration. These are marked, nonetheless, by a greater vitality of surface—red brick with a contrasting spare use of light stone in the foundations and trimmings. The effect of a conspicuously lighter tone for the most emphatic members is striking. Stone sills and keystones at Gilpin stand out in sharp though shallow relief. At Whittier and Ebert, four horizontal courses—two at sill level in stone—both further enliven the brick surface yet the banding also reinforces its compact unity. In a further variation of this linear ornament, a string course at Ebert serves as lintels above the windows and disrupts the decorative moldings of the arches at the first-story level. A cornice of fancy

Figure 3–8
Gilpin School
Denver, 1881
CHS F44844

brickwork, either graded horizontally or laid in a sawtooth pattern (a minor theme in Denver architecture and a leitmotif in Roeschlaub's work generally as a low-cost alternative to terra cotta or carved stone), girdles these schools and adds to the dry, incised effect. Brettell notes the distinct planes and sharp edges of these buildings; white mortar made each brick stand out in precise relief.[24] Roeschlaub introduces relief arches with decorative brickwork to the center projec-

tions of Ebert and Longellow. He frugally expands the use of this ornament at Ebert to the tympanum of the first-story windows. At Whittier brick trim, laid in dark red mortar, appears more extensively. But in these works Roeschlaub always confirms structural truth: ornament is integral with the surface of the building.

The technique of transforming the name and date of the school into an elaborate decorative plaque first occurs at Whittier. At Whittier, too, is a significant new

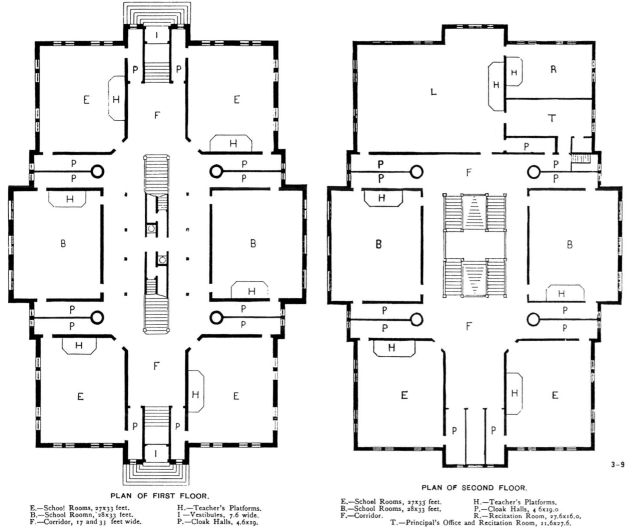

PLAN OF FIRST FLOOR.

E.—School Rooms, 27x33 feet.   H.—Teacher's Platforms.
B.—School Roomn, 28x33 feet.   I —Vestibules, 7.6 wide.
F.—Corridor, 17 and 33 feet wide.   P.—Cloak Halls, 4.6x19.

PLAN OF SECOND FLOOR.

E.—School Rooms, 27x33 feet.   H.—Teacher's Platforms.
B.—School Rooms, 28x33 feet.   P.—Cloak Halls, 4 6x19.0
F.—Corridor.   R.—Recitation Room, 27.6x16.0.
      T.—Principal's Office and Recitation Room, 11.6x27.6.

Figure 3–9
Gilpin School, 1881
Floor plans

3

addition to his decorative repertoire—gingerbread patterning of alternating light and dark stone voussoirs. Roeschlaub uses them again in the expansion of Ebert in 1892 and at the Lafayette (Maria Mitchell) School in 1898 and 1901. He gets the maximum decorative effect by such simple means.

In this group, Ebert and Delgany are distinguished by their tall, acutely tapered mansard roofs with crests and dormers. Ebert is especially distinctive

In plan, each of three schools—Gilpin, Whittier, and Emerson of 1884 (Figs. 3–12 and 3–13)[25]—offer an alternative on the theme of building in the round. All of Roeschlaub's schools had open space on ample lots for play, a functional consideration which set them back from the street and, incidentally, added to the perception that these were special monuments. In the mid-1880s he seized the opportunity offered by these unencumbered sites for multidirectional orientation to

3–1

in its verticality. Roeschlaub here pulls out the simple projection, caps it, and thus bestows an impressive entrance pavilion on a building that is otherwise very close in plan to Longfellow. These neatly organized, if somewhat brittlely detailed buildings of the early to mid 1880s reflect the values of honesty, economy, and dignity that Denver prized at the time in its school system. For Roeschlaub, appropriateness was a prime architectural virtue.

the city. At Gilpin the staircase, although narrow, has pride of place at the center, surrounded by eight iron posts that carry an open gallery; Roeschlaub was to perfect these two features as part of his repertoire for celebrating the building's core and circulation around it. As there are six rooms to each story, not the four of the Broadway model, an elongated plan was logical. Roeschlaub separates out the middle room from the main rectangular block with a new depth and empha-

Figure 3–10
Whittier School
Denver, 1883
CHS F44848

sis. He even adds an intermediary break in the massing of the lateral facades by flanking the midsection with cloakroom-corridors and expressing them on the exterior. Gilpin is a series of staggered, plain blocks that increase in height toward the center. Thus there is the suggestion of elliptical movement through, around, and over the building.

Elaboration, both decoratively and in plan, link Whittier School to Roeschlaub's schools of the late 1880s. Whittier is a dynamic departure and the beginning of a new prototype based on convex and concave shapes. The architect has rethought his previous solution to a first-story plan of six rooms, abandoning the block in favor of an elongated cross consisting of two rooms on the long facades and a wing of one room at each short end. This creates a void at the corners. Gilpin and Emerson retained two entrances lined up at midblock, as in Roeschlaub's earliest schools. At Whit-

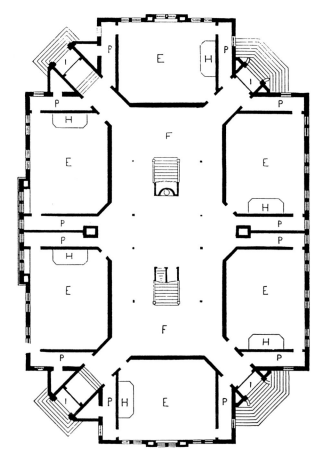

PLAN OF FIRST FLOOR.

E.—School Rooms, 28x33 feet.
F.—Corridor, 38.4x83 feet.
H.—Teachers' platforms.
I.—Vestibules, 8.7 wide.
P.—Cloak Halls, 4.6x18.

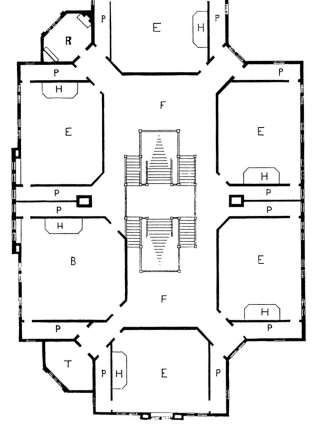

PLAN OF SECOND FLOOR.

E.—School Rooms, 28x33 feet.
B.—School Room, 35 6x33.4 feet.
F.—Corridor, 38.4x83 feet.
H.—Teachers' Platforms.
P.—Cloak Halls, 4.6x18.
R.—Principal's Office and Recitation Room, 13x19.
T.—Recitation Room, 13x19.

3-11

Figure 3-11
Whittier School, 1883
Floor plans

tier four entrances are set catty-corner at the transition from one facade to another. A great X-shaped path unfolds from the entrances through a series of vestibules. This bold organization is further refined: the circulation paths that extend from the corners do not quite cross; they actually form two V's pulled apart rather than a simple X. The apex of each V meets at one of two interior staircases in the communal central hall, which is fitted, like Gilpin, with a two-story gallery.

3-12

Thus the architecture works to draw one into the school.

For further spatial complexity, four classrooms at Whittier form a square at the school's center. Roeschlaub employs his familiar device of slicing off the innermost corners of these four rooms. Thus he takes what could have been a simple cloakroom-corridor set perpendicular to the long sides of the building and spatially implies an elongated hexagon at the center, which creates a minor elliptical path across and counter to the major circulation route around the hall. There is thus an intense propelling directional pull and a series of choices in this plan—in and out towards the exits, to the internal staircases, and around and

across the hall and gallery. Overlapping, yet individually distinct, dramatic spaces characterize the whole. There is a curious affinity between this Colorado architect and characteristics of spatial organization typical of the late eighteenth-century European architecture of certain churches and palaces, reinterpreted, with no stylistic borrowings, in a new land and for a democratic school system.[26]

Whittier is nearly symmetrical, consistent with all of Roeschlaub's schools, but not static: it seems to unfold in space. Thus the architect states of his building in the 1885 annual report of the school board: "Unfortunately, the building fronts the east (away from the city), so that the approach is towards the rear, making it necessary to go some distance *beyond* the building to obtain a view of it.... The finest view of Denver and the surrounding country may be obtained from the roof of this building, consequently many applications to go on the roof are made by visitors. To protect the roof, a broad walk is provided for their accommodation."[27] The highest and broadest of Whittier's many gables establishes the primacy of the elevation facing the city street. This combination of prominent gables and incipient corner pavilions, as well as its plan, establishes Whittier as an early version of an important Roeschlaub school type that he perfected at Corona (now Dora Moore).

Emerson School, too, shows Roeschlaub's interest in the building as an object in the round. The view of, and from, Emerson in 1884 was noted in the *Rocky Mountain News*: "The sight is a commanding one on Capitol Hill, far above the mass of the city, overlooking the town and facing the mountains."[28] In plan Emerson is still related to Roeschlaub's early blockish eight-room schools: "[It] will be somewhat larger than the Longfellow building, and is planned on much the same basis."[29] But Roeschlaub cautiously experimented with the concept of irregularity at Emerson and thus offers an alternative to the Gilpin-Whittier model. He treats Emerson not as a cube but as a series of four blocks slid out from the center, each of which has a different orientation to the compass. The beginning of a sense of rotation is created, as though each block were the spoke of a pinwheel anchored to the small but hexagonally shaped hall. The placement of the four corner towers and stairwells at Roeschlaub's Trinity Methodist Episcopal Church three years later would be the mature realization of this concept (Fig. 2–9).

Emerson School is unique. The asymmetrical organization of its elevation is as far as Roeschlaub goes towards expressing a romantic, picturesque point of view in his school buildings. A brick structure above a foundation of Colorado lava stone, Emerson exhibits

eclectic here; his sources take second place to his own character as an architect. Emerson, as at his other schools from 1880 to 1885, is a work of taut, precise lines on a contained surface.[32] Soon after its construction the *Colorado School Journal* commented on the novelty of the school: "The plan is entirely new and original, an outgrowth of the experience of Captain Roeschlaub, the architect of the Board, the members of the Board of Education, and Aaron Gove, the superintendent, in the

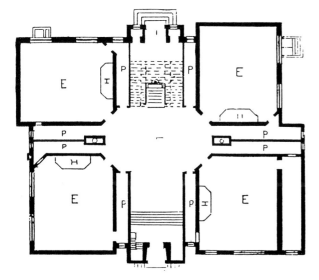

PLAN OF FIRST STORY.

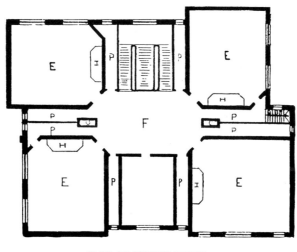

PLAN OF SECOND STORY.

E.—School Rooms.
H.—Teacher's Platform.
P.—Cloak Halls.
F.—Corridors.

3–13

virtuoso work in the design and execution of its extensive brick trim. The outstanding features are the entrance portal, a plaque on the west elevation with the date 1884, and the *pièce de résistance*, an immense sundial of stone on the entrance front, probably the first in Colorado.[30] The style is best described as neo-Tudor, a historical period that mixed Gothic and early Renaissance motifs, but it is more accurately "the Roeschlaub middle-period school style."[31]

The stolid portal, a singular occurrence in his school work, is gothic in outline and houses a doorway of simple Renaissance profile. Roeschlaub is creatively

erection of the many school buildings…in the district during the past ten years. In the planning of this building care was taken to introduce no feature that would produce aesthetic effect alone, and which would be detrimental to the convenience or comfort of the occupants of the house, or would in any way interfere with the work of the school."[33] The sundial was educational, no doubt. However, one may conjecture that Roeschlaub and Gove could not bring themselves to justify the pretty details of Emerson on the ground of their obvious intrinsic charm.

The picturesque point of view, revealed in details

Figure 3–13
Emerson School, 1884
Floor plans

91

at Emerson, recurred in isolated instances. For example, Roeschlaub incorporated a false-fronted, double-curved brick pediment into his school work once, at the one-story Free Kindergarten of 1890 (Fig. 3–14). The single documented example of his use of a stepped gable was for the Liller School (1884), the first brick school in Colorado Springs.[34] Perhaps these elements, common coinage in contemporary architecture of the 1870s and 1880s, were too frilly for Roeschlaub's taste. It

3–14

was more time-efficient to refine his school types rather than to start from scratch with each of his numerous commissions.

The architect's search for exemplary models included a subgroup to which he returned from time to time—schools with open belfries. The Washington School in Eaton, Colorado (1884), was a two-story white brick structure with a hipped roof and a gabled vestibule that served as the bell tower. The belfry itself was a light, simple affair.[35] On the other hand, the belfry at the Hinsdale School (1883) (Fig. 3–15) was an elaborate, Queen Anne extravaganza. It consisted of Stick Style bracing of ornate woodwork in Gothic arches and a steep pyramid roof complete with decorative dormers inset with carvings or plaques of a sunburst design. Whether or not they were necessary as timekeepers to summon their pupils, these belfries were effective symbols of the period when the school and the church were closely associated in men's minds. The school bell was a source of community pride.

The main line of Roeschlaub's development continued

with East Denver High School, his grandest school composition of the early and mid 1880s. Its site, obtained by former congressional representative Thomas M. Patterson, a client of Roeschlaub's, was on donated federal government land between Stout and California and Nineteenth and Twentieth streets. As evidence of its importance to the East Denver board of education, the board held a competition to choose the school's architect. Not surprisingly, considering the

3–15

confidence Aaron Gove had in him, Roeschlaub received the commission.

Although Roeschlaub planned the high school building as a whole in 1881, it was built in two stages that spanned nearly a decade. The first block (Fig. 3–16), which housed eight schoolrooms, was occupied by June 1881. A year later, the *Rocky Mountain News* stated that "among the elegant and substantial structures now in process of erection may be named the

Figure 3–14
Free Kindergarten School
Denver, 1890
CHS F49948

Figure 3–15
Hinsdale School
Pueblo, 1883
Pueblo Public Library

new high school building.... The era of tumble-down structures is happily past."[36] The erection of the main building (Fig. 3–17) was begun in February 1886 and partially occupied in September 1887. In March 1889 the *Western Architect and Building News* reported that the building was nearly finished.[37] The work was completed about January 1890.

The key to the stylistic treatment of the high school was its conception as a palace of learning,[38] a High Renaissance palace. The style of the first block was indicative of the whole, "finely proportioned [and] classic in design" (Fig. 3–18).[39] The repeated stone arches that surround the fenestration of the second and third stories have a weight and correct detailing new to Roeschaub's interpretation of the Renaissance. The school is adorned with full balustrades, medallions, and other manifestations of a classical vocabulary. Yet the jaunty rhythm of the spacing between the windows, the many inflections of the blocks, the inconsistency between the first-story detailing and the upper stories, and especially the stacked-up miniaturization of the dormers on top of the main block reflect an anticlassical, eclectic, High Victorian point of view.

The school was a major civic monument. One of the most important of the city's institutions, the public library, was housed on the first floor of the new building (Figs. 3–19 and 3–20)—the first separate structure for this purpose in Denver.[40] The library block had its own entrance and autonomy, and the formality of its entrance, consisting of granite steps leading up to three arches—a ceremonial portal similar to Trinity but reinterpreted in a classical vocabulary—bespoke the importance of this Denver institution (Fig. 2–31). Similarly, an assembly hall for school events was located on the second floor. This wing functioned, too, as a geological museum and a small astronomical observatory.

The high school and public library occupied an entire city block (Figs. 3–21, 3–22, 3–23, and 3–24). Landscaping was extensive for this building—the first time Roeschlaub enjoyed such luxury in his school buildings—and it is the only one of his Denver schools that was raised on a terrace.[41] Superintendent Gove thought of the high school building as an important

backdrop to public spectacle. The terrace wall, he stated, afforded "a convenient and comfortable seat for those who often frequent this 'breathing place,' and for the crowds who here congregate to witness the processions which invariably make this the turning point in their route."[42]

Roeschlaub redefines the meaning of appropriateness in school architecture with his East Denver High School, and it is a fitting symbol of the new era of

3–16

prosperity for Denver in the late 1880s. It was not only the most expensive school that he had done to date but the most costly building under construction in Denver in 1887. In its year-end review of building projects, the *Denver Republican* noted that "among the big buildings completed or commenced in the city during the year, the Denver High School is the most expensive. This structure is said to be the largest of its kind in the United States and cost close on to a quarter of a million dollars."[43]

Figure 3–16
East Denver High School
First wing
Denver, 1881
CHS F31201

The architecture of the new high school also symbolized an academic elite. It was designed to be the epitome of East Denver's educational system. One passed through the grand archway of the main, or northeast, entrance on Stout Street to an ample vestibule. Like the library, the administrative offices on either side of the vestibule could function as an autonomous wing. The north-south entrances formed a cross-axis to the heart of the school (Figs. 3–25 and 3–26),

3–17

which was a long hall, 122 by 60 feet, surrounded by a 6-foot-wide gallery extending around the walls and across the building's center. The large-scale, luxuriant spaciousness of the work was immediately communicated.

Because of the length of this building, Roeschlaub came up with a diversion from his prototype of the centrally planned school and interiors bathed in light. The direct view up to the coved ceiling of the high cupola is blocked by the bridge of the galleries, which divides the building in half. The soaring space of the building, then, is organized around two light wells. Especially effective is the way the staircases can be seen through the open galleries as though suspended in air, weaving their way through the three stories of the central block. By the varied intensity of light and partial views through a screen of iron colonettes, one is invited to explore. As Brettell has aptly written of the high school, "Roeschlaub was obsessed with movement. Going between classes and entering the library

were more important to him than actually being anywhere within the building, and he glorified the staircases and hallways."[44]

The high school building could also be called an architecture of light. In Roeschlaub's schools from 1875 to 1884, the practical improvement in natural lighting explains various design features. The dictum of the period—that lighting should come from behind and to the left of the pupils' desks—was taken seriously. At

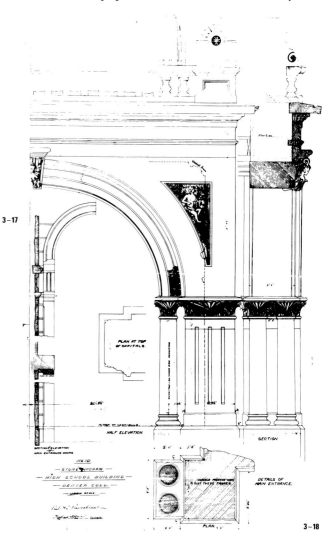

3–18

Figure 3–17
East Denver High School
Denver, completed 1890
CHS F49631

Figure 3–18
East Denver High School
Main entrance, portal detail
CHS F49927

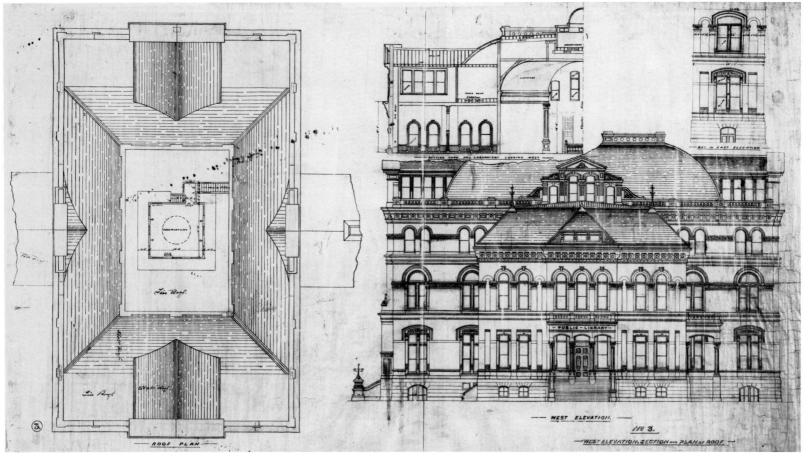

— WEST ELEVATION. № 3.

"WEST ELEVATION, SECTION and PLAN of ROOF"

ROOF PLAN

the Broadway School, Roeschlaub believed his lighting to be defective in three rooms because its source came from the right of the pupils. The Twenty-fourth Street School was supposedly "a great improvement" because desks were oriented in all cases to receive light from the back and left; at Emerson, too, the relationship of the teachers' platforms to the windows elucidates the plan.[45] From Longfellow and Ebert on, windows were large and high. The ceilings of the classrooms at Emerson were sixteen feet high, at the high school a full twenty feet. Light flooded the two stairwells and the many corridors of the high school's interior from the sides and from skylights above. Roeschlaub's technique for providing direct and indirect natural light is

3-20

Figure 3-19
East Denver High School
West elevation and roof
CHS F49925

Figure 3-20
East Denver High School
Interior, Public Library reading room
CHS F4905

95

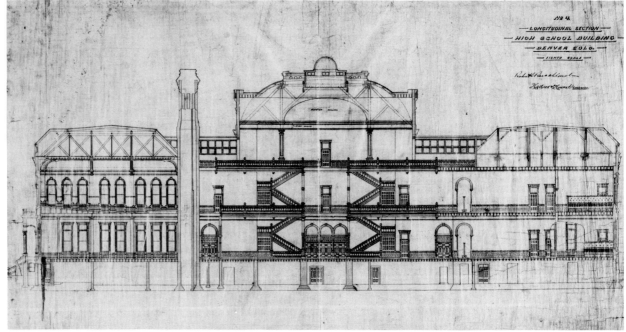

Figure 3–21
East Denver High School
Exterior view, California Street
Courtesy Peter A. Dulan

Figure 3–22
East Denver High School
Longitudinal section
CHS F49928

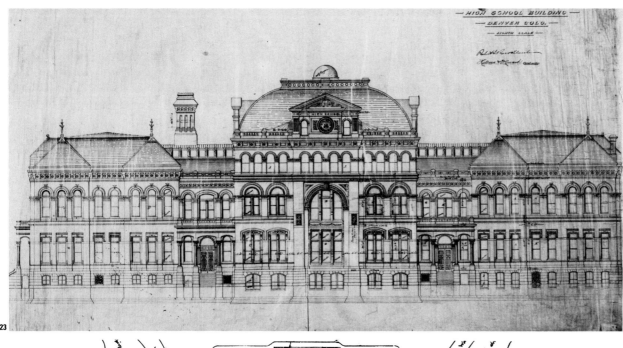

3-23

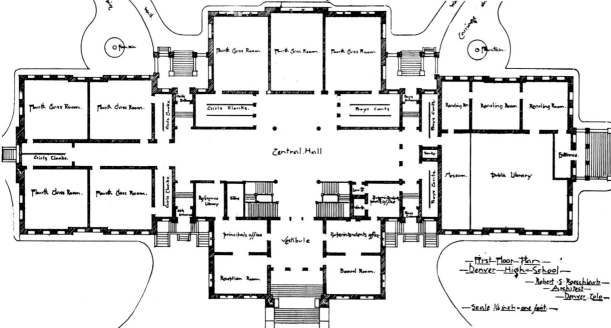

3-24

Figure 3-23
East Denver High School
South elevation
CHS F49923

Figure 3-24
East Denver High School
First floor plan

here taken to a higher level of architectural expression.

There is richness, even opulence, in the school's appointments. A marble-tiled hall in a light-and-dark checkerboard pattern ran the entire length of the first floor. The vestibule was furnished with Arts and Crafts stenciling in stylized flat patterns of leaves and flowers in the vestibule (Fig. 3–27). The building was finished throughout in polished black walnut and butternut. Drawings show that Roeschlaub was responsible for

the overall point of view of these schools, especially Hyde Park and Corona, as a series of shifting silhouettes. They are characterized by wild bursts of ornament on bold masses. Decorative terra cotta is used lavishly at Hyde Park, Corona, and Wyman for capitals, friezes, capstones, and spandrels over the doorways in a celebration of the experience of entrance. The rich color of these buildings depends on the intrinsic quality of their materials, unpainted in their

3–25

3–26

every detail of the design of the abundant, high-quality woodwork. A molded frieze beneath the ceiling was used throughout the public spaces of the first floor and in the assembly hall. One cannot be certain that this is Roeschlaub's design, but it unites the varied spaces, and its lush, dense quality provides a nice contrast to the open, central corridor.

The grand scale, spacious central hall, and expensive decoration of the high school were features that continued in the designs of Roeschlaub's most exuberant schools—those of the late 1880s. This group includes the Hyde Park (now Wyatt) School of 1887, Corona (now Dora Moore) of 1889, Wyman (1890–91), and Columbine (1892–93). In a major departure from Roeschlaub's earlier work, ornamentation is often in high relief and deeply shadowed, which underscores

original state—rose lava stone foundations and trim, a deep, dark red brick structure above, the red-orange of the terra cotta, and a combination of tin and slate roofs. In style the decoration is mostly based on freely interpreted Renaissance sources, from the langorous delicacy that recalls sixteenth-century Mannerist work above the portals of Corona to seventeenth-century references in the lusty, winding vegetation of the corner tower frieze of Wyman School.

However, Roeschlaub is at his best when, as in Trinity Methodist Church, he reinterprets nature directly. He does this, for example, in the terra-cotta plaque that combines the words "Wyman School" with a spraylike vine. Seminaturalistic Arts and Crafts details can also be noted on the drawing of Corona's west elevation, such as in the terminations at the corners of the gables and the terra-cotta band on the chimney. These schools are characterized, too, by enor-

Figure 3–25
East Denver High School
Second floor hall
CHS F49633

Figure 3–26
East Denver High School
First floor hall
CHS F49629

3-27

3-28

Figure 3-27
East Denver High School
Vestibule
CHS F49632

Figure 3-28
Hyde Park (Wyatt) School
Denver, 1887
Courtesy Peter A. Dulan

mous, high, pyramidical roofs; important gables; Richardsonian brick arches; and bulbous onion domes that cap prominent square pavilions.[46] A new bravura is exhibited at Hyde Park and Corona as this vocabulary is used to continue the Whittier prototype of architecture-in-the-round and to refine movement through interior spaces.

At Hyde Park (Figs. 3–28, 3–29, and 3–30) there is a preferred view: that of the fully three-dimensional

3–29

PLAN OF SECOND FLOOR.

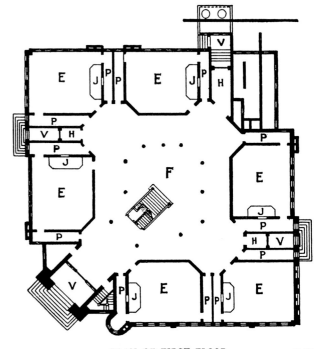

PLAN OF FIRST FLOOR.   3–30

entrance, which is delineated by a majestic pavilion set diagonally to the rest of the building at the corner of the site. The plan is thus split bilaterally. The elevations and circulation pattern radiate out from the entrance. Roeschlaub's experimentation is at his most playful at Hyde Park. The plan can be read as two somewhat triangular components aligned at the interior staircase. Roeschlaub did not quite reproduce one segment in mirror image but rotated it 180 degrees. Thus the control and geometry typical of his work prevails, but in elevation Hyde Park seems whimsical due to the

Figure 3–29
Hyde Park School, 1887
Interior
Courtesy Peter A. Dulan

Figure 3–30
Hyde Park School, 1887
Floor plans

staggered organization of its gables. The tall, round *tourette* of Romanesque derivation placed at one side of the main entrance, which Roeschlaub used at the Delgany School two years previously, is a true asymmetrical element. The plan identifies it as a nook inserted for pure delight rather than utility (Fig. 3–31).[47]

The interior of Hyde Park School is a dazzling combination of central staircase, backlighted by a large,

glazed area, and an octagonal gallery carried on slender colonettes. The plan of Hyde Park reads clearly as a centrally organized work because of its nearly equilateral proportions. In a variation of this Whittier-Corona model, which only appears at Hyde Park, four subsidiary, somewhat elliptical shapes overlap and further enliven the interior and accentuate a dynamic push outwards that typifies the schools of this series. There is intimacy to this space as well as changing vistas. As far as design can influence behavior, this architecture provided its pupils with an image of a school free of boredom.

Corona (now Dora Moore) School (Figs. 3–32, 3–33, 3–34, and PLATES 9, 10, 11)) exploited every possibility latent in the Whittier model of theatrical, sculptural architecture. Built between March and October 1889 and occupied in September 1890, it dominates the cityscape even today.[48] The by-now-familiar themes of a commanding site; a high, pyramidical roof and large gables; accentuated towers and onion domes; use

of fine materials; and care in heating, ventilation, and lighting were noted at the time.[49] The four entrance foyers at Whittier are reworked into full pavilions of three stories in the style that first appeared at Hyde Park. The interior spaces located on the second story of these towers were large enough to be used for the principal's office, a teachers' room, a library, and a recitation room; they were special spaces expropriated for the privileged people and activities of the school. Roeschlaub's dramatic changes in planes are thus accomplished by a manipulation of architectural mass and space. Stained glass, well-preserved in the transoms at Corona, was indicated on Roeschlaub's drawings for other schools, such as the high school.

Roeschlaub's drawing of the cross-section of Corona (Fig. 3–35), the only one for this group of schools that has survived, shows the central rotunda form typical of his schools of the late 1880s. Note the coved ceiling above an interior hall with ceremonial stairs. As at Whittier the stairs are centrally placed, an example of how Roeschlaub delights in crisscrossing space. One can see in the cross-section the glazed roof of this rotunda, exposed to a light shaft from the sides.[50] Roeschlaub's plan of the roof (Fig. 3–36) shows the elegant symmetry that controls the abandoned detailing, broken skyline, and general plasticity of Corona. This final drawing of the Corona series also reveals the elaboration of the roof truss structure and the full collection of the ventilation and exhaust ductwork to the two cupolas. Exposed mechanical equipment, such as pinnacles, cupolas, and gratings were fully integrated into the aesthetic expression of all of the architect's buildings,[51] but at Corona School these details are particularly attractive.

A tendency to straighten out the wavelike plans of Hyde Park and Corona can be detected at Wyman (Fig. 3–37) and Columbine (Fig. 3–38). Wyman exhibits strongly delineated end pavilions with onion domes, but they are lined up parallel to the main block. The school's static, noble quality is strangely akin in organization (but, except for the roofs, not in style) to French Baroque chateaux of the seventeenth century, such as

Figure 3–31
Delgany School
Denver, 1885

101

3-32

Figure 3–32
Corona (Dora Moore) School
Denver, 1889
W. H. Jackson photograph
CHS 3261

Figure 3–33
Corona School, 1889
Floor plans

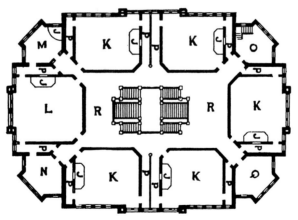

PLAN OF SECOND FLOOR.

K.—School Rooms
L.—School Room
M.—Recitation Room
N.—Principal's Room

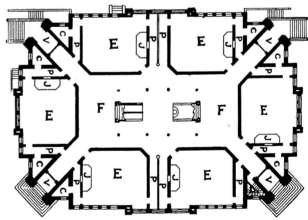

PLAN OF FIRST FLOOR.

E.—School Rooms
F.—Hall

3-33

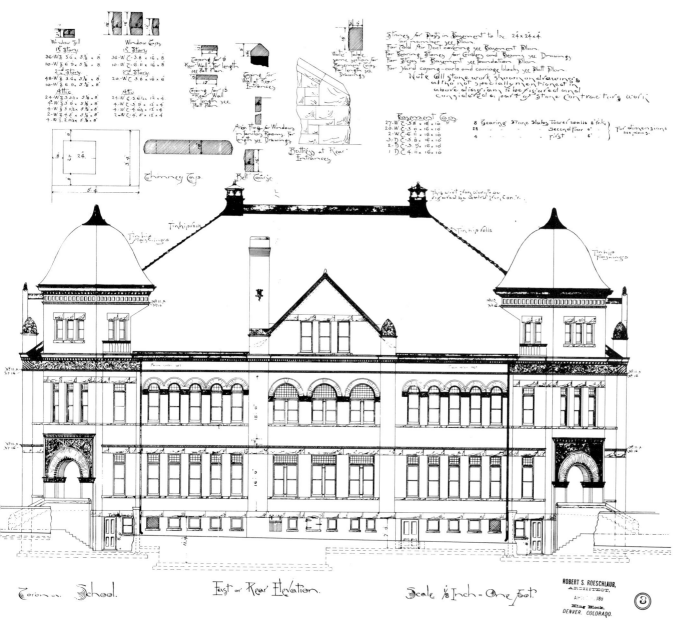

Corona School.

East or Rear Elevation.

Scale ⅛ Inch = One Foot.

ROBERT S. ROESCHLAUB,
ARCHITECT.
APRIL 189
King Block.
DENVER, COLORADO.

Figure 3-34
Corona School, 1889
Floor plans
Kenneth R. Fuller

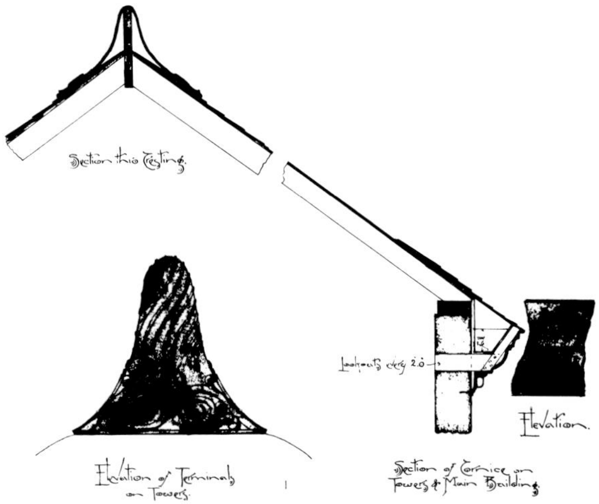

Half Transverse Section.
at E-F.

Section
thro' Tower Roof

Elevation of Vent and
Cresting on Main Roof
and Hip Rolls.

Elevation showing Truss
at Towers.

Elevation of Terminals
on Towers.

Section of Cornice on
Towers & Main Building.

Elevation.

Half Transverse Section.
at A-B.

Scale ⅛ Inch = One Foot.

Half Longitudinal Section
at C-D.

Corona School.

ROBERT S. ROESCHLAUB,
ARCHITECT.
APR 1889
King Block
DENVER, COLORADO.

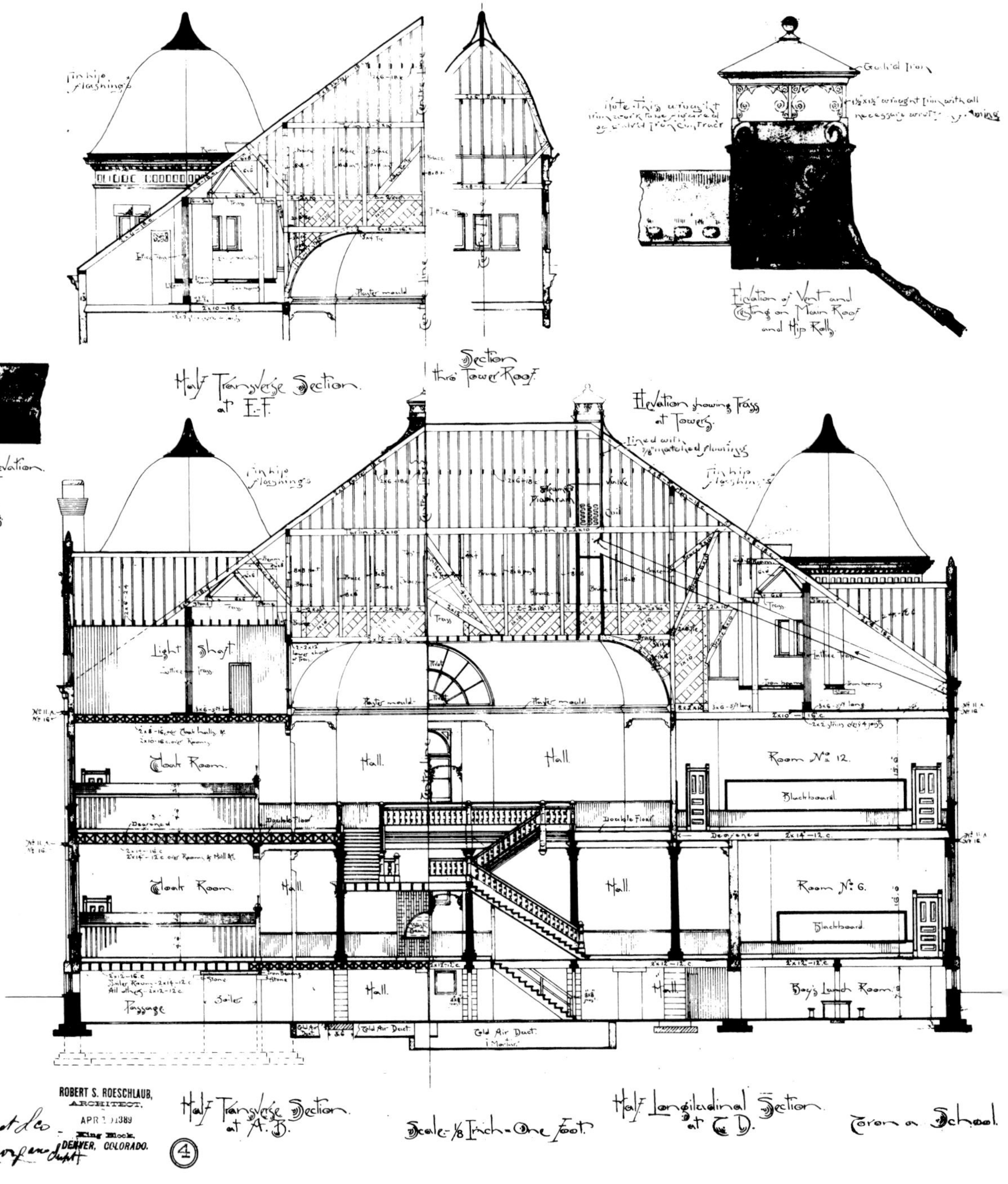

Figure 3–35
Corona School, 1889
Cross-section
Kenneth R. Fuller

3–35

104

Vaux-le-Vicomte. Columbine has a deep entrance vestibule angled to the main hall and exuberant, high roofs into which is inserted the only occurrence by Roeschlaub of the whimsical slit "eyebrow" window popularized by H. H. Richardson. But the bulbous domes are gone. The entrance pavilion is one story, not two or three. The largest block of Columbine is a plain wall of neo-Romanesque arches. Indeed, Roeschlaub's original design for Wyman was neoclassical (Fig. 3–39).

In the unbuilt version, the broken roofline and sections that step up to the center show a restlessness in keeping with his other work of the late 1880s, but the style anticipates the Beaux-Arts schools that Roeschlaub built after 1900.

In the 1890s Roeschlaub built additions to at least five of his schools of the 1880s. He designed a temporary portable schoolhouse (Fig. 3–40) that was used at Whittier and other sites to relieve the pressure of an

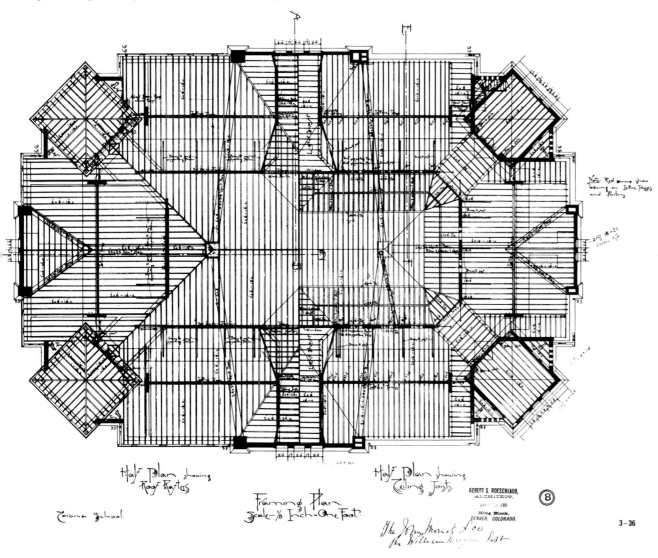

Figure 3–36
Corona School, 1889
Plan of roof
Kenneth R. Fuller

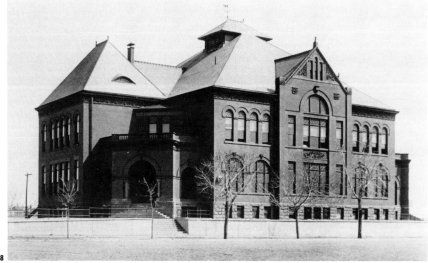

3-38

Figure 3-37
Wyman School
Denver, 1890
W. H. Jackson photograph
CHS J2057

Figure 3-38
Columbine School
Denver, 1891
Courtesy Peter A. Dulan

3-3

increased student population until these expansions were completed. The theme of incrementation was carried out very graciously. Duplication was one formula, established at East Denver High School. In this process, also used at Longfellow, the original block was cloned. Note the modification to Roeschlaub's methods of enlargement by comparing the Washington School in Colorado Springs of 1894 (Figs. 3–41 and 3–42) to the Lafayette (Maria Mitchell) School of 1898 and 1901 (Fig. 3–43). Washington and the early section of Lafayette were a sort of vernacular interpretation of the complex massing of the late 1880s. At Lafayette an open exterior platform staircase enables the school to be approached from two directions. It is typical of a type of exterior stairway commonly associated in the history of architecture with English neo-Palladian works of the early eighteenth century, such as Chiswick House.

Roeschlaub recognized the potential of this element as a staccato, distinct episode of spatial ambivalence that augmented his own architectural personality.

If such high-style analogies seem overpowering when made in reference to this workaday Denver public school, a study of Roeschlaub's school designs has demonstrated that he was capable of just such an understanding of the underlying principles of architecture. When he expanded Lafayette, he preserved the original block and added a long wing behind it, caboose fashion. At Whittier, he kept the 1883 building intact and added low flanking wings, an obvious approach to expansion (Fig. 3–44). Ebert, however, was enlarged by engulfing the 1880 school. In 1892 Roeschlaub eliminated its mansard and built out on two sides and over the original structure (Fig. 3–45). Indeed, a study of Ebert reveals that the high roofs of

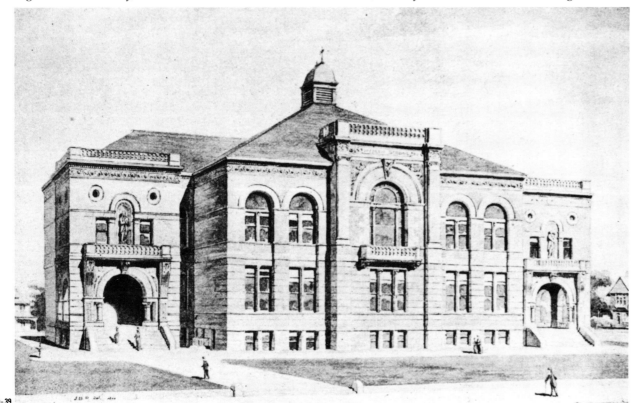

Figure 3–39
Wyman School
Project, c. 1890
CHS F44820

107

the late 1880s took their shape primarily as a result of Roeschlaub's search for better performance in heating and ventilation.

Ebert School of 1880 was the first schoolhouse in Colorado to use steam heating. The apparatus was supplied by John Davis and Company, which had recently opened a branch in Denver. An article of 1881 describing the Davis system in detail comments, "In designing this building the practical experience of the architect has been used to advantage."[52] Gary Long notes that the "overhaul of Ebert [in 1892] was major in its physical appearance as well as in its mechanical system, and style and function are beautifully integrated."[53] The roof of the 1880 Ebert was truncated, a modified mansard, while the roof of the expanded complex in 1892 was a high pyramid. Its renovated heating and ventilation system represents a fully developed gravity ventilation technology just before the introduction of powered fan systems.[54]

Roeschlaub's handling of gravity ventilation in many of his schools, including Corona, prior to 1893 is basically that of the later Ebert. The principle behind

this is that the greater the distance between basement and the exhaust cupola on the roof, the greater the draft for the gravity force; hence, the high, pyramidal roofs. The 1893 expansion at Gilpin (Fig. 3–46) marks a switch to a central fan-powered ventilation and pressurized exhaust system. The two fans and their electric motor are Sturdevant equipment, perhaps the first in

3–4[

3–41

3–42

Denver. "The 1894 addition to Whittier," states Long, "is one step ahead of Gilpin with two supply fans plus a central exhaust fan pulling all building exhaust down to the basement thence to the outside up a shaft alongside the boiler stack. Again, as with the other schools of the series, the original roof is Mansard, changed to a pyramidal form in the additions."[55]

The long-held prejudice of the board of education against the establishment of trade schools was reversed in the early 1890s, and the Manual Training High School, designed by Roeschlaub, opened in 1894 (Fig. 3–47). This school looks modern to twentieth-century eyes, accustomed to large areas of glazing in a plain brick cube, long and low. Roeschlaub's plan reflects aspects of the curriculum: foundry, forge room, and machine shop on the first floor; drawing rooms, carpenter and pattern shops on the second; and sewing room, cooking room, and physical and chemical laboratory on the third. The photograph of his school, taken from the rear, also reveals the division between the shop block and the administrative offices to the front. The facades of the administrative wing were divided into bays of two and three windows by colossal pilasters. The building thus expresses Roeschlaub's lifelong belief in a hierarchy of importance between building types and in the nineteenth-century difference between building and architecture.

The Clayton (Stevens) School of 1900 (Fig. 3–48, PLATE 16), Roeschlaub's last documented public school in Denver, is a huge barn of a building with a gabled roof plan in the shape of a Lorraine cross. It belongs to no particular type, but the marked use of skylights and the high roof, topped by a pinnacle, shows that Roeschlaub continues to deliver a well-lit, commodious interior. Its style is transitional. The buff-colored brick reflects a national change in taste, after Victorian riotous red, to neutral, subdued tones (Roeschlaub also used this material to face one of his commercial buildings in Denver, the Hover Wholesale Warehouse of 1902). However, the image conveyed by blank walls with little ornament for relief is one of paucity. There are episodes of classicism: the Federalist Style portals

consist of Doric engaged columns, an entablature with graceful Adamesque swags and festoons, and heavy keystones above a large lunette set in a brick frame. In contrast is the dynamism of the two flights of exterior stone stairs on the principal facade, which are set at an angle to the outer wings of the building. They continue the investigation of movement through space of Roeschlaub's buildings of the 1880s. One is actively drawn into the school by round, boulder-like stone

3–43

3–44

Figure 3–40
Temporary schoolhouse
Denver, c. 1883
CHS F49934

Figure 3–41
Cascade (Washington) School
Rendering, c. 1894
CHS F44823

Figure 3–42
Washington School
Colorado Springs, 1894
*Denver Public Library
Western History Department
P1669*

Figure 3–43
Lafayette (Maria Mitchell) School
Denver, 1898 and 1901
Courtesy Peter A. Dulan

Figure 3–44
Whittier School expansion
Denver, 1894 and 1897
(Compare Fig. 3–10)
CHS F49942

3-45

Figure 3–45
Ebert School expansion
Denver, 1892
(Compare Fig. 3–7)
Courtesy Peter A. Dulan

Figure 3–46
Gilpin School expansion
Denver, 1893
(Compare Fig. 3–8)
CHS F49441

3-46

appendages which splay out from the stairs; this swirl of the banisters recalls H. H. Richardson at his most Art-Nouveau. In a less pronounced form, the exterior steps to Chamberlin Observatory of 1890 were given a similar treatment, but at Stevens Roeschlaub exploits the device fully for the first time in his work. He remained inventive in his various solutions to the problem of procession.

After the great Columbian Exposition in Chicago of 1893, the academic norms of design and architectural education offered by the French École des Beaux-Arts increasingly dominated American architectural consciousness. During the first years of the new century, Roeschlaub and Son designed two schools of a monumental classicism. There is a Roman grandeur to Central High School (1905) in Pueblo (PLATE 19). As

3-47

3-48

Figure 3-47
Manual Training High School
Denver, 1893
Courtesy Peter A. Dulan

Figure 3-48
Clayton (Stevens) School
Denver, 1899–1900
Courtesy Peter A. Dulan

large as East Denver High School, it, too, was surrounded by a graded lawn and extended a full city block. Roeschlaub's preferred design, as illustrated in the drawing, had a central portico and dome. He used a heavy, colossal Ionic order for the two-storied portico. Although the high dome was a powerful visual device, it was a luxury and soon disappeared from studies.

The final design of Central High was more austere and substituted for the tall attic of the domed scheme a

of rigorous academic detailing, such as niches with classical statuary. There was a semicircular pavilion at either end with giant two-story, engaged pilasters of a Corinthian or Composite order.

The Greeley High School (1911) was designed after Robert K. Fuller joined the firm, as evidenced by his signature on the perspective rendering (Fig. 3–49). It, too, is a dignified Beaux-Arts building. The decorum of a small, eighteenth-century French palace, or *hotel*

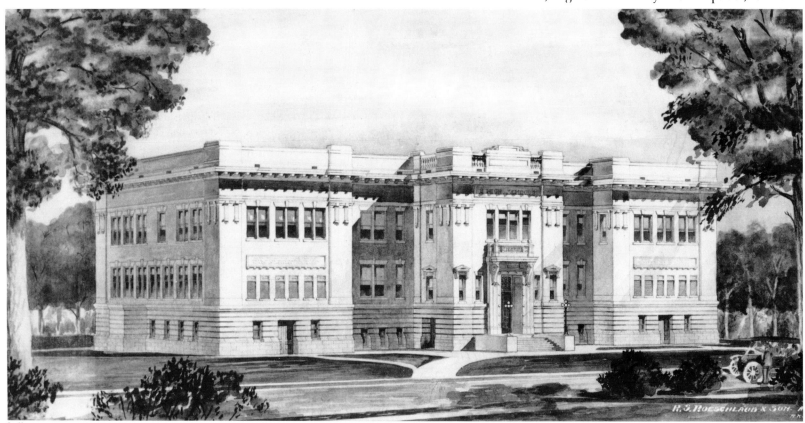

3–49

uniform crown consisting of a low balustrade. In the revised version, two and a half stories were fitted into the central portion. Rectangular openings replaced the arches of the main elevation, underscoring the sense of rectitude and the even rhythm of the building. By these small changes in the executed work, the central section was transformed into a broad block, flanked by wings

echoes in its horizontal line with a characteristically neoclassical insistence on plane surfaces, symmetry, and geometric precision. However, the short, vertical strips placed around the three evenly projecting sections of the building are not orthodox elements in the classical language of architecture. The severe doorway and most of the detailing are academically correct.

Figure 3–49
Greeley High School
Greeley, 1911
CHS F49630

Roeschlaub was primarily an architect of public institutions. His buildings, other than commercial or industrial structures, constituted the city's monuments. They were usually freestanding, like schools and libraries, or buildings of distinct appearance and self-contained purpose, such as churches. If these were the public symbols necessary to any cultural definition of a "city," however, the commercial work formed its fundamental spatial element—the streets. In this respect, Roeschlaub mostly produced filler structures and two, perhaps three, buildings of genius. Nevertheless, that quiet work helped to give Denver its urban character.

While Frank E. Edbrooke is rightfully known as Denver's commercial architect, the importance of Roeschlaub's commercial and industrial work has been underrated, largely because it was practically unknown before the 1980s. Richard Brettell, writing in 1973, states that Edbrooke "was almost singlehandedly responsible for the architectural maturity of Denver's downtown in the late 1880's and 1890's. A master of street architecture, he designed office blocks, street buildings and warehouses which transformed a commercial area...into a grand, large-scaled, and beautifully articulated grid."[1] Yet Roeschlaub, too, realized an opportunity to translate the two-dimensional, neutral pattern of the street grid, imposed on land to measure out most towns of the American West, into a three-dimensional texture.

In addition to twenty-four stores and forty-seven other business houses, Roeschlaub designed or improved at least ten factories or related buildings associated with Colorado's heavy industry, including powerhouses, soap works, breweries, malt houses, and tanneries. Of these, the Boston and Colorado Smelter (1878) at Argo in North Denver (Figs. 4–1, 4–2, and 4–3) is unique visual evidence for what was a substantial part of the architect's practice.[2] In architectural imagery, the Argo plant is an industrial city, its administrative center the sole "monument" amidst the "streets" of the surrounding barracks-like buildings. The starkness of the long industrial blocks has the sober beauty of unadorned utilitarianism.

The administrative building at Argo is distinctive. Its minimal architectural vocabulary emphatically con- veys the building's importance and a function apart from the industrial processes that surround it. A rectangular plan of one and a half stories in stone, it has a curious Latin cross plan at roof level.[3] Thus by the curt and reductivist means of an inflected facade on all four elevations—two centrally organized, two pushed asymmetrically to the back of the building—and a tower, which is Early Christian in origin but of the plainest octagonal formation, Roeschlaub singles out

4–1

his work. There is little stylistic pretension here, and the inherited architectural codes that Roeschlaub brought with him to the new West begin to emerge. The cultural shorthand of this little building was indiscriminately applied as well to Roeschlaub's early schools and residences of the 1870s.

While Roeschlaub's industrial buildings reflect the state's railroad and mining glory, his commercial blocks illustrate the shifting economic profile of Colorado's cities. For example, in 1873, according to a recent study of Denver's urbanization and planning history, the young city followed a stagecoach transportation model, its commercial heart lying along Larimer and Lawrence streets parallel to the South Platte River.[4] Thereafter, with the growth of the city to the east, Roeschlaub's

Figure 4–1
Boston and Colorado Smelter
North Denver (Argo), 1878
Administration Building
CHS F6646

commissions for office blocks helped to define the architectural development of a new center of commerce, especially of business, banking, and retail trade. From the late 1870s to about 1890, rail and tramway lines along Fifteenth, Sixteenth, and Seventeenth streets gave impetus to a progressive expansion and shifting of the business district towards Broadway. In a parallel development, Roeschlaub's many stores, warehouses, and manufacturing establishments, erected

The pattern was repeated by other architects throughout the West.

Two examples of Roeschlaub's early commercial work, the William A. Hamill Office and Carriage House in Georgetown (1879–80), are in several respects exceptions (Figs. 4–4 and 4–5). Georgetown became the commercial hub and service center of an extensive mining region in the wake of silver discoveries in 1864. The peak of the boom was reached in 1877 when five

4–3

thousand people lived in the valley; that year the town was connected to Denver and ultimately the East by the Colorado Central Railroad. "Throughout the 1880's the town enjoyed an opulent stability. . . . Fine brick buildings were constructed to replace some of the more temporary wooden ones. Flagstone sidewalks, granite walls, and a city park were further signs of refinement and permanence."[5] Prosperity lasted until the silver crash of 1893. William A. Hamill's wealth and influence grew tremendously during the 1870s, and in 1879 he sold to investors several mining properties which had become extremely valuable."[6]

In addition to improvements to his residence,[7] Hamill "purchased sufficient land on the west end of his house lot to begin construction of a 2½ story granite office building and a large two-story stable and carriage house."[8] The Hamill Office and Carriage House complex, at the present-day address of 305 Argentine Street, is a charming miniaturization of nationally popular styles. They relate strongly to each other as a

4–2

between 1875 and 1905 in the older center, or what came to be known as Lower Downtown, confirms that area's emergent, and then dominant, architectural character. Whether considering Roeschlaub's architecture of elaborately modeled facades, such as the Times Building, or plainer buildings such as the King Block, he was one of the first, and one of the few, architects responsible for the emphatic definition of the physical fabric of Denver's central business district, a dense core of brick and stone brought to a height of four or more stories.

Figure 4–2
Boston and Colorado Smelter
Unknown rendering
CHS F31202

Figure 4–3
Boston and Colorado Smelter
W. H. Jackson photograph
CHS J2069

group and show Roeschlaub's increased confidence in his design repertoire.

The office is an "unusual building in a remarkable state of preservation, a rare artifact of Colorado's mining history."[9] The high profile of the truncated hip roof and especially the black cresting, a decorative enhancement ordered from a commercial catalog, identify "French Chateau," as it was concurrently being employed in full orchestration at the Tabor Grand Opera House of 1879–80. But Roeschlaub evokes the memories of high culture almost generically. Irregular quoins seam the edges of the building, a device typical indeed of the Henry IV style but used in exactly the same manner as at the early Broadway School, which was Palladian, not French. Segmental arches of three stones over the doors and windows, and dormers and wood brackets (which have nothing French about them) under the pronounced wood eaves produce a work of great civility. The formal quality and Roeschlaub's sense of hierarchy is enhanced by the east front, the most important facade, and side elevations, which receive regular coursing of ashlar granite masonry over brick, contrasted with an irregular rubble wall to the rear.[10] The dormer woodwork on the east elevation is oversized and cut to look like stone. Borrowing the greater value of stone over wood by this representational device had an honored history in American architecture going back to colonial times; within ten years, Roeschlaub's change in architectural philosophy to "truth to materials" would forbid such innocent trickery.

While the exterior of the Hamill Office is very fine, the interior design and detailing make it a spectacular architectural work (Figs. 4–6, 4–7, and 4–8). The ground floor plan shows Hamill's private office, which was never finished, and a public office with a magnificent banking counter and matching grand stair and vault from which he ran his mining operations. Elaborately designed woodwork, paneling, and stairways were installed, though some were never painted or papered; perhaps Hamill ran out of money and was persuaded to finish his residence first. Details of the newels, balusters, and handrails of the stair are standard manufactured woodwork in American black walnut,

bought from catalogs.[11] However, nearly all of the other woodwork was custom-made on site for the mine owner; Roeschlaub's superior talent for woodwork design is demonstrated here. The work, cut and assembled in place, is made of native species of walnut and butternut ("white walnut") and finished with veneers of walnut and English burl. The style is a "hybrid of Eastlake and [Georgian] Renaissance Revival."[12] Of an exquisitely balanced Georgian composition of applied pilasters and a full entablature

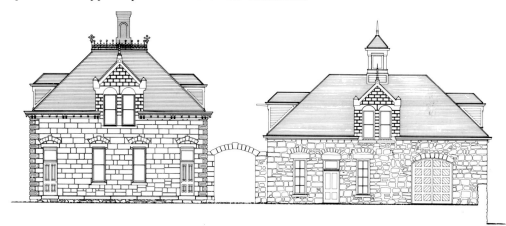

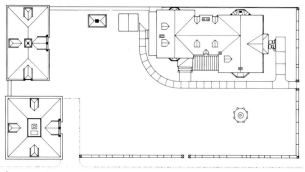

4–5

complete with broken pediment are eleven 12-foot-high window and door frames situated on the main floor. While these all match in detail, each is slightly different in dimension (further evidence that they were individually carved on the site). Of Eastlake inspiration is the whimsical, even eccentric, compilation of architectural motifs at the foot of the stair with a squat column

Figure 4–4
Hamill Office and Carriage House
Georgetown, Colorado, 1879
Courtesy Long-Hoeft Architects

Figure 4–5
Hamill Office Building, 1879
Site plan
Courtesy Long-Hoeft Architects

115

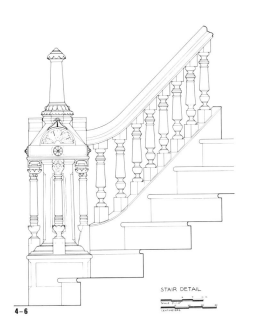

STAIR DETAIL

4-6

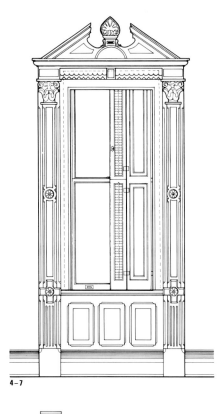

4-7

4-8

4-9

as its towerlike apex, so three-dimensional as to be an experimental model of a mini-building.[13] Roeschlaub did not adapt Eastlake's underlying principles of rationalism towards materials here or in his commercial work until the Central Block of Pueblo (1889), but stylistic motifs were taken up immediately. Indeed, it was Roeschlaub's accepting attitude towards rich interior decor and ornament that was to shape his architectural work in the early 1880s.

The Hamill Carriage House, the only identified survivor of Roeschlaub's nineteen stables and barns, is located at the rear of the Hamill House property, adjacent to the office building. "It has some similar design elements with the Office Building, but it is differently proportioned and its stonework is less refined."[14]

These were free-standing buildings; simultaneously, Roeschlaub developed his street-front, common-party-wall blocks typical of towns larger than Georgetown. In his commercial and industrial architecture, the idea of transformation within an easily identifiable type—office block or warehouse —is paramount. His work of contiguous partition walls keeps the unity of the grid and continuity of the street but without monotony. Not every one of his commercial works stands out, and properly so; the beauty and human quality of the pre–World War I city derives from the predominance of the street over the individual building.[15] The chronology of Roeschlaub's

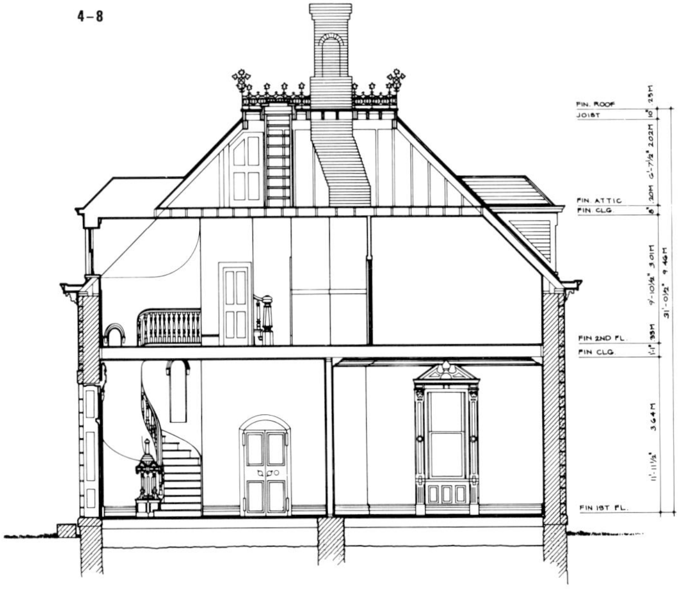

Figure 4-6
Hamill Office Building, 1879
Detail of stair
Courtesy Long Hoeft Architects

Figure 4-7
Hamill Office Building, 1879
Window elevation and section
Courtesy Long Hoeft Architects

Figure 4-8
Hamill Office Building, 1879
Section
Courtesy Long Hoeft Architects

Figure 4-9
Chever Block
Denver, 1879
CHS F31250

116

work in Denver points to the economic boom of 1879 to 1882 as his peak for commissions of this type; the doldrums of the mid-eighties are followed by active years between 1889 and 1891 and again, at a lower level, in 1901–2 (Fig. 1–37). Unfortunately, one often knows more of Roeschlaub's clients than of the appearance of his buildings, and written descriptions are more abundant than visual documentation.[16]

The Charles G. Chever Block, built for $21,000 at Seventeenth and Larimer streets in 1879,[17] expresses in a fancified way the basic Denver commercial formula that had been established in the 1860s (Fig. 4–9). The early Denver blocks have aptly been described as eventless: two-story brick buildings with a repetitive rhythm of arches or cast iron and plate glass fronting the street, identical windows placed equidistant, and flat cornices.[18] Later views of Larimer Street, from about 1880, show three and even four stories—the height of the Chever Block—as the norm. Contemplating this building, one might miss its virtues—a lack of fussiness and an absence of cultural pretense. Roeschlaub applies ornament like icing; the double cornice with brackets seems like appliqué work, yet the overall impression is one of several facades of increasing liveliness, in keeping with High Victorian taste.

Roeschlaub's problem here, and the underlying theme that makes sense of his commercial blocks up to 1882, is to define the relationship of increasingly large buildings to the street and to human scale. The task is exacerbated by the conflict between the horizontal emphasis of stacked stories and vertical expression. The Chever Block is best read as a series of facades divided by thin, vertical, nonstructural engaged half-columns, some of which may be rain spouts. The potential of this feature to express verticality is a theme the architect developed most fully in Pueblo's Central Block. Each of the main facades above the shops has a dominant central feature of tripartite window and narrow flanking windows; the side of the building has five vertical bays that widen toward the center. There is some argument in arrangement between an even division into bays and a central emphasis. But ornament meant luxury and success, a coming of age for Denver. This was the general direction of American architecture

and the line Roeschlaub's commercial architecture was to follow for the next few years.

The King Block, begun on December 5, 1879, and finished in late summer of 1880, was located on the west side of Lawrence between Sixteenth and Seventeenth streets. The first built version (Fig. 4–10), three stories high with a basement, Roeschlaub redesigned in 1889 for an additional two stories, though this addition was not constructed until 1902 (Fig. 4–11).[19] It

4–10

Figure 4–10
King Block
(From advertising card, Denver City Directory)
Denver, 1879
CHS F31247

occupied six lots. The architect divided up the long footage of 150 feet to read as a row of small blocks. The occasional narrowing of a bay and the architrave, dated "1880," which rises above and relieves an otherwise even roof line, are devices to achieve diversity within unity. The street, once again, is more important than the individual block.

Above the building's six ground-floor storerooms with iron and plate glass fronts, the detailing is "dry,"

4–11

in low relief as at the Chever Block. Fenestration composed of Gothic lancets decorates the second floor; the reduced architectural vocabulary, effective nonetheless as a cultural symbol, is revealed in the mere triangular forms above the third-floor windows, which represent pediments. Roeschlaub, as usual, was

concerned with lighting, ventilation, and heating. Stated the *Rocky Mountain News:*

> On the second and third floors there will be a number of offices *en suite*, with hallways twenty-two feet wide, extending from end to end, parallel with the street, and to be lighted by a skylight twenty-two feet wide and ninety-six feet long, arranged for ventilation as well as light. The building will be heated by steam. Above the store fronts the brick will be entirely concealed by

4–12

elaborate work in Morrison red sandstone, Castle Rock lava (pink and purple), and gray rock from Manitou. The King block will be owned by Messrs. H. H. and F. G. King, who are contributing largely to Denver's growth and importance.[20]

When he added the two stories, Roeschlaub terminated the building with dormers and Flemish gables. The remodeling was an effort by a later owner, J. M. Johnson, to reaffirm faith in the lower downtown as a business district. He saw "favorable symptoms" indicating that "the up town movement so far as many classes of business are concerned, is coming to a halt.... The [Capitol] hill trade is not the whole thing.... [The King Block's] rooms are spacious and suitable to the display of samplers. They are in demand

Figure 4–11
King Block expansion
Designed c. 1889
Completed 1902
CHS F44837

Figure 4–12
Laramie State Bank
Laramie, Wyoming
CHS F44819

for that purpose now as soon as an elevator is put in the building: It is on the border line of the wholesale and retail quarters, a line of demarcation that promises to be permanent."[21]

Reflecting Colorado's need for rapid capitalization in the Age of Enterprise, Roeschlaub's offices included at least seven commissions specifically for banks. The

simple device of cutting through the corner edge of the building at a slant, the grid of the city is interrupted by a cross-axis. Augmenting this counter-rhythm is the extension of the diagonal facade above the line of the cornice.[23]

The Moritz Barth Block (1882), at 1210 Sixteenth Street on the northwest corner of Lawrence, and the Union Block, begun in 1881 and finished in 1882 at the southwest corner of Arapahoe and Sixteenth streets,

4–13 4–14 4–15

corner of the Chever Block originally housed the Exchange Bank; Charles Chever, its financier, was in the real estate and investment business.[22] The Laramie (Wyoming) City Bank (Fig. 4–12) is a transitional work related to the early type by its mere two stories, since smaller cities tended to repeat Denver's progression in architectural scale at a later date. Its exterior shows a greater degree of light and shade. The Italianate fenestration on the second story is crowded, plastic, and tense. A startling feature of this otherwise ordinary work is the termination of the decorative piers of the second floor, which appear at intervals of one or two windows; they stop abruptly at keystone level above the fenestration, perhaps an unwitting expression of dismay at the irresolution of the work. Whatever its date, it belongs to a group of business blocks that address the street in a different way: by the

gain credibility as extensions of this urbanistic type. The Denver streetscape, ever grander, had now reached four stories—of stone, not brick. In an 1880s photograph of Sixteenth Street (Fig. 4–13), the mansarded ranges of these two works, one behind the other, punctuate the even rhythm of the relentless city grid, exuberant objects against the sky, marking street intersection and building entrance.

Roeschlaub's first version of the Barth Block (Fig. 4–14) had a true tower, a spindly structure that rose a full story above the dormers, much like Richard Morris Hunt's Tribune Tower in New York (1873), a widely published paradigm for office tower design. As built, the "economy package" (Fig. 4–15) had far less exterior ornament than the Union Block (Fig. 4–16). The corner treatment above the cornice in both buildings of this type is Second Empire, especially the deeply shadowed

Figure 4–13
View of Denver's Sixteenth Street, looking northwest. The Union Block is on the left and the Barth Block is behind (1880s).
W. H. Jackson photograph
CHS J2033

Figure 4–14
Project, Moritz Barth Block
Denver, c. 1882
CHS F31246

Figure 4–15
Barth Block
Denver, 1882
CHS F44829

119

oeil-de-boeuf which breaks through the cornice at the Union building; this "small cupola defined the top of the bank."[24] The rest of the Union is more accurately Queen Anne. What both styles have in common—the former based on French Renaissance and Baroque sources and the latter on Jacobean and eighteenth-century motifs—is a point of view: late Victorian extravagance of ornamentation, loaded surfaces, and top-heavy elevations, the glory of inventiveness.

4-17

4-16

Indeed, the Union Block is a work of fragments, and the advantage of the Queen Anne was its flexibility. The architectural theme is the transformation of the facade within the uniformity of the street. Roeschlaub conceived of this work as four separate buildings, which, in fact, represent the reality of its functions. Contemporary criticism referred to it as four-in-one, the whole standing as the Union Block but differentiated into 1) the Union Bank; 2) the Gottesleben jewelry store and office (the entire building being owned by the Peter Gottesleben family); 3) a section of general rented office space and residential apartments; and 4) the *Denver Republican* newspaper plant and its administrative offices (Fig. 4–17). The Republican's entrance, skewed between Sixteenth Street and the alley, recalls that of the main intersection but is accorded a different treatment. Thus a loose unity is restored.

The native stone of the Union Block contributed to a warm coloration typical of Queen Anne, but, as Brettell notes, the massive character of the material, roughly dressed, is at odds with the episodic character of the building.[25] However, the very materials of the Union Bank were seen to symbolize its purpose and gave a distinct regional identity to the otherwise common parlance of an Anglo-American architectural vocabulary. "The Union Bank building," states a contemporary publication, "is of solid granite. . . . Its safe deposit department has two large vaults in the basement, constructed of railroad iron and other material—the very personification of strength—and finished in superb style. They are positively fireproof, and are burglarproof to the extent that no gang of that gentry could possibly make an impression upon the bolts and bars before they would be discovered at the work, and are so pronounced by the best experts."[26] A great novelty in Denver, these were safety deposit vaults for individual clients. "In every particular, the Union Bank structure was built for the purposes to which it is now devoted, and in all its adjuncts, appointments and accessories is simply perfection for its uses."[27]

Architecture that addressed the needs of the street with forms such as quaint Dutch broken pediments could also serve the precise functions dictated by newspaper production. The Republican portion of the Union block was not only "one of Denver's. . . ornaments" but a "peculiarly convenient and well arranged one for the printing business."[28] In a spacious and deep basement were heavy cylinder presses and a steam engine. The first floor had "beautifully frescoed" offices to the front and job and mailing rooms to the rear. On the second floor were two immense rooms for newspaper composition and make-up. Above them, on the third floor in front, were the editorial offices; the other half of the upper floor was used for the bindery and other mechanical operations. There were both freight and passenger elevators. All through, the offices were placed towards Sixteenth Street, the production units along the alley—a duality that conforms to the hierarchy of the city and to the architectural composition of the building itself.[29]

Figure 4–16
Union Block
Denver, 1881–82
CHS F31221

Figure 4–17
Republican Building
(Part of the Union Block)
Denver, 1881–82

The *Denver Times* office at 1547–51 Lawrence Street of 1881 (Fig. 4–18) is the happiest of Roeschlaub's highly modulated and charged facades of composite style: Queen Anne sunbursts, medieval pointed arches, and squat half-columns on the top floor, and Italianate quoining and symmetry. It, too, exhibits the strident polychromy favored nationally: "The Denver *Times* has the handsomest building of any newspaper within a radius of many hundred miles," stated a contemporary article. "It was constructed of four kinds of Colorado stone, viz: the Morrison red, Trinidad blue, Castle Rock lava, and a red granite from the South Platte." Functional as well as beautiful, the "building is as nearly fireproof as possible, and its internal finish is every way equal to the outer. The woodwork is polished oak, and the floors tile."[30] The elevation is built up of elements in ever-increasing relief. This point of view, which enlivens the building as it seems to project into and over the street, is a hallmark of later neo-Gothic architects. For all that, Roeschlaub's detailing is still small-scaled and conventional in the Queen Anne manner compared to the boldness of a Frank Furness or even less exceptional architects such as Ware and Van Brunt.

The Times type was popular in Denver—a block with a strong central emphasis achieved by an inflected bay, voussoirs that disrupt and push up the cornice to erupt in a flamboyant broken pediment, as here, or with a gable. It combined disciplined organization with the exuberance of a city and an architecture pleased with itself. If the Union Block is a paradigm for corner elements, this is an updated version of the type that faced the street straight on.

By the time Denver's building boom of 1879–82 was over, Roeschlaub had played an important role in the spread of the new business district towards Broadway and Capitol Hill. When his 1880 Bancroft Block on Stout and Sixteenth streets was torn down in 1902, a reminiscing article in the *Times* encapsulated the change: "The old [Bancroft] block was the finest thing of the kind uptown about twenty years ago. All the old citizens who had homes on Sixteenth street a quarter of a century ago were enriched within fifteen years by the growth of business up that street."[31] In 1899

Roeschlaub renovated the building for the Preis clothing company which "remove[d] from their old establishment on Larimer street [to] take possession of their new quarters in the Bancroft block.... [A] desire to keep in closer touch with the people, to be where the people want to come, and to keep in line with the upward trend of the commercial life of the city, necessitated the present move to the Sixteenth street establishment."[32]

4–18

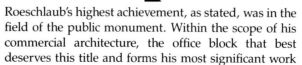

Roeschlaub's highest achievement, as stated, was in the field of the public monument. Within the scope of his commercial architecture, the office block that best deserves this title and forms his most significant work

Figure 4–18
Times Building
Denver, 1881
CHS F44834

121

in a cityscape was not built for his own city of Denver. Instead, his masterpiece, the 1889 Central Block for Mssrs. Thurlow and Hutton, was erected in Pueblo, Colorado, "the city of forges, furnaces and factories...this hurrying, bustling, industrious Pittsburg [*sic*] of the West" (Figs. 4–19 and 4–20, PLATES 14 and 15).[33] Here Roeschlaub realized a cathedral of commerce in an age when the office block began to rival the church as the most prominent building type in the

to each shop individually; shoppers were not accorded entry to the building itself but redirected outward towards city life. The rotunda began on the second level; a special entrance penetrated into the office building through a vestibule which led immediately by stair or passenger elevator one story up. For the select group whose business took them inside, the rotunda (which predates by a few months the famous galleried well of Frank Edbrooke's Brown Palace Hotel in Denver)

4–19

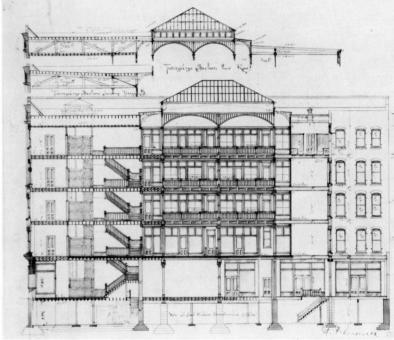

4–20

American city—indeed, the type that *defined* the city.

A five-story masonry building with a central glass-roofed well of spatial majesty, the Central Block continues the development of the interior courts favored in several late nineteenth-century building types. The nineteenth-century city typically stressed the differentiation of public and private spaces, or between entry and circulation, and the Central Block exemplifies these distinctions. Its facade, with shops on the first floor, served the street, while the central well became an intermediate zone between public and private business. The building offered the public access

served as an enclosed semipublic plaza.

The Central Block, a major work of the architect, rivals anything in Chicago at the time. In organization of plan and structure—external walls of bearing masonry, interior glazed lobby, and internal metal skeleton—it is closest to Chicago's Rookery Building (1888) by the architects Burnham and Root. Specifically, Roeschlaub erects an exterior bearing wall and nine-inch cast-iron columns vertically stacked on the interior. These columns are set on an irregular grid, responding to the variety of spans and interior spaces Roeschlaub desired. Eight-inch-wide exposed cast-iron

Figure 4–19
Central Block
(Thurlow and Hutton Building)
Pueblo, 1889
CHS F44936

Figure 4–20
Central Block, 1889
Elevation

colonettes support the balconies in the rotunda. The I-beams, which rest on the cast-iron columns, are of twelve-inch steel; the Second Street elevation indicates structural steel lintels, which are left exposed above the ground floor. Roeschlaub did the calculations for the building himself as his notations on the drawings for the Central Block demonstrate.

Indeed, the Chicago connection is even more pronounced. The directness of the facade has another

4-21

source. This is Roeschlaub's first commercial edifice to be modeled closely on H. H. Richardson's Marshall Field Wholesale Store of 1885–87 (Fig. 4–21) and on the recent work of the master of skyscraper design, Louis Sullivan—namely, the Chicago Auditorium Building, designed in 1886 and built in 1887–89 (Fig. 4–22). Sullivan's first really great work, the Auditorium Building, in turn, derived largely from Richardson's Marshall Field Store, at least in regard to the exterior.[34]

"Chicago architects," states William H. Jordy, "were variously affected by the austere force of [Richardson], none more so than Sullivan. And none better learned the lesson of Richardson's example than he. So much was this the case that, as [Sullivan] grasped the power of Richardson's box—solely articulated as it was by the repetitive motifs of its openings, and by moldings and textural changes integral with the quarry-faced ruggedness of its masonry walls—Sullivan radi-

cally altered his own preliminary schemes for the elevations of the Auditorium."[35] Roeschlaub was equally impressed. He kept illustrations of all of Richardson's designs and of the Auditorium Building in his clippings, and he had already worked the previous year with Sullivan's chief interior decorators, Healey and Millet, on Trinity Church in Denver.

Expressing the grandeur of scale and regularity of Richardson's Marshall Field Store, Roeschlaub's Central

4-22

Block testifies to the influence of Richardson's late work. Here Roeschlaub exchanges the prettiness of his earlier Italianate and Queen Anne business buildings for a blockbuster. In a first version of the Central Block, published in April 1889, filials rise above the roof line in a wavy broken skyline favored by the picturesque Queen Anne (Fig. 4–23).[36] Yet, as executed, the building is all solidity—the cornice flat and severe like Richardson's monument (although the diapered or checkerboard-set brick in this harsh terminus is based on the Rookery). The concept of unifying a tall building beneath vertical arcades of several stories is a lesson drawn from both the Richardson and Sullivan examples, and five stories established a new phase of grandeur and height in the urbanization of Pueblo.

The exterior of the Central Block, considered "very handsome" by the local press, was built of the best materials.[37] The color of the building, in three-toned

Figure 4-21
H. H. Richardson
Marshall Field Warehouse
Chicago, 1885
Chicago Historical Society
ICHi 01688

Figure 4-22
Louis Sullivan
Auditorium Building
Chicago, 1886–89
Chicago Historical Society
ICHi 18768

red, was as strident as any of Roeschlaub's Queen Anne work, and the terra-cotta detailing retained the love of freely interpreted nature, which makes it very much a part of the international Arts and Crafts mentality. The difference, as we have seen, is in its strict order. The piers and entrance in the first story—the jambs, arches, buttresses, and trimmings—were of hard, red sandstone. The four upper stories were built of hard, red, pressed brick laid in red mortar. The belt

4–23

courses, panels, terminals of buttresses, and cornicing were of ornamental terra cotta designed and made especially for this work. The look of the rough-hewn stone is Richardsonian, but Roeschlaub shaped the vertical organization of the business block from the Sullivan model of the Auditorium Building. It is one of a successive ascending svelteness of exterior surface, from a brusque ground story to smooth upper stories.

The depressed arch of the Central Block's main entrance derives indirectly from the Richardsonian "Romanesque" (actually the Early Christian in Syria, as Hitchcock showed long ago), but this is not present at the Marshall Field Warehouse. Roeschlaub's earth-hugging doorway seems to express the burden of the building's weight. It is similar to Sullivan's portals at the

Auditorium Building and, significantly, to the last of a row of ground-story arches in the nearby Pueblo Opera House on Union and Fourth, under construction by Adler and Sullivan at the same time as the Central Block (Fig. 4–24).[38] Adler and Sullivan made frequent, extended visits to Pueblo from June 1888 through September 1890.[39] Formally, Roeschlaub's office block resembles their Chicago work, the opera house hardly at all. But given the concentrated building activity in downtown Pueblo at that time, the relatively small population, the close circle of leading citizens and patrons of architecture, and the architects' history of mutual acquaintances, it is not inconceivable that Roeschlaub became acquainted with Adler and Sullivan.

In its own way this office block, amongst all of Roeschlaub's commercial buildings, acknowledges the brute power and vigor of American capitalism, tempered by sentiment and feeling represented by the lush naturalism of exterior ornament. Roeschlaub was uniquely inventive in the use and design of the "anchors," as he refers to them on his drawing of facade details (Fig. 4–25). Wiry cast-iron pieces of Celtic inspiration, these decorative caps, centered on the third floor of every major pier, act like screws that hold horizontal steel tie rods in tension to prevent the masonry wall from buckling. Leafy terra-cotta plaques band the third and fourth floors; in style they are commonplace for 1889, similar to those of the poly-chromatic and playful Corona (Dora Moore) School and Trinity Methodist Church. Such soft ornament against mass was a preoccupation of Richardson—not at the Marshall Field Store but in a variety of other works known to Roeschlaub, like the boldly orna-mented work of Peter B. Wight (1838–1925). The dif-ference here is a more disciplined placement. The plaques fit into recessed spandrels, thus delineating each bay—as well as glazing from solid, and subsidi-ary mullions from major piers. Roeschlaub's design is poised in tension between the commercial building as mass, indicated by wall treatment, and the commercial building as an articulated skeletal structure.

In his ideas about the relationship of vertical organization to ornament, Roeschlaub takes from the

Figure 4–23
Central Block, 1889
First version
*Denver Public Library
Western History Department*
07264

Richardson–early Sullivan model but offers a fascinating deviation from it: the facade of the Central Block reads as the interior elevation of a medieval cathedral turned inside out. Slender "shafts" run from the springers which mark the vertical extension of each major pier, attenuating what would otherwise be a mostly horizontal emphasis. These members terminate at attic level with a burst of loose, three-dimensional vegetation. This interpretation implies the line at which

4–24

a medieval cathedral roof of segmented arches would begin, an imaginary canopy crossing over the street— another device which enables this work to act as both a self-contained block and a building facing outwards toward Pueblo's commercial center.[40]

During this period of economic prosperity and growth, the Central Block, the new opera house, and a dozen other buildings redefined the monumentality of Pueblo around 1890. Of the Central Block the *Pueblo Chieftain* stated: "Its location is admirable and its appearance imposing from any part of the city" (a detailed description of the building's interior appears in this article).[41] Nearly all the new residences in this period were going up on the south side of the city, while the business structures rose on the north side.

An article entitled "Architects and Builders" in 1891 stated:

> The rapid and extensive growth of Pueblo has given a wonderful impetus to the building trade. The city presents many handsome models of architecture the construction of which has required the very best of material, the most careful direction and the most skilled workmen, giving Pueblo architects and builders an experience far ahead of many cities of a larger population. It has always been a marked characteristic of Pueblo that her citizens, her capitalists, her business men and her mechanics have ever been alive to the development of the city and have been equal to the demands made upon them by the city's growth. This trait has been especially marked in the case of the builders and architects, who have by their successful work gained a reputation that is second to none, and left massive monuments of imperishable stone to convey to succeeding generations the record of their skill, industry and ability.[42]

Skyscraper slab design had already become characteristic in Chicago by the late 1880s—the quadrangular plan of the Central Block and the Rookery is exceptional and old-fashioned. Louis Sullivan, in the years of the mid-1890s, immediately after his Pueblo Opera House commission, continued as master architect of the American office building. He focused on the creative possibilities latent in the frank structural expression of the new type of steel skeleton construction with its emphasis on tall proportions and the successful integration of architectonic and decorative elements.[43] Roeschlaub did not follow this path of the commercial slab as a hollow cage, perhaps realizing instinctively that such treatment would obliterate the subtle range of distinctions between inside and outside that characterized the spatial organization of the nineteenth-century urban core. To Roeschlaub, whether from timidity of imagination or by conviction, these traditional civic values remained paramount to architecture.

The Holzman and Appel Store (Figs. 4–26, 4–27, and 4–28), completed in its first phase in September 1891 and located in Denver on Sixteenth Street between

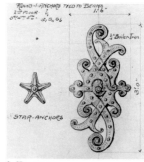

4–25

Champa and Stout, is a display of Roeschlaub's love of glazed terra cotta. Stylistically it is an early if schematic example in Denver of the Renaissance Revival as practiced by such national architectural giants as McKim, Mead and White and introduced to the city's commercial district by the firm of Andrews, Jacques and Rantoul of Boston. Gone is the Richardsonian boldness of great arches and contrasting textures that characterized the Central Block. This, instead, is the

4-26

Figure 4-26
Salomon's Bazaar
(Holzman and Appel Store)
Denver, 1891
CHS F44836

beginning of a taste for restraint, different from earlier verbose, Italianate styles. The cream-colored terra-cotta details, however, are lushly Roman. A frieze of garlands in exceptionally high relief graces the architrave. (These appeared beneath a cornice, since removed; the brickwork of the attic and the total modification of the

first two stories date from the 1940s.) Deeply modeled to a profile of about ten inches are symmetrical plaques of antique derivation in the spandrels and coarse but appealing vegetation, Roeschlaub's hallmark during the latter part of his career. Although round arches appear on the upper level, unified by the light and shade of horizontal striations above stringer level, they read as the last story of a commercial *palazzo*.

This building was suited for stores and offices. The greater part was utilized at first by A. Z. Salomon and Company as a large, fancy dry goods establishment.[44] "Salomon's Bazaar" was originally a four-story block 75 by 100 feet, of four bays. Constructed at a cost of $54,000 of salmon-colored brick with terra-cotta trim, it was built by Hallack and Howard, the contractors for Trinity Methodist Church and other Roeschlaub works. The corner was added in 1902—three bays along Sixteenth and five along Stout Street, in replica of the original, to form the present block. In this building, street making remains paramount: all architectural treatment—cornice, terra cotta, bay rhythm—ends abruptly a few feet into the alley, along the northern lateral wall of the block. Roeschlaub had come a long way since the superficial surface articulation of the Chever Block. His analysis of the relationship between voids and piers in the composition of the second and third stories relates this work to the Hover Warehouse built ten years later, his last major commercial enterprise.

The flagship of Roeschlaub's buildings in lower downtown Denver was the W. H. Hover Wholesale Drug Warehouse (now the Bromley Building of the University of Colorado–Denver) on the corner of Fourteenth and Lawrence streets (Figs. 4–29 and 4–30).[45] But in keeping with Roeschlaub's nineteenth-century sense of appropriateness and hierarchy of building types in the urban landscape, he tells us that this edifice has two functions. It is both humble Building + Architecture—a warehouse, storage, and shipping facility in addition to the firm's office headquarters. This he indicates on a series of drawings dated February 8, 1901, on which he calls the commission a "Business House."

The Hover Block is the Holzman-Appel Block

carefully rethought. The plain buff or tan-colored brick facade recalls the "mill buildings" of a long tradition of factory-type architecture developed in Europe and America since the late eighteenth century. In contrast, the heavily decorated Roman cornice and vigorous brackets announce that architecture is more than structure. The first version of the Hover Block had terracotta plaques of lush acanthus-like leaves in the middle of each bay above ground level and swags under the

4-27

cornice. Instead, Roeschlaub delineates the spandrels with a picture frame of molded brick. These elements bestow a dignity appropriate to a business block which lifts it above the mere warehouse type (at least in Roeschlaub's representational vocabulary). The architect's design principles, even in this seemingly straightforward work, differentiate between the interior and the obligation of architecture to present an exterior facade with public import. As always, Roeschlaub's architecture contributes to the life of the city street. The building has been built right up against the property line.

The Hover Block is a harmony of rectangles. The City Beautiful movement, popularized by the Chicago World's Fair of 1893, had provided architects and planners with easily identifiable images of institutions—white classical vessels of civic decorum. Roeschlaub

reserved the full play of that vocabulary for schools, libraries, and theaters in this last phase of his career. In 1901 the unified tone of the tan brick block reflected the change in architectural style from elaborate Queen Anne to a monochrome, subdued, and disciplined architecture. Gone are the dynamic corner elements that accentuated the diagonal of the city's grid blocks during the 1880s and 1890s, and there are no Dutch gables. Bays are no longer set off by rolling round-

4-28

headed arches of the Richardsonian-Sullivanesque period illustrated in Roeschlaub's Central Block of Pueblo. Instead, he presents a rectangular aesthetic. The corner pier is carried around both Fourteenth and Lawrence streets and emphasizes the concept of the building as a cube. Straight-edged piers mark off seven bays on the long Fourteenth Street front (which bore the sign "Wholesale Drugs. W. A. Hover & Co.") and three bays on Lawrence Street.

In this more humble urban building type, two versions of classicism are at work. The first is that of the

Figure 4-27
Salomon's Bazaar
(Holzman and Appel Store)
Detail of upper stories
David Diaz Guerrero

Figure 4-28
Salomon's Bazaar
(Holzman and Appel Store)
Denver, 1891 with 1902 expansion
David Diaz Guerrero

127

hierarchy described above. The cornice is a sign that illustrates Roeschlaub's shorthand and minimal but effective use of a classical vocabulary—that is, one that signifies a building of worth. As evidence of this, his cornice appears only on the two street sides; "architecture" is reserved for the urban face. His treatment of the private alley along the back, off Lawrence Street, is in his own terms "unarchitectural": there is no underlying formal scheme at all. This was quite a common

The second definition of the new classicism at the turn of the century is in the simplicity of the block itself—a feeling for abstraction. As in the French architect Auguste Perret's definition of a modern spirit of a classicizing aesthetic, in Roeschlaub's Hover Block architecture is in the proportions. Between the piers at the level of the third floor are spandrels set at varying vertical planes. Each bay of the second through fourth stories is divided by a tripartite window frame with

4–29

practice in the late nineteenth century; Roeschlaub also did this on the back of the Engineering Hall for the School of Mines. One of the few features to which Roeschlaub gives attention on this lowly side are two gates (one folding iron gate and a wrought-iron gate) and "indoyant lights," the frosted, opaque glass on the lower levels of a stairwell, a device supposedly meant to deter people from breaking into the building.

recessed slender colonettes engaged to square-set supports, all of cast iron. On the fourth and last story, three small-scale piers in brick are substituted for the cast iron and brought forward to the outer plane of the building. One is made aware of the horizontal division of the building by means of a secondary cornice in masonry at the floor level of the second and fourth stories. Commonplace in warehouse design, there is a

Figure 4–29
Hover Wholesale Drug Warehouse
(Bromley Building)
Denver, 1901
Rendering
CHS F31248

slight dimunition in the height of each story which reflects the decreased loads carried by each floor and the corresponding dimunition in the girth of the structural steel columns. However, unlike Perret and the imperative of truth to materials and construction techniques—which became a byword of twentieth-century modernism—Roeschlaub conceals more than he reveals.

The Hover Warehouse is a work of state-of-the-art

4–30

service systems and ingenious construction, but it is also a conservative building. Roeschlaub never refines structuralism into his exclusive architectural statement. In this he differs from the best of the Chicago School architects, whose work he knew well. There is a strong similarity between the Hover Block and Adler and Sullivan's preliminary design for the Meyer Wholesale Store (1893) in Chicago, which appeared in the *Inland Architect* in 1892 (Fig. 4–31).[46] Sullivan's scheme, though of skyscraper construction, comes close to articulating a traditional masonry wall. Roeschlaub's facade is load bearing but uses Sullivan's aesthetic to give traditional construction a new clarity.

The look of industrial buildings and processes became an inspiration to architects, especially European, in the years immediately before and after World War I. To Roeschlaub, however, all buildings were not

to look like factories. Rather, the Hover Block was a pragmatic answer to the special needs of the client. W. A. Hover's old building sat diagonally across the street from the new site on Lawrence Street. In a state of near collapse from the heavy load of stored bottles, medicines, and chemicals required for his trade, it was finally finished off by fire. Roeschlaub's building, then, was an improvement upon and critique of the inadequacies of this previous headquarters.[47] Designed for

4–31

the terribly heavy loads of shelving and to facilitate the production sequence of Hover's business, Roeschlaub's means of fulfilling the program—that is, the client's main needs—were by structure and organizational process. The building is immensely strong. It is an exterior wall-bearing structure with interior built-up steel columns and beams reinforced with large steel brackets. Roeschlaub's drawing of a longitudinal section shows the steel columns set on a foundation of concrete spread footings. The four longitudinal structural bays of about fourteen feet, in keeping with Roeschlaub's concept that architecture does not derive exclusively from structure, do not line up with the

Figure 4–30
Hover Wholesale Drug Warehouse
(Bromley Building)
CHS F44935

Figure 4–31
Preliminary design
Meyer Wholesale Store
Adler and Sullivan
Chicago, 1893
(From *Inland Architect*)
Art Institute of Chicago

129

rhythm of the three bays on the Lawrence Street facade.[48]

The building is all muscle yet presents a face of elegance to the city of Denver. As for the steel columns, because they fulfill different conditions throughout, they are built up of differing sections.[49] On Fourteenth and Lawrence streets the cast-iron mullions for the windows are actually intermediary supporting columns. Roeschlaub's drawings show that they continue through the depth of the wall for the full height of the story, tied back with a cast-iron wing. They add a highly pleasing ornamental contrast in texture and color to the surrounding brick in addition to their structural function. Even in the delightful detail of the flagpole on the roof, Roeschlaub has to pay special attention to bracing, a difficulty presented by the often fierce Colorado winds. Made of cast iron, the pole is stuck through and below the galvanized iron cornice. As a visual device it harnesses the energy of the corner and indicates the public entrance to the building, a more discrete coding substituted for the flamboyant gable of the 1880s. Within the outer masonry walls lies a final detail of strength: at floor level in every bay are bearing plates.[50] The Hover business house is, in fact, quite a particular and unusual application of warehouse construction.

The plan was obviously determined by the requirements of the business. In the basement was a "sponge room"; the rest was storage of undefined purpose. A bank vault of two stories went through the basement and first floor. "Prismatic lights," or glass bricks, let daylight into the basement. The first floor at street level shows the advantages of the open plan. Various irregular enclosures provide for a general office area and a shipping room: this floor is divided between "clean" and "dirty" functions. The sequence of services is generated by the revolving-door entrance, which was placed at the street corner. Because the public entered here, office functions are placed nearest to it. Close to the revolving door along Fourteenth Street was the "city department," furnished with a counter and desks, an area of paperwork for customers in Denver to get their orders filled. Along Lawrence Street towards the alley was a private office for Hover, then the bookkeep-

ing department with the two-story vault opening off the accounting department further along the back of the building.[51] One of the more eccentric tasks Roeschlaub solved was the storage of cigars, which needed to be kept moist in a high humidity environment.[52]

These civilized functions gradually gave way to those typical of behind-the-scenes packing and shipping. Logically placed on the private alley to the back was the shipping department with a "sundry room" next to it. More prosaically, the freight elevator was directly off the alley at the southwest end of the block. Placed between the "dirty" and "clean" functions, and thus convenient both to shipping and the servicing of walk-in trade, was a "bottle room." In addition to the freight elevator, the circulation system consisted of two main and several secondary stairways which went up one floor to another department.

Why the heavy construction of the building was needed is made clear by the second-story plan. It shows a double-decked room loaded with and subdivided by shelving. Galleries, catwalks, and balconies are hung on rod supports from the ten-foot ceiling. Little stairways give access to the walkways, and hung cubicles, like library stacks, were stocked full of racks and cases of chemicals, medicines, and drugs, transported by dumbwaiters. The third and fourth floors were open, general storage areas.

The "scuppers" or spouts, holes through the wall at floor level in the second, third, and fourth stories on the Lawrence Street side, were drains for water overflow. There was therefore an early sprinkler system in the building. Roeschlaub tried to sooth Hover's understandable anxiety about chemical accident or fire, which destroyed the client's previous building, and incidentally added a piquant aesthetic note.

The paradigm of a smoothly running industrial plant, which Roeschlaub created here, was to become a seductive image for twentieth-century architecture. Roeschlaub took such task-oriented solutions for granted. However, in his own definition of architecture he did not make time-and-motion studies the criteria for all good architecture, nor did he mistake the efficient workplace for the ideal universal habitat.

In addition to his reputation as a designer of public schools, Roeschlaub was the architectural founder of several new or expanding institutions of higher learning in Colorado between 1888 and 1907. Except for buildings that he designed in the central city for the University of Denver, these colleges and universities were, as Ellen Micaud has described them, potential communities "alone on the prairie."[1] Roeschlaub was given the opportunity to stake out the most important symbolic building, the traditional "Old Main," or main institutional building, for three universities: the University of Denver's new suburban campus, the State Normal School (University of Northern Colorado) at Greeley, and the Colorado School of Mines in Golden. University trustees called upon his technical expertise to design a variety of college buildings devoted to the humanities, the sciences, engineering, and astronomy. His two university libraries, built in the first decade of the twentieth century, are supurb examples of the dignified classicism of that era, and one is a representative of the Carnegie Library movement.

Under the name of the Colorado Seminary, the University of Denver, originating in the heart of Denver at Fourteenth and Arapahoe streets, was the first chartered school for advanced education in Colorado. The seminary's first structure, built in 1864, had been replaced in 1880, but even this had become inadequate less than a decade later. Although nondenominational in its acceptance of students, the university was the educational branch of the Methodist Episcopal Church, and Roeschlaub's relationship with this denomination as architect of Trinity Methodist Church gave him the commission in 1887 for the Haish Manual Training School of 1888 (Fig. 1–34). This structure, the gift of an Illinois benefactor, Jacob Haish, was built at the cost of $40,000 on the southeast corner of Fourteenth and Arapahoe, across the street from the first university building. In addition to its manual training course for adolescent students over the age of fifteen, it housed various university departments at one time or another—the schools of medicine, business, law, and dentistry.

Flexibility, dictated by expansion and change in these professional schools, was the key to the building's open plan. In fact, it had more in common with the architect's commercial blocks than with his structures on suburban campuses. In the law library, iron structural posts were left exposed in wide unencumbered bays—the same treatment that Roeschlaub gave to several of the building's lecture rooms and laboratories.[2] On the exterior, however, he adopted a generic castellated style, one that he often used to give artistic expression to simple and relatively inexpensive institu-

5–1

tional works.

Haish Manual Training School is a four-story block. The ground floor, with its neo-Romanesque arched portals and trim, is of lava stone. Irregular bays of one, three, or four windows, arcuated on the highest story (as at the Holzman-Appel Store), are subdivided by brick piers. Roeschlaub thus reserves most of the stylistic elaboration of this work for the fourth story and above. Corbelling, cornice, and parapet cap the work. To Roeschlaub, except for warehouse buildings, a block needed to be "finished." Once again, the street, and the facade presented to it, takes precedence over the structural expression of what is in reality similar stacked stories of gradually increasing heights.

In 1886 the university decided to expand far outside the limits of the city. A large, eighty-acre tract of donated real estate in Southeast Denver came to

5–2

Figure 5–1
University Hall
University of Denver
Denver, 1890
David Diaz Guerrero

Figure 5–2
University Hall, 1890
Detail of column
David Diaz Guerrero

131

be known as University Park, the permanent home and center of a new residential suburb developed by the university. Fortunately Roeschlaub's work was commenced before the university suffered financial difficulties consequent to the Panic of 1893.[3] His campus buildings of around 1890 represent the first phase of this involvement with the University of Denver at University Park. They symbolize the reconciliation of education in science, or secular knowledge, and

5-3

5-4

religion. Indeed, the cornerstone of his University Hall reads "Pro Scientia et Religione." For the earliest of these campus buildings, Roeschlaub was not the architect of the Iliff School of Theology, but he designed several others, among them University Hall (1890), which faces Iliff across a quadrangle; Cottage Hall (probably Wycliffe Cottage), a home for women students (completed in 1891); Chamberlin Observatory (1888–91); and a smaller student observatory (1890–91).

A typical campus Old Main, University Hall (Fig. 5–1, PLATES 12 and 13), the flagship of the new suburban campus, was opened for classes in the fall of 1892. Architectural historian Ellen Micaud asked, and then answered, the question, "What was Old Main?": "Within this structure," she states,

all the activities of the fledgling institution were housed....Physically it was a large stone, or some-

times brick, building set on the highest point possible and signaling its institutional status by turret or belfry. Functionally it was a sturdy enclosure for a variety of needs—chapel, preparatory school, president's home and student dorm, chemistry lab and music school, library and gymnasium, classrooms, recitation halls, and offices. Symbolically it was the epitome of all the activities that made up the early college, public or private.[4]

Except for a separate president's house and school of music—at that time still in central Denver—this is an accurate description of the University of Denver's Old Main hall.[5]

The most impressive surviving examples of Roeschlaub's Richardsonian work are at the University of Denver. The hall is a large and imposing edifice of three and a half stories, faced completely with volcanic lava stone ashlars set in irregular courses. Old photographs showing the open prairie to its rear enhance its still-apparent clifflike quality. The plan is bilaterally symmetrical, a feature typical of Roeschlaub's work, yet, as Brettell states, "the facade of the University Hall...pulls in and pushes out simultaneously.... Multiple entrances enable the student or faculty member to enter from any part of the campus. University Hall and Roeschlaub's schools of the later eighties were buildings intended to be the centers of their respective communities. They related to their environment in multiple directions."[6] The exterior, though smaller and far more orderly, recalls the severely handsome facade of Richardson's Allegheny County Courthouse and Jail (Pittsburgh, 1884–87). Shallow round arches vertically unite the fenestration of several stories, as at Richardson's Marshall Field Store and Roeschlaub's Central Block in Pueblo.

With its two round stairwells, expressed clearly on the exterior, the hall demonstrates one of the most memorable massing of towers in Roeschlaub's architecture and is close in spirit to the monumental grouping of the true Romanesque. It is an example of Roeschlaub's most extreme stripped-down aesthetic, yet as at the Central Block and Trinity Church, the rose Colorado stone and its treatment provide a warm and lively surface. Here, too, there are discrete episodes of

Figure 5-3
Chamberlin Observatory
Denver, 1889
Interior with telescope
CHS F49628

Figure 5-4
Chamberlin Observatory
First version, 1889
Courtesy University of Denver

salient ornament that contrast sensuously with the bold, broad exterior walls. Roeschlaub's versatility in designing capitals can be seen in a comparison of the lacelike, backlit foliage of Byzantine inspiration at the hall (Fig. 5–2) with the freely interpreted Arts and Crafts Gothic flora of the D. D. Seerie Residence in Denver of 1890 (Fig. 5–24). As usual, the building is appointed with the most up-to-date heating and ventilating systems: "Roeschlaub designed 56,000 gross square feet of flexible space...fitted with what was vaunted at the time as a 'perfect system of heating and ventilation, the air in rooms being entirely changed every ten minutes,' and all this for $80,000."[7]

The Chamberlin Observatory (Fig. 1–43), along with what was known as the "baby observatory,"[8] a gift of Humphrey B. Chamberlin, a Trinity Church trustee as well as a Denver real estate agent and amateur astronomer, was considered to be one of the best equipped in the country at the time of its construction. The ground-breaking ceremony took place in 1888, and the building was completed in 1891. It was erected to contain a first-class telescope, a twenty-inch equatorial refractor made by Alvan G. Clark of Massachusetts (Fig. 5–3). The telescope's installation in 1894 was delayed, since it had been on display at the 1893 World's Columbian Exposition in Chicago. The observatory's location on an isolated and beautifully landscaped isolated plat of fourteen acres in University Park was selected precisely because it was remote. The entire subdivision had to be replatted to avoid traffic vibration.[9]

Roeschlaub's preliminary design for the observatory was a cylindrical building (Fig. 5–4) supposedly modeled on the Carleton College observatory in Northfield, Minnesota (1886–87), which had recently been featured in the *American Architect and Building News.*[10] The final version is a building of massive red Colorado sandstone with added short wings flanking the central cylinder. It is crowned by a great, delicately balanced iron dome weighing twelve tons, which is supported by the building's outer walls. The foundation was constructed independently of the deep piers that supported the telescope—again, a necessary precaution to eliminate structural vibrations that might

influence the instruments. Thick walls were designed to maintain a constant temperature, sustaining a greater accuracy in the time recording apparatus. Herbert A. Howe, who served as its first director and commissioned a residence for himself from Roeschlaub directly west of the observatory, insisted that all of the stones making up the 320-ton foundation be the same color to ensure that the foundation would expand and contract equally everywhere.[11]

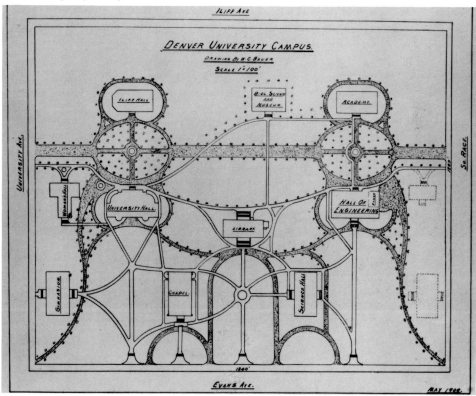

5–5

Roeschlaub managed these specifications with great finesse. One is led into the building by stairs with stone rails which curve invitingly—a motif the architect was to develop later at the Stevens School. Delicate iron grills of a walkway or balcony were originally set off against the rugged stone. As at the Central Block in Pueblo, the iron terminals of the tie rods are a cause for decorative celebration; they anchor the stone as though pressing into flesh. All these are Richardsonian

Figure 5–5
University of Denver
Campus plan, 1906
Courtesy University of Denver

133

touches; the soft-hard contrast brings a note of sensuality to this scientific project.[12]

In the second phase of his work for the University of Denver, from 1906 to 1908, Roeschlaub proposed and attempted to enact a comprehensive campus plan (Fig. 5–5) that included various buildings based on the aesthetic idealism and classicism of the French Ecole

5–6

Figure 5–6
Carnegie Library, 1906
Interior
Courtesy University of Denver

Figure 5–7
Carnegie Library
Preliminary project
University of Denver
Denver, 1906
Courtesy University of Denver

des Beaux-Arts. In this he worked once again with Henry A. Buchtel, former minister of Trinity Methodist Church, governor of the state, and now university chancellor, but this time the association was only partially successful for the architect. The university ostensibly accepted the plan of Roeschlaub and Son for the north campus, but the firm built only one work, the Carnegie Library, in 1906 (Figs. 5–6 and 5–7, PLATES 17 and 18). The background to Roeschlaub's new concept was the White City of the World's Columbian Exposition, which had been held in Chicago in 1893 and planned under the direction of the *doyen* of eastern architects, Richard Morris Hunt. Roeschlaub possessed a full series of engravings of the Exposition.[13] In

addition, an international competition in 1897–99 for the Phoebe Hearst architectural plan for the University of California at Berkeley echoed the ideas of the White City; and Roeschlaub had a copy of these competition requirements among his papers. They read in part:

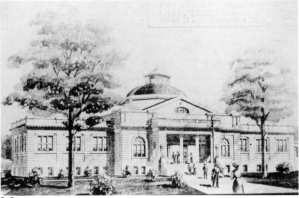

5–7

> It is a city that is to be created.... All is to be left to the unfettered discretion of the designer. He is asked to record his conception of an ideal home for a University assuming time and resources to be unlimited.... He is to plan for centuries to come.... [I]t is believed to be possible to secure a comprehensive plan so in harmony with the universal principles of architectural art, that there will be no more necessity of remodeling its broad outlines than there would be of remodeling the Parthenon had it come down to us complete and uninjured.[14]

Roeschlaub wrote similar sentiments to Buchtel in more prosaic language on June 22, 1907:

> In working up so vast an enterprise as the [university's] housing and placing, with proper settings,...it is necessary to look far ahead into the years to come with their possible requirements.... The buildings, and general lay out at the Chicago Worlds Fair, have to this day been conceded as near perfection.... This was the result of that stupendous work being under the direction of one mind.... One architect, who by his training, experience, the powers conferred and responsibility placed upon him, was enabled to give the *whole* scheme direction.... The designing and placing of every building...was under his supervision, harmonizing the varying ideas and producing a beautiful tout

ensemble out of what otherwise would have been the prevailing "patch work."[15]

According to Roeschlaub's campus plan, the 1906 Carnegie Library was intended as the centerpiece of the new north campus. It fronted a planted quadrangle facing Evans Avenue, which was to be closed by a new science hall on the west and the new Buchtel Chapel on the east, both eventually built, but not by Roeschlaub.[16] As Micaud has observed, "the Carnegie Library is essentially a pavilion, its prototype buildings like the French classical garden pavilions at Versailles. A closer source is undoubtedly the many libraries designed by McKim, Mead and White. A key feature of such buildings is the predominance of the long "French" windows over all other design features."[17] Roeschlaub used the pavilion type for the Greeley High School and the Carter Library, which no longer stands, at the University of Northern Colorado at Greeley. As at the classical Central High School in Pueblo, his preferred design had a prominent dome, which was abandoned in the final design.

Since the library at the University of Denver was among the last gifts with which Andrew Carnegie was personally involved, it is possible that he may have approved the design and plans. Carnegie's secretary, James Bertram, notified Chancellor Buchtel in April of 1906 that the university had been granted $30,000 for a library contingent on its raising matching funds for an endowment for the building and its collections.[18] Early Carnegie libraries were not standardized in style. Roeschlaub's design is significant because it so accurately foretells the typical Carnegie library of years to come.[19]

In 1907 Roeschlaub built one more pavilion for the university as an annex to the Haish Building in central Denver. A little two-storied work, the Dispensary Building of the Denver and Gross College of Medicine, between Thirteenth and Fourteenth streets on Arapahoe, is billboard neoclassicism in which only the street facade was elaborated (Fig. 5–8).[20]

In 1890 Roeschlaub was commissioned to design an addition to the Old Main or administrative hall at the Colorado School of Mines in Golden. To the first two blocks, of 1880 and 1882 respectively, he added a short linking corridor and an irregular block that in itself was as large as the original two wings. The principal characteristic of his addition, which is a variation of his rugged Richardsonian work, is its adjustment to the marked change in grade of the site. Although the main hall was on open, high terrain, it presented a different architectural problem from that of the Old Main at the

5–8

University of Denver. Here the three wings were lined up in a row, and, linked by a dramatic terrace, the complex had one preferred vantage point. This was from a meandering path which took account of the hilly site by occasional flights of steps (Figs. 5–9 and 5–10). Roeschlaub seized the opportunity to create an impressive entrance of his own which led from this terrace. His work consisted of a long flight of stairs and a nearly free-standing vestibule, an exaggerated version of his entrance at the Wyman School; the mammoth round arch of the entrance portal thus became the most authoritative element of the entire suite of buildings. In further accommodation to the sloping site, Roeschlaub divided his addition into a three-and-a-half-story block with library, reading rooms and offices, and a four-and-a-half story block that housed laboratories and a lecture room. The latter has more three-dimensional play, and, by a slight projection on the lateral facade, ends the composition.

Figure 5–8
Dispensary Building
University of Denver
Denver, 1907
Courtesy Peter A. Dulan

This use of materials—a high base and trim in lava stone with brick above—Roeschlaub repeated in his 1894 Hall of Engineering, which faced the main hall (Fig. 5–11). Although it stands isolated today among twentieth-century campus buildings, Engineering Hall was designed as a pendant oriented to the Old Main. This explains its prominent and strongly articulated facade and the relative neglect of the rear elevation, which looks onto a service road. The Engineering Hall

5–9

is a compact three-story block, steeply graded like its counterpart, with sharp, precise linear detailing of the same character as Roeschlaub's school buildings of the early 1880s. However, the stylistic vocabulary has changed. An example of Roeschlaub's personal eclecticism, this building combines a fortress style (typified by the corbeling and parapet), a stepped gable, and a portal that demures to classicism by its keystone and cornice. Yet the architect integrates his sources into a sober and simple red building, relieved by sharply edged virtuoso brick detailing and sinuous stone mold-

Figure 5–9
Executive Hall (Addition)
Colorado School of Mines
Golden, Colorado, 1889
*Denver Public Library,
Western History Department
F40848*

Figure 5–10
Colorado School of Mines
Campus plan, c. 1889
Courtesy Colorado School of Mines

ing and decorative foliage which frames the entrance arch.

At Greeley, trustees of the State Normal School (now the University of Northern Colorado) commissioned one of the most significant Old Main buildings in Colorado, known as Cranford Hall (Figs. 5–12, 1–45), which has unfortunately been demolished. Designed

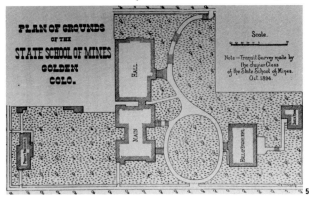

5–10

in its entirety in 1889, it was built in stages, beginning with the two-storied east wing;[21] the central three-storied block dates from 1893 and 1895.[22] It was completed in 1903 with the addition of a west wing that duplicated and balanced the first.[23] On the building's central block Roeschlaub realized his first true neo-classical portico. Giant pairs of Corinthian columns and engaged Doric piers carry a prominent, straight, full entablature deep enough to serve as a balcony to the third story. Its grandeur looks forward to the Beaux-Arts classicism that typified the architect's last works.

Constructed of pressed brick and stone, Cranford Hall retains the Palladian organization—the high, hipped central roof and side wings—of East High and other schools for which Roeschlaub built additions in the 1890s, rather than the low, even line of his late pavilions. There are also some intrusions, such as the sawtoothed brickwork of the third story that are foreign to a correct classical vocabulary. Yet Roeschlaub has given up episodic quotations of classical motifs, as typified by the Times Building and his early schools, for the essence of classicism, which is the integration of every part in an immutable composition. As contrasted with East High, Cranford Hall is tightly organized both vertically and horizontally by paired engaged Doric piers of brick. In Cranford Hall, states Micaud, Roeschlaub

> gave an able demonstration of the full potential of the classical language of architecture. The orders—which were correctly used—organized, controlled, and gave sculptural interest to the long facade of this impressive

5–11

building. More important, they evoked the image of the great public architecture of Europe and of a cultural tradition that stretched back five centuries. Without question, Cranford Hall was designed with a strong didactic intention, for in choosing to communicate in the language of the long tradition of humanism, the architect made it his responsibility to pass this tradition along to succeeding generations.[24]

The library at the Normal School (1906–7), now also gone, most fully realized Roeschlaub's idyllic arcadian classical ideal.[25] Set in a formal garden with a

reflecting pool, it was his sole garden pavilion built with a dome as well as a portico, probably in emulation of Thomas Jefferson's Monticello (1770–1809) and (as at the Carnegie Library at the University of Denver) the university libraries built by the architectural firm of McKim, Mead and White.

In addition to his college and university buildings, Roeschlaub built two theaters that represent the beginning and final periods of his architectural practice—the Central City Opera House (1878) and the Isis Theater (1912) in Denver.

The Central City Opera House was among two or three edifices that established the civic identity of that Colorado mining community (Figs. 5–13 and 1–18). The town boasted of having the best musical society in the state, and after Central City's near destruction by fire in 1874, the undertaking of the erection of an opera house was a sign of its indomitable spirit, or, in the language

Figure 5–11
Engineering Hall
Colorado School of Mines
Golden, Colorado, 1894
*Denver Public Library,
Western History Department*
F40847

of the time, "vim and vinegar."[26] An opera company was formed, and Roeschlaub was engaged to design the theater in 1878.

The opera house is at once ambitious and so simplified as to be an abstraction of grand European opera houses on which it is modeled. Its style owes as much to provincial German Renaissance opera houses as to current French Second Empire architecture. "The exterior," stated a journalist for the *Rocky Mountain*

5-12

News, who had been given a tour by the architect in March 1878, "is massive masonry, plain but imposing."[27] Its very plainness lent—and lends—a vigor and honesty appropriate to Colorado. As Brettell has rightly observed: "Roeschlaub eschewed the opportunity to cover the building in ornament. He divided the facade into three blocky masses, a central area with a mansard roof flanked by two towers, and succeeded in giving the building a great deal more solidarity and depth than its neighboring street buildings.... There is little waste, and the whole building has a tightness of execution typical of Roeschlaub's best buildings."[28] Contemporaries had a high opinion of the contribution that the Central City Opera House made to the region:

Figure 5-12
Cranford Hall
University of Northern Colorado
Greeley, Colorado, 1889
CHS F44842

Figure 5-13
Central City Opera House
Central City, Colorado, 1878
CHS F1478

"[W]e...will have by far the best and most convenient opera house in the west,...a first-class [building], with all the modern improvements, thereby making it comfortable and pleasant for our amusement-loving public."[29]

As in all of Roeschlaub's architecture, movement within the opera house is carefully thought out and, in this work, straightforward. The four outer doors lead to a foyer that spans the entire width of the building.

5-13

From the foyer two stairways provide access to the balcony, or gallery; the original box office was in the center under the stairs. To the right and left of the vestibule a short flight of steps leads to the two large entrances of the auditorium.

The auditorium is a simple box with a balcony at the back, yet overlapping symmetrical spaces and other devices of spatial elaboration—characteristics of Roeschlaub's architecture developed throughout the 1880s and 1890s—are evident in rudimentary form. A coved plaster ceiling is suspended from the conventional truss roof, and the resulting curved joining of the walls and ceiling obscures the spatial boundaries of the room. Thus the line between objective reality and fantasy is softened. The sides of the balcony project forward slightly at a wide angle in a three-sided shape that is reiterated by the diagonally set walls which flank the proscenium stage. An elongated octagonal space in between the two elements results, a three-dimensional octagon-within-a-rectangle that was a favorite Roeschlaub architectural device.

The simple interior was further transformed into a theatrical illusion by the ornately decorated ceiling in

5-14

full High Renaissance style[30] which includes a convincing version of the centuries-old device—a painted view of an open dome surrounded by a balustrade in false perspective depicting sky and clouds. This conventional motif, executed by a San Francisco artist named Moseman, whom the architect had brought to Central City for the work, was given a local interpretation: "[O]ne can almost imagine...looking through the roof at the sky overhead, with angry clouds hurrying by en route to Georgetown and Pike's Peak direct without change, as the railroad guides say."[31] The stenciled frieze that encircles the room has an unsophisticated and very un-Parisian charm.

The great, central gas-lit chandelier (which has

since been replaced) was similar to the one in Roeschlaub's Central Presbyterian Church of 1876 for which Moseman also provided the frescoing. Other decoration included allegories of the various arts, paintings of rearing horses to the side of the proscenium, and a representation of a Rhine scene between parted *trompe l'oeil* drapery, a fitting reference to German opera, painted on the fire curtain of the 42-by-53-foot stage. The bowled orchestra—called the

5-15

Figure 5-14
Isis Theater
Denver, 1912

Figure 5-15
Isis Theater
Frieze

parquette, or floor, at the time—had a raised dress circle to the rear. Plain spindle-backed wooden chairs at orchestra level gave a unique frontier character to the opera house. The site lines and acoustics were, and are, particularly good. Contemporary critics praised Roeschlaub for every aspect of the opera house, including the provision of ample room backstage: "Indeed, stated one, "the most striking feature of the opera house is its generous proportions as compared with

5–16

most western and suburban theaters."[32]

The Isis Theater (1912), the first Denver edifice built exclusively as a motion picture theater (Fig. 5–14), was the work of Roeschlaub and Son, along with the full collaboration of Robert Fuller. It was located in the dazzling urban theater district along Curtis Street, which was distinguished by buildings whose facades were extensively lit by decorative electric lights in the metropolis that called itself the "City of Light."[33] Even in this company, according to an account in the *Rocky Mountain News*, the Isis held its own: "[T]he most illuminated theatre in the world [glistens] above all other glows on that most lighted of Denver thoroughfares...like an architectural diamond in the Den-

ver street of illumination."[34] Indeed, light bulbs were embedded everywhere on the three wide bays of the theater's front elevation. Its gaudy and overblown ornament, based on the French Renaissance School of Fontainebleau of the sixteenth century (a historic period known for its crowded surface decoration), is typical of the Edwardian theaters and cinemas of the decade preceding World War I. In the elaborate frieze, colossal terra-cotta caryatids are bedecked with gar-

5–17

lands of fruit (Fig. 5–15), and a central sunburst motif flares out from a horrific mask of Tragedy embellished with harp, garland, and langoring female allegorical figures. It is a festive classicism, not the serious, restrained Parnassian ideal of the Greeley High School or Roeschlaub's university buildings.

Robert K. Fuller, a specialist in mechanical engineering, was responsible for the theater's splendid motor-powered heating and ventilation system. Because a great quantity of air could be introduced, heated, and expelled very quickly—50,000 cubic feet per minute—the main entrance doors remained open in winter, a novel feature by which the building's very architecture helped to attract customers. Meanwhile the interior of this entertainment palace was furnished with a Wurlitzer organ which had a tremendous console of four keyboards. The organ was equipped with a unit orchestra manufactured by Hope-Jones:

Figure 5–16
Bell Terrace
Denver, 1890
CHS F44832

Figure 5–17
Sopris Duplex
Denver, c. 1886
CHS F44758

when certain keys were played, it could reproduce the sound of a live orchestra.

In his domestic architecture, Roeschlaub's terraces, small apartment houses, and mixed-use blocks are the equivalent of work in other American cities that appeared in professional journals to which the architect subscribed; examples from New York, Boston, Cincinnati, and Chicago seem to have been the most frequently illustrated. The important difference was that of scale. Denver terraces were often of a single story, rarely exceeded three stories, and sometimes had their entrances at street level (like Roeschlaub's M. L. Smith Duplex of 1890); Chicago work, on the other hand, was commonly three or four stories high.

The terrace, a row of individual units with contingent party walls, is an urban form whose usefulness is in the creation of density and of residential units that underscore the importance of the street. Denver terraces, partly because of their lack of height, remained isolated fragments in the city, even in areas like Capitol Hill where many fascinating late nineteenth-century rows still stand. The quality of one coherent urban element made from consistent, repeated units is found in Roeschlaub's E. B. Light Terrace of 1890 (Fig. 1–29) in a Gothic style similar to his commercial King Block. The Richardsonian Bell Place, or Seven House Terrace of 1890 (Fig. 5–16) has houses with bow windows in mid-block and broad townhouses on each corner, forming an exceptionally strong, unified composition typical of the best Chicago terraces.

The uniformity of the terrace, its prime characteristic since the first Georgian prototypes of the eighteenth-century English city of Bath, began to bore the Victorians. Even Roeschlaub, who had a disposition for symmetry, designed multiple dwellings like the Sopris Duplex (Fig. 5–17), probably of the late 1880s, in the Queen Anne style, consisting of projecting open porches, varied facades, and tall decorative chimney stacks. Two fine examples of his small apartment houses, the H. J. Kruse Duplex of 1890 (Figs. 5–18 and 5–19) and the Ady Terrace of 1889 (Fig. 5–20) represent, respectively, a shallow U-shaped block set parallel to

the street and a nearly L-shaped variation of the building type with flat roof and parapet, which creates a forecourt and sense of privacy. Intricate diapered brick in the spandrels above the plain round-arched windows of the third story lends interest to the Kruse block, which also features a terra-cotta plaque of a Chinese masque in the center of the facade, the most exotic detail in all of Roeschlaub's work[35] and typical of the general enthusiasm for things Oriental in the arts

5–18

5–19

of the time. The Ady Terrace, now an apartment house, is basically Richardsonian with terra-cotta foliage and an elegantly curved iron stairway leading to the entrance, a horseshoe-shaped masonry arch.

Although Roeschlaub earned his reputation as Denver's institutional architect, his list of plans shows that he designed almost two hundred private residences for clients who were leaders in government, education, and business. Not only that, he built houses for some of his contractors and subcontractors, such as Geddis and Seerie, a sure sign of confidence in his work among members of the building trades. Just as his commercial blocks established the continuity of the street in an emerging city, most of his houses contributed to the

Figure 5–18
H. J. Kruse Duplex
Denver, 1890
David Diaz Guerrero

Figure 5–19
H. J. Kruse Duplex, 1890
Detail of ornament
David Diaz Guerrero

general character of Denver's middle-class neighborhoods, that of free-standing dwellings with green space in front and back. In this sense, quantity and a standard of good quality was as important as the occasional masterpiece.

Roeschlaub's domestic work is primarily a survey of popular styles of the time. One of his earliest houses, built for John Church in Georgetown in 1876–77, is an outstanding example of the Gothic Revival architecture

further refinements in the provision of thermal comfort.

In 1879 Roeschlaub expanded and radically overhauled another Georgetown house, built in 1867, for his friend William Hamill (PLATE 1). It is an example of upper-class life of the period; everything about it has an aristocratic air. Roeschlaub had an opportunity to include a conservatory as an element of his design vocabulary. Of the first house, only the front Gothic

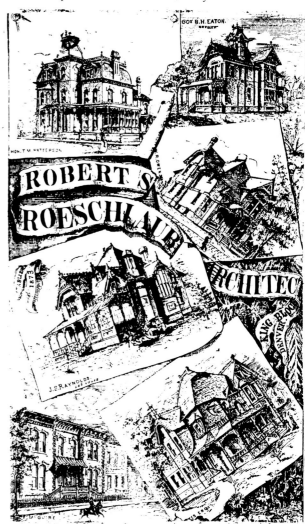

5–20

prevalent throughout the small mountain town. This two-story frame house is noteworthy for its rhomboid brackets at the eaves and its steeply pitched roof.[36] The house also "indicates an off-hand sensitivity to the advantages of passive solar heating,"[37] which is not present in other Georgetown houses but is in keeping with Roeschlaub's general interest in technology. The plan has been arranged so that the main rooms of the house face to the south, as do most windows. There are

Figure 5–20
Ady Terrace
Denver, 1889
David Diaz Guerrero

Figure 5–21
Six Roeschlaub residences
Advertising card
CHS F44841

5–21

facade remains intact. Gary Long has written, "As in the Church house, Roeschlaub gives the [Hamill] house, by dint of the addition, a southern exposure complete with additional bay window sun-catchers. A central convection heating system was installed with a furnace in a new basement. The conservatory is prominently placed in the middle of the southern facade, at the juncture of the dining room and library."[38]

Among its many fine features, the main staircase

5-22

ascends to the second floor from a central hallway, and light penetrates the space through a pointed-arch tracery window. An Italian tile fireplace in the parlor and additional fireplaces on the second and third floors supplement the heat from the furnace and give a sense of hearth and home. Gold-plated doorknobs also add to its elegant atmosphere.[39] It is among Roeschlaub's most imaginative and richly appointed houses.

The R. S. Little Residence (1884), named for its owner, was the grandest house in the town of Littleton because it was the first stone house in the community. Yet it is merely a vernacular masonry construction of several gables, a hipped roof and at least one projecting gabled "L."

An advertisement of the period shows five eclectic Victorian houses by Roeschlaub which are more generous in scale, built between 1881 and 1885 (Fig. 5–21). All are studies of discontinuous elements. Heightening

this multiplicity, each element has its own roof shape: among these are the Hon. T. M. Patterson Residence, which has a cupola and a variety of dormers in a French Renaissance style, and the Greeley residence of Governor Eaton with a Queen Anne belfry and Stick Style bracing under the eaves. The irregular forms of these houses probably reflect internal functional arrangements (although there are no plans to verify this), yet the effect is calculatedly chaotic. Roeschlaub

5-23

puts a wide veranda on his houses of this period; the closed-in porch of the J. S. Raynolds Residence (Fig. 1–25) of Las Vegas, New Mexico, is the most interesting. The Gottesleben Residence in Denver (1888) has the push and pull and multidirectional organization of a massive sculpture in the round (Fig. 5–22) that relates it to the University of Denver's University Hall. Every protruding volume corresponds to another; the deep bow on one corner refers to an octagonal tower; and one porch relates to another. The rough-cut lava stone

Figure 5–22
Peter Gottesleben Residence
Denver, 1888
CHS F31209

Figure 5–23
Rev. C. M. Sanders Residence
Denver, 1891
David Diaz Guerrero

gives the work a Richardsonian unity and grandeur that has established it as Roeschlaub's most impressive residence.

In the Rev. Clarenden M. Sanders Residence of 1891 (Fig. 5–23), this near abstraction is retained in a work of no particular stylistic derivation. The T-plan of this small two-story house, rather, forms a subgroup within Roeschlaub's domestic work in which his personal preference for symmetry is reasserted. The long central

5–24

5–25

suite of rooms ends in a three-sided bow. A conical, sectioned roof is set neatly against the hipped roof of the rear block. A truncated variation of this plan was used by Roeschlaub at the residence of Mrs. D. H. (Elizabeth) Price of 1889.

A variation in the architect's design of stone houses is the picturesque D. D. Seerie Residence (Figs. 5–24 and 5–25) which in its eclectic way has nonstructural half-timbering under the principal gable. The squat piers of the deep porch are of either granite or marble, and each of the capitals is designed differently. Indeed, the details are the best aspects of this house, which has extensive carved woodwork within. The

Addison J. Fowler Residence of 1890 (Fig. 5–26) is typical of Roeschlaub's Victorian vernacular double-gabled narrow and vertical designs. It is a two-and-a-half-story corner house with a cross gable roof and half-timbering in the gable faces. The dimensions of the house, 34 by 47, were considered large for the period. The decorative pediment was ordered from a commercial catalogue.

The H. A. Howe Residence of 1891 in University

5–26

Park (Fig. 5–27) is a crisply detailed and refined example of Edwardian vernacular. Slim posts carry a wrap-around porch typical of the period. The house is classicized in front and similar to Queen Anne in its asymmetrical massing towards the informal garden elevations. Shingles—some scalloped and shaped—and modillions contrast with the brick surface. It is a delicately detailed, pleasant work.

On a smaller scale and sharing some features of

Figure 5–24
D. D. Seerie Residence, 1890
Detail of porch
David Diaz Guerrero

Figure 5–25
D. D. Seerie Residence
Denver, 1890
David Diaz Guerrero

Figure 5–26
Addison J. Fowler Residence
Denver, 1890
David Diaz Guerrero

5-27

5-28

the more personalized Howe Residence are Roeschlaub's many Foursquare houses. The A. A. Blow Residence of 1892 (Fig. 5–28) is an early example. As *A Guide to Colorado Architecture* states, "One of the most commonly found styles in Colorado after 1900, the Foursquare is easily recognized by its square plan and overall simplicity.... The typical Foursquare is a two-story hipped roof structure with central dormer, minimal decoration, broad overhanging eaves with brackets

5-29

or modillions, classical frieze with dentils, and a porch with hipped roof supported by simple Doric columns or square posts."[40] The asymmetrically placed porch and scalloped shingles of the Blow House recall the Queen Anne, but one can see the predominance of the Foursquare type.

This brief survey of Roeschlaub's domestic work ends with an unidentified project for a Colonial Revival house (Fig. 5–29), a counterpart to the Beaux-Arts schools and university buildings with which he passed on his practice to a younger generation. Roeschlaub's earlier interest in expressing function has been exchanged for an artistic ideal of dignified nostalgia.

Roeschlaub's domestic architecture consisted mostly of background buildings in the townscape. But a survey of his institutions—churches, schools, colleges, universities, and theaters—has demonstrated that his architecture was very much in the foreground of the cities of the emerging West.

Figure 5–27
Herbert A. Howe Residence
Denver, 1891
David Diaz Guerrero

Figure 5–28
A. A. Blow Residence
Denver, 1892
David Diaz Guerrero

Figure 5–29
Project for Colonial Revival house
Denver, 1890s

Notes

◀▮▬▬ Chapter One: Life and Career

1. See, for example, Hajo Holborn, *A History of Modern Germany, 1840–1945* (New York: Alfred A. Knopf, 1969), and Chester Penn Higby, *The Religious Policy of the Bavarian Government during the Napoleonic Period*, vol. 85, Studies in History, Economics, and Public Law (New York: Columbia University, 1919). The prescription in Michael Roeschlaub's handwriting is in the possession of his great-granddaughter, Virginia Roberts, Denver.

2. The limited facts about Michael Roeschlaub's life can be found in two documents: *The History of Adams County, Illinois…containing…Portraits of Early Settlers and Prominent Men* (Chicago: Murray, Williamson & Phelps, 1879), 685, and David F. Wilcox, *Quincy and Adams County: History and Representative Men*, vol. 1 (Chicago and New York: Lewis Publishing Co., 1919), 390. The two accounts disagree with the recollections of Michael Roeschlaub's granddaughter, Alice Roeschlaub Williams, who believed that he had, like his own father, been dean of the medical school at the University of Munich (handwritten biographical account of Robert S. Roeschlaub, January 1944, Colorado Historical Society, hereinafter referred to as Williams recollections, CHS). No further information about Michael Roeschlaub's son Andrew has come to light, although the 1879 *History of Adams County* stated that he was still living. He is not mentioned in the Wilcox account.

3. Alice R. Williams recollections, CHS; *History of Adams County*, 448–49. Information about the cholera epidemic and slavery issue as they bore upon the Roeschlaubs' arrival in Quincy was kindly provided by Allen Oakley, former editor of the *Quincy Herald-Whig*, in a November 3, 1987, letter to Kenneth R. Fuller.

4. George Christ, "Quincy Political History," in *People's History of Quincy and Adams County, Illinois*, ed. Rev. Landry Genosky, O.F.M. (Quincy: Jost & Kiefer Printing Co., [1973]), 234. For Twain's quote see *Life on the Mississippi*, chapter 57.

5. Although their years of birth are not known, it is probable that the three elder children were born in the first four or five years after the Roeschlaubs' arrival, and the fourth much later. The birth order of the Roeschlaub children may be surmised from identical listings in *History of Adams County*, 685, and Wilcox, *Quincy and Adams County*, 390. Their approximate ages may be determined by other records.

For example, Henry, the youngest male, is listed in *History of Adams County*, 563, as having been a private in the Union army. Assuming that he was very young when he went into the service, and that he entered late in the war, he might have been eighteen when mustered out in 1865. That would put his birth at 1847. Similarly, the same source mentions that Jessie married Dr. L. H. A. Nickerson in 1880; assuming that she was of marriageable age, around twenty, this would put her birth close to 1860.

6. Williams recollections, CHS.

7. Robert S. Roeschlaub, "The Pioneers' Trail," *Sons of Colorado* 1 (May 1907): 33.

8. Ibid., 34.

9. *Denver Tribune–Republican*, June 16, 1885.

10. Roeschlaub, "The Pioneers' Trail," 34.

11. Ibid., 35.

12. Roeschlaub (hereinafter RSR) tellingly reveals his identification with the earliest pioneers of Colorado—and indirectly with his father—in the repetition of a single phrase that appears in an article he wrote for the *Western Architect and Building News* (*WABN*) of February 1890 and in his address to the Sons of Colorado in 1907. In the first instance, speaking of the strides that Denver had made in its architecture, he points to the "visible monuments which mark the stages of our advancement and progress from the mining camp of '59 to the city of enterprising and cultured people of '90" (180), this, he states, "we have accomplished…within a period of little more than twenty years"—that is, approximately from the time of his arrival in the early 1870s. Here he is speaking quite clearly of the second-generation city-builders who turned Denver from a supply town for the mining camps into a large metropolis. In the 1907 article, speaking of the Fifty-niners, he states: "In twenty years they had given to the world, through their zeal, what other cities were hundreds of years in acquiring" ("The Pioneers' Trail," 35). Suddenly the contributions of the forerunners and latecomers merge into one, and the son's efforts became an extension of the father's.

13. Although a number of civic biographies and newspaper articles about RSR mention his war service, the most reliable information can be found in his *Personal Military and Civil History*, a record compiled by the Soldiers and Sailors Historical and Benev-

olent Society in 1908, probably at RSR's request and with his assistance (original document in possession of Virginia Roberts, Denver).

14. Almost nothing is known about the origins of RSR's interest in architecture or his plan to enter the field as a career, and available accounts are contradictory. Alice Roeschlaub Williams, his daughter, states that he "was looking forward to beginning his medical studies" prior to the Civil War (Williams recollections, CHS); similarly, a biographical portrait in *The City of Denver: Its Resources and Their Development* (Denver: Denver Times, [1891]), 41, states that he was "taking an academic course, preparatory to the study of medicine, when the war broke out." In contrast, a short biographical piece in the *Rocky Mountain Herald* of April 24, 1909, mentions that he "studied and practiced the profession of architecture in Quincy, Ill., before and after the war." An earlier source (Henry Dudley Teetor, "Architecture in Denver: Captain Robert S. Roeschlaub," *Magazine of Western History* [1890], 177) appears to support this notion but is ambiguous in its phrasing: "At the time [of the war] he was preparing for his profession, and his enlistment was under one of his professors." The confusion could merely be a consequence of inaccuracies in reporting; but it could also reflect shifting professional allegiances in RSR's own mind once he had gotten into the Quincy academy.

15. Robert S. Roeschlaub, "War Reminiscences: A Sixty Days' Race with Hood's Army," *The Great Divide* (July 1894): 170.

16. Ibid., 171.

17. Ibid., 170.

18. Ibid., 171.

19. This unsigned oil painting, probably done by RSR himself in his later years, is a part of the collection of the Colorado Historical Society, donated by the architect or his family, along with other Civil War artifacts, in the 1920s. In 1982 it was fully restored and placed on exhibit.

20. Quincy City Directory, 1866.

21. Letter from Robert Handschin, Robert Bunce's great-nephew, to Carl Landrum, Quincy historian writing for *The Quincy Herald-Whig*, August 3, 1983 (in the possession of Kenneth R. Fuller, Denver).

22. *The Workshop: A Monthly Journal Devoted to Progress of the Useful Arts*, edited by Prof. W. Baumer and I. Schnorr, began publication in New York City in 1868.

A striking example of the formal classicism and idealism that affected academic thought and emerged, finally, in the White City of the World's Columbian Exhibition of 1893, this journal featured on its pages lovingly ornate engravings of classical ornament, traditional furniture, and interior decoration. RSR's five extant copies, dating from the first issue into the mid-1870s, can be found among the materials of the Roeschlaub-Fuller Collection at the Colorado Historical Society.

23. Other evidence that RSR began working in Bunce's firm at least as early as 1868 is a biographical statement in *The City of Denver*: "At the close of the war he took up the study of architecture, and entered an office in Quincy, Illinois, where he remained till his removal to Denver in 1873" (42). Although not specific, the phrasing implies that RSR began his architectural training within a year or two after becoming a civilian, which would correspond to Bunce's arrival in Quincy between 1866 and 1868.

24. Carl Landrum, "That Building at Sixth and Maine," *Quincy Herald-Whig*, November 3, 1968.

25. Thomas E. Tallmadge, *Architecture in Old Chicago* (Chicago: University of Chicago Press, 1941), 100. Tallmadge makes the interesting point that Burling's Chamber of Commerce Building was "damned with faint praise" because it was "not overloaded with ornament and the architectural bombast and fussiness regarded in the sixties as fashionable" (91).

26. Some speculation has it that the architect's later level of sophistication might be attributed to a European education. While this is tempting to consider, it does not square with RSR's rapid transition from Civil War captain to Quincy draftsman. Moreover, even if the space of time between the end of the war and RSR's employment with Bunce allowed him to receive a European education, he would undoubtedly have mentioned this fact in one or another of the several biographies and newspaper articles about his career that were published in his later life. It is possible, however, that his steadfast adherence to the classic principles of utility, convenience, and simplicity of design came not only from Burling but also from his father, who was educated in the arts in Munich during a time when that city, under the hands of the otherwise despised Ludwig I, flourished in its development of the arts and architecture. The first scholar to point out RSR's independence from the vagaries of late-nineteenth-century eclecticism of taste was Richard Brettell in *Historic Denver: The Architects and the Architecture, 1858–1893* (Denver: Historic Denver, Inc., 1973), 94–121.

27. Allen Oakley, former editor of the *Quincy Herald-Whig*, to Kenneth R. Fuller, August 1, 1983 (letter in the possession of Kenneth R. Fuller). Carl Landrum, "Jewish Congregation Formed in 1856," *Quincy Herald-Whig*, September 25, 1983, gives a complete description of the temple and its history.

28. Carl Landrum, "When Pranksters Had Their Day," *Quincy Herald-Whig*, January 11, 1981.

29. For a comprehensive account of the evolution of the nineteenth-century architectural office, see Bernard Michael Boyle, "Architectural Practice in America, 1865–1965: Ideal and Reality," *The Architect: Chapters in the History of the Profession*, ed. Spiro Kostof (New York: Oxford University Press, 1977), 309–44.

30. This book is a part of the Roeschlaub-Fuller Collection of the Colorado Historical Society.

31. For Denver's population in 1871, see Jerome C. Smiley, ed., *History of Denver, with Outlines of the Earlier History of the Rocky Mountain Country* (Denver: Denver Times/Times-Sun Publishing Co., 1901), 667; for Quincy's population in 1870, see *Gray's Atlas of the United States* (Philadelphia: Stedman, Brown & Lyon, 1874).

32. Nathaniel Pitt Langford, *The Discovery of Yellowstone Park: Journal of the Washburn Expedition to the Yellowstone and Firehole Rivers in the year 1870* with a foreword by Aubrey L. Haines (Lincoln: University of Nebraska Press, 1972), 117–18.

33. Lyle Dorsett, *The Queen City: A History of Denver* (Boulder, Colo.: Pruett Publishing Co., 1977), 59.

34. Isabella L. Bird, *A Lady's Life in the Rocky Mountains* (New York: G. P. Putnam's Sons, 1879; Norman: University of Oklahoma Press, 1960), 137.

35. RSR's first impressions of Denver can only be surmised from a later article (*WABN* 1 [February 1890], 180–82) but, given his veracity in other respects, it can be taken as a fair assessment of his reaction to the development of the city some thirty years earlier.

36. For a detailed description of the transformations that took place in a two-block area of Denver on either side of Fifteenth and bounded by Lawrence and Arapahoe streets, see Bill Brenneman, *Miracle on Cherry Creek: An Informal History of the Birth and Re-Birth of a Neighborhood* (Denver: World Press, Inc., 1973). A paean to one company's urban redevelopment plan, this history also celebrates the social life of central Denver, but has less to say about the historic buildings, now gone, that gave visual character to that life. More than one RSR building occupied a portion of these two blocks, among them the Union Block, the Times Building, the King Block, and the Haish Manual Training School.

37. Today the entire block on which the Roeschlaubs lived is occupied by the new offices of the *Rocky Mountain News* (*RMN*), a Denver institution that, despite its contemporary look, originated above a saloon in the same year that Michael Roeschlaub, Robert's father, joined the Pikes Peak gold rush.

38. In a letter to his mother, Margaret Roeschlaub, dated January 2, 1876, RSR states that he has paid a third on "a piece of ground 75-ft. front and 100-ft. deep, on the hill corner of 13th St. and Colfax avenue." Though he seems interested in the speculative value of the land, his intention to stay is clearly expressed in his desire to "build in such a way that the house will [meet] the demands of a growing family like ours" (original in the possession of Virginia Roberts, Denver, as are all personal RSR letters hereinafter cited).

39. Kenneth R. Fuller, "Background History of AIA Colorado," part 1, *Field Report* (newsletter of the Colorado AIA), 1985. This building was later replaced by another, more substantial block of the same name, which was in 1919 remodeled to become the Granite Hotel.

40. Several historians have pointed out that the Panic of 1873, although severe in its effects on the nation at large, had less impact on Colorado and on Denver in particular, which maintained its economic stability from the revived production, transportation, and processing of ores—all due in large part to the circumstantial combination of the railroads reaching Colorado and the development of new and more effective methods of milling and refining. See, for example, Robert Athearn, *The Coloradans* (Albuquerque: University of New Mexico Press, 1976), 135, and Smiley, *History of the City of Denver*, 459.

41. RSR to Margaret Roeschlaub, May 17, 1874.

42. Williams recollections, CHS.

43. Evidence of RSR's work before 1875 comes only from his 1874 letter to Margaret Roeschlaub and as yet unconfirmed buildings whose plans, many of them undated, he preserved in the office's files over the course of his forty-year career in Denver. The original list of these drawings, most of which are not extant, will hereinafter be referred to as the RSR inventory of plans (CHS). Compiled and typed on legal-sized sheets of paper and amended in pencil sometime after RSR's retirement, the list is part of the Roeschlaub-Fuller Collection at the Colorado Historical Society (Box 19, file 30).

44. RSR to Margaret Roeschlaub, September 5, 1875.

45. In his list, for example, RSR includes improvements of $400 for W. M. Clayton (home or business), an addition to the Turner Hall for $2,490, improvements on the grounds of the Phillips home for $500, improvements on the George W. Clayton store for $785, and an odd reference to "Bancrofts Book [case?]" for $125. "Improvements," while a nondescript part of the architect's professional vocabulary, could change the entire character of a storefront or transform an older residence into a new, quite different looking building, much as RSR did with the residence of William A. Hamill in Georgetown.

46. Frank Hall, *History of the State of Colorado*, vol. 4 (Chicago: Blakely Printing Co., 1895), 49. Specifically, Hall states, when the Central Presbyterian Church was built, "it was believed by many that the congregation would not go to so distant a point to worship."

47. Ibid., 29–30.

48. District 1 annual report (1885), 21. The original of this and all other District 1 annual reports cited may be found in the collections of the Stephen H. Hart Library, Colorado Historical Society.

49. Ibid.

50. Ibid., 47. Speaking of having discovered a schoolhouse in Laramie, Wyoming, that was a copy of his Twenty-fourth Street School (itself a close adaptation of his own Broadway School), RSR states that "it is not meet to *copy* even what is considered a good building, as copies are always inferior to the original." He goes on to explain, with barely concealed disdain

mixed with a little pride: "No one who had visited the Twenty-fourth Street School building, and had studied or enjoyed its conveniences, would for a moment think that the school-house at Laramie was a copy of it, and yet this is a fact. That is, it was copied as near as *could be* from the cuts in a former school report. The general arrangement of rooms and exterior appearance are similar, but hundreds of minor arrangements and conveniences that go to make such a house perfect are omitted. The same may be said of a number of other houses throughout the country, which are believed to be copies of Denver schools."

51. RSR to Margaret Roeschlaub, January 2, 1876.

52. RSR to Margaret Roeschlaub, December 20, 1877.

53. RSR to Margaret Roeschlaub, October 20, 1878.

54. Smiley, *History of the City of Denver*, 464–65.

55. James E. Fell, *Ores to Metals: The Rocky Mountain Smelter Industry* (Lincoln and London: University of Nebraska Press, 1979), 49–54. For a discussion of RSR's role in the planning of the Boston and Colorado smelter, see page 137.

56. See Charlie H. Johnson, Jr., *The Central City Opera House: A 100 Year History* (Colorado Springs: Little London Press, 1980) for a detailed account of the building and subsequent history of the opera house. This booklet, however, is not without errors, such as attributing to RSR the design of the Boston and Equitable buildings in Denver (9).

57. Not only an object of great beauty and rich history, the opera house has also inspired its share of Colorado lore. As one rumor has it, "Put those walls to an assay test and it would show that the gold recovery would more than build a brand new opera house—with money left to spare."

58. Williams recollections, CHS. A comparison of the original building plans, held by the Central City Opera House Association, with the final structure supports her assertion (see Johnson, *The Central City Opera House*, 9–17).

59. Perhaps written for the revival opening of the Central City Opera House in 1932, this poem, though an amateur effort, testifies to the importance that Alice Williams believed the western setting had on her father's work. So far as is known, RSR himself never acknowledged any influence, whether geographical, professional, or stylistic. The idea that RSR's architecture emulated characteristics that he found in the spirit and geography of the West may have been concocted wholly by his daughter, but such a misreading of her father's intentions seems unlikely. The typewritten poem, undated but signed in her own hand, is entitled "The Builder" (CHS collection).

60. Actually, at $25,340, including architect's fees of $1,082, the Twenty-fourth Street School cost more than the $23,000 opera house at Central City. In both cases the clients wanted modest but substantial-looking structures, and this necessity may also have played a part in the look of RSR's buildings of the "new and simple West."

61. Ibid., 19. See also *RMN*, November 10, 1881, p. 4.

62. District One annual report, 1881, 10–12. The collapse of the Tabor Grand, which was being built under the supervision of Frank Edbrooke, a recent arrival from Chicago, may have made things temporarily difficult for its architect-superintendent, but it was found to have been caused by a failure in safe construction practices rather than a flaw in the design of the building. Edbrooke, who weathered the investigation and publicity, went on to become Denver's most esteemed commercial architect and the nationally known designer of the Brown Palace Hotel. The collapse of the Straus Building led to a coroner's inquest and to a call for the appointment of a building inspector; however, its architect, F. C. Eberly, continued to prosper, like Edbrooke and RSR, throughout the 1880s and survived the panic of the early 1890s (*RMN*, March 9, 10, 11, and 17, 1881).

63. Besides his contribution to the Colorado Chapter of the American Institute of Architects from 1892 until his retirement in 1912, RSR previously served on a committee to establish building codes and improve standards of construction (*WABN* 1 [May 1889]: 1).

64. *Denver Times*, January 8, 1902, p. 11.

65. The bulk of these commissions are announced in the January 1 issues of *RMN* for 1880 and 1881. A few others may be found in the issue of February 17, 1880. The practice of celebrating the new year with a published list of new construction, along with the architects responsible, unfortunately declined after this period. The information in these lists reflects quite accurately RSR's projects at the time as indicated on his office inventory of plans.

66. *RMN*, January 1, 1880. The architects were: Emmett Anthony (with a total construction value of $279,000), W. W. Goodrich ($123,600), W. H. J. Nichols ($107,500), RSR ($106,415), and L. Cutshaw ($103,000).

67. Ralph Roeschlaub is not, for example, mentioned among the children who celebrated their parents' fiftieth anniversary in 1919; indeed, the San Diego newspaper that interviewed the Roeschlaubs on this occasion mentioned only six children, a clearly wrong count. In the family records, his name appears, but not his date of birth; yet the same records show that he died at the age of fifty-six on September 18, 1936 (*Personal and Military History*, in the possession of Virginia Roberts of Denver).

68. Judith Brunvand, "Frederic Albert Hale, Architect," *Utah Historical Quarterly* 54 (Winter 1986): 7.

69. *East, 1875–1950: Past and Present* (East High School pamphlet), 23–24 (copy in the collection of the Colorado Historical Society). According to the pamphlet, Ella Catherine Matty graduated in 1900 from Anne Brown's School in New York City and married Frederick B. Orman of Pueblo. She took an active interest in social and benevolent organizations, including the Polio Foundation, the Exceptional Child Division of the Board of Managers, and the Colorado Congress of Parents and Teachers. She died in the late 1970s.

70. Ezra M. Cornell, according to *The Denver Post* of February 8, 1929, had been RSR's supervisory architect for all of the East Denver school buildings and at the time the article was written filled the same function for the United States Treasury Department. An 1879 graduate of the old Arapahoe High School, Cornell is listed in the 1881 Denver City Directory as a member of RSR's staff, and his business card, along with that of Fred Hale's, was found among the items discovered in a small lead box under the cornerstone of old East High when the building was demolished. Cornell outlasted Hale in RSR's firm by some three years, ending his employment in 1885. He later tried his hand as an architect in partnership with Alexander Cazin (1886) and worked for a time as an architect for the construction firm of Hallack and Howard.

71. District One annual report, 1885, 25–50.

72. Brettell, *Historic Denver*, 98. Although Brettell attributes the Ashland School of 1874 to RSR and discusses it in some detail, its architect has since been found to be J. L. Mitchell (*RMN*, March 22, 1874, p. 1). Nevertheless, it does have characteristics that are similar to RSR's schools of the early 1880s, particularly in the brickwork.

73. Aaron Gove correspondence (letters received, July 1879 to April 1880), Western History Department, Denver Public Library.

74. District One annual report, 1885, 26.

75. One exception, a family story that has the ring of authenticity, was RSR's refusal to design a home for Colorado silver king H. A. W. Tabor and his young wife Baby Doe. Horace Tabor's machinations in obtaining a divorce from Augusta, his wife of twenty-six years, and his insistence on flaunting his new bride-to-be in a Washington, D.C., marriage attended by the president and Tabor's fellow senators, scandalized Denver society and was boycotted by the senators' wives (Duane A. Smith and David Fridtjof Halaas, "A Fifty-Niner Miner: The Career of Horace A. W. Tabor," *Colorado Heritage* 1983, Issues 1 & 2: 31). RSR's supposed refusal to build the home for the celebrated couple may have reflected either the Roeschlaubs' moral values or social standing at the time, or both; in any case, his scruples applied only to Tabor's house, for his inventory of plans includes an entry for an H. A. W. Tabor barn.

76. For a discussion and illustration of the Hill Residence, see Sandra Dallas, *Cherry Creek Gothic: Victorian Architecture in Denver* (Norman: University of Oklahoma Press, 1971), 41; for the Bancroft Building, see Smiley, *History of Denver*, 955.

77. Biographical references to these clients may be found in Smiley's *History of Denver*, but RSR's clients over the course of his career appear in all of the standard Colorado histories. A good study, perhaps a master's thesis, awaits the researcher who can examine the matrix of business, professional, and social ties of RSR's clients in the manner of Glen M. Leonard in "William Allen's Clients: A Socio-economic Inquiry," *Utah Historical Quarterly* 54 (Winter 1986): 74–87.

78. See especially Richard Brettell's criticism of the Union Block in *Historic Denver*, 114–15.

79. Hall, *History of Colorado* 4:30–31.

80. The arrangement of windows at Emerson allows light to enter only from the left, along one wall. This treatment may have been a response to the concern among

educators that light coming from other sources posed a distraction and possible danger to the students as well as the teachers. RSR states in the District One annual report for 1885, for example, that Emerson School "is quite a departure from the plans of the older buildings, in that the teacher's [*sic*] desks are placed at the *end* of every room…[T]he teachers are not troubled with a direct glare of light while at their desks, which past experience teaches is very injurious to the eyes [and] there are no cross lights" (46).

81. *Denver Tribune-Republican*, December 25, 1884, p. 4.

82. Unconfirmed buildings on the RSR inventory for 1884, 1885, and 1886, include homes for Mrs. S. W. Madge, R. S. Little (both in Littleton), J. W. Bowles, H. E. Luthe, Mrs. Mary Mortimore, Dr. R. Tucker, Lieut. W. S. Brown, James G. Dingwell, Walter Dunning, R. W. Hockaday, Judge Merrick A. Rogers (double residence), S. T. Sopris, T. G. Lyster (assistant cashier of the First National Bank), Dr. C. N. Guyer, and R. T. Binford. Other unconfirmed buildings for this period are the F. W. Crocker and Company Store, Bigger Livestock Company ranch house, Lincoln School in Colorado Springs, Mrs. Smiley Block, the Las Animas Hotel, the Patterson and Thomas stores, and the H. H. Symons Building in Laramie, Wyoming.

83. Unfortunately, RSR had little to donate to what became the Colorado Historical Society of his own or his father's contribution to the state. During RSR's tenure as curator—actually a term that was equivalent to a member of the board of directors—the Society's collecting practices were highly eclectic, and the only items eventually donated by the architect were some of his Civil War relics. From modesty, perhaps, he did not donate any of his plans and drawings, which were fortunately preserved in the offices of his successor firm, Fuller Fuller and Associates, and now constitute a valuable collection of early Denver architecture.

84. Denver City Directory, 1880–91.

85. See, in particular, Kathleen Hoeft and Peter Snell, *Pioneer Greek Revival Log House* (Denver: Long Hoeft Architects, 1981), a historic structures report on an early log house in the possession of the Colorado Historical Society.

86. Andrew Jackson Downing, *The Architecture of Country Houses* (D. Appleton & Co., 1850; New York: Dover Publications, Inc., 1969).

87. *WABN* 2 (February 1890): 181.

88. Denver City Directory (1886) and Fred Hale scrapbook, Utah Historical Society, Salt Lake City. Hale has remained a relatively little-known Colorado architect despite nearly a decade of work in the state, from 1881 to 1889. He is much better known in Utah, where he spent the bulk of his career as one of Salt Lake City's most respected architects. Some of the buildings that Hale featured in a portfolio of works—part of the Hale collection at the Utah Historical Society—were built in Pueblo, Colorado, and may have been due to RSR's professional ties to that city.

89. The dates of employment in RSR's firm for all of these assistants, and for Fred Hale, are approximate, for the Denver City Directory usually came out in the fall of the year and thus in many cases could be considered almost a year behind the fact.

90. The relationship between RSR and Frank Edbrooke is one of the most intriguing yet elusive in Denver's early architectural history. RSR never commented publicly on Edbrooke's buildings, nor did Edbrooke indicate, in his reminiscences, *Frank E. Edbrooke* (Denver: Egan Printing Co., [1918]), his attitude toward RSR. Yet both knew that the other was a major figure in the development of late nineteenth-century Denver architecture. For a good discussion of the role each architect played in Denver's commercial and institutional growth, see Brettell, *Historic Denver*, 33, 94.

91. The original drawings for the opera house belong to the Central City Opera House Association, but photocopies are held in the Roeschlaub-Fuller Collection at the Colorado Historical Society.

92. Several brief letters from Aaron Gove to RSR illustrate the burden of detail that lay upon the school architect—from broken fixtures to disposal of garbage (Gove correspondence, Western History Department, Denver Public Library). For RSR's resignation, see *RMN*, February 15, 1891, p. 7.

93. *WABN* 2 (April 1890): 19.

94. One architect's criticism of another's architecture cannot, by itself, be considered unprofessional except by choice of words and the forum chosen for the criticism. Every architectural student's design at one time or another undergoes professional criticism in a public setting, and visiting architects often express their dissatis-faction with everything from a city's unplanned development to the individual characteristics of buildings designed by local or out-of-town architects who are responsible for the apparent chaos. What separates Rosenberg's comments from those of contemporary critics is his highly charged, personal, and vindictive stance— an important criteria for determining unprofessionalism in any occupation today. More and more, the freedom to criticize architecture seems to have become the domain of the architectural historian or social commentator.

95. *WABN* 1 (November 1889): 128.

96. *RMN*, February 15, 1891, p. 7.

97. For his part, RSR, who was no longer the architect for the East Denver schools, put up a wry and energetic defense. Someone had cut a nineteen-inch hole in the base of the chimney, he stated, to ventilate a new set of bathrooms, and the size of the ventilating hole seriously weakened one of the chimney supports. "Almost anyone should have known better than to undermine the chimney in this way," he stated, "but it was as bright an idea as it was to carry the foul air from the water closets into this shaft, which connects with the schoolrooms, thus emptying this foul air into those rooms at times" (Ibid.).

98. *RMN*, February 16, 1891, p. 2.

99. *WABN* 1 (November 1889): 128.

100. *WABN* 3 (March 1891): 198.

101. For a full account of Jesse B. Dorman and the *Western Architect and Building News*, especially of the journal's role in "guiding the course of the building boom" and developing a strong sense of professional responsibility among Denver's architects, see Brettell, *Historic Denver*, 26–30.

102. *WABN* 2 (December 1890): 153–54.

103. See the address of Richard Morris Hunt, president of the American Institute of Architects, reprinted in the *WABN* 1 (December 1889): 155.

104. Later the members contemplated joining the Western Association of Architects, based in California, but decided instead to apply for a charter in the older organization. At the time of Hunt's address in 1889, both the American Institute and the Western Association were contemplating a merger, but this had not occurred when the Colorado Association members made their decision two years later. That decision is significant in that it implies a rejection of regionalism and an affirmation of unity among the nation's architects.

105. *WABN* 3 (May 1891): 1.

106. See Ellen C. Micaud, "Alone on the Prairie: Old Main on Colorado Campuses," *Colorado Heritage* 1983, Issue 4: 13–15, for a comparison of the University of Denver and Denver's Westminster College, two institutions that dared to build on speculation far outside the city and came to quite different ends.

107. Henry Dudley Teetor, "A Chapter of Denver's History: H. B. Chamberlin's Visit in Search of Health and What Came of It," *Magazine of Western History* 10 (June 1889): 149.

108. Brettell, *Historic Denver*, 174; David Gebhard and Tom Martinson, *A Guide to the Architecture of Minnesota* (Minneapolis: University of Minnesota Press, 1977), 299.

109. Hall, *History of Colorado* 4:551–52.

110. Micaud, "Alone on the Prairie," 14.

111. See, for example, Gove's argument against vocational education in the District One annual report for 1890, 41–44, in which he concludes that "with the exception of the manual dexterity acquired, little discipline comes to the attendant of the typical manual training school that is not acquired by industrial and free hand drawing, intelligently taught. The establishment of manual training schools is a legitimate field for private enterprise." The necessity for such a statement of philosophical and educational principles in an annual report, however, implies that there were those on the school board who thought differently. By 1893, when the Manual Training High School was completed, their views had obviously won out.

112. For an intriguing suggestion of RSR's conception of space and movement in his buildings, see Brettell, *Historic Denver*, passim.

113. Aaron Gove to RSR, September 4, 1901, Gove correspondence, Western History Department, Denver Public Library.

114. RSR to Henry Buchtel, June 22, 1907; Buchtel to RSR, June 25, 1907, Roeschlaub-Fuller Collection, CHS.

115. Rodd Wheaton, National Register nomination form, Office of Archaeology and Historic Preservation, Colorado Historical Society (unpublished, 1987).

116. Robert K. Fuller graduated from Colorado A&M (Colorado State University) with a degree in engineering, worked in his father's office, and then attended Cornell University in Ithaca, New York, receiving his Bachelor of Architecture degree in 1908.

117. RSR to members of the Triangle Club, January 24, 1920 (letter in the possession of Virginia Roberts, Denver).

118. Thomas J. Noel and Barbara S. Norgren, *Denver: The City Beautiful and Its Architects, 1893–1941* (Denver: Historic Denver, Inc., 1987), 1–27.

119. Robert S. Roeschlaub died in San Diego October 25, 1923. Annie, his wife of fifty-five years, died on March 22, 1930. Both are buried in Fairmount Cemetery in Denver.

120. *The WPA Guide to 1930s Colorado*, intro. Thomas J. Noel (Lawrence: University Press of Kansas, 1987), 79–82.

 Chapter Two: Churches

1. George L. Hersey, *High Victorian Gothic: A Study in Associationism* (Baltimore and London: Johns Hopkins University Press, 1972).

2. James H. White, ed., "The First Hundred Years of Central Presbyterian Church, Denver, Colorado, 1860–1960" 25, 30 (clipping files, Western History Department, DPL). "Plans for a new church" states this account, "became an immediate consideration and in May four lots, 100 by 125 feet, were purchased on the corner of Eighteenth and Champa streets....A building committee to cooperate with the board of trustees was selected. Plans for the new church building were prepared by Architect R. S. Roeschlaub and adopted (except the spire and finishing of the auditorium, which was let to Kelsey and Evans in October, 1875."

3. Sandra Dallas, *Cherry Creek Gothic: Victorian Architecture in Denver* (Norman: University of Oklahoma Press, 1971), 173–74; RSR to Margaret Roeschlaub, September 5, 1875, states that the church would cost $49,000.

4. *RMN*, January 1, 1892, p. 15.

5. Ibid.

6. *Central Presbyterian Church: Pioneers through the Years*, n.d. [after 1950], 9 (clipping files, Western History Department, DPL). After the church burned down, some of its remaining stones were used in the foundation of the Montview Boulevard Presbyterian Church in Denver (see Dallas, *Cherry Creek Gothic*, 173–74). RSR's projected spire was not built, either in the building's first or second incarnation, despite the fact that it is illustrated in a rendering in *RMN*, January 1, 1892, p. 16.

7. Richard Brettell, *Historic Denver: The Architects and the Architecture, 1858–1893* (Denver: Historic Denver, Inc., 1973), 96.

8. Phoebe B. Stanton, *The Gothic Revival and American Church Architecture: An Episode in Taste, 1840–1856* (Baltimore: The Johns Hopkins Press, 1968), 235.

9. Ibid., 115, 288. Notman traced the drawings of the spire from R. C. Carpenter's All Saints' (Brighton, 1846).

10. Mary Papo, "Pueblo's Single Episcopal Church Evolved from Merger of Parishes," *Pueblo Chieftain*, December 21, 1957.

11. *WABN* 2 (April 1890): 21 (illustration). The church was probably designed earlier, between 1887 and 1890.

12. A history of Trinity and its congregation is given in a series of articles written by its first historian, Peter Winne, in *The Trail* from February 1915 to April 1916. In particular, see "Events in the History of Trinity M. E. Church" (February 1915): 10–14; ibid. (December 1915): 17–23; ibid. (January 1916): 10–18; ibid. (February 1916): 16–21; ibid. (March 1916): 16–20; ibid. (April 1916): 17–24. Winne, for years superintendent of the Sunday School, was a trustee and member of the building committee for the new church. A new history of Trinity is scheduled for late 1988 publication.

13. The Lawrence Street Methodist Episcopal Church is illustrated in Isaac Haight Beardsley, *Echoes from Peak and Plain; or, Tales of Life, War, Travel, and Colorado Methodism* (Cincinnati: Curts & Jennings; New York: Eaton & Mains, 1898), 361. See also J. Alton Templin, Allen D. Breck, and Martin Rist, eds., *The Methodist, Evangelical, and United Brethren Churches in the Rockies, 1850–1976* (Denver: Rocky Mountain Conference of the United Methodist Church, 1977).

14. Minutes of the Meetings of the Board of Trustees of Lawrence St. M. E. Church, January 1–September 28, 1891 (daybook), 27–147, Trinity United Methodist Church Archives, Denver.

15. *Rocky Mountain Advocate*, December 27, 1888, reprinted in *The Trail* 8 (April 1916): 20. The trustees, who originally projected the cost of the building at $60,000, agreed to a magnificent church at the then-high sum of about $173,000, including the organ (Beardsley, *Echoes*, 363).

16. The parsonage, financed by H. B. Chamberlin as a memorial to his mother, was built on Sherman Avenue.

17. RSR's foundation plans of March 1887 correspond to the final construction scheme of August and do not include a parsonage.

18. Beardsley, *Echoes*, 363. For this work RSR earned 5 percent, or $6,584 (with a possible 1-1/2 percent on extra changes); from this fee he paid a "voluntary" contribution, stipulated in his contract, of $1,400 to the building fund (Minutes, Board of Trustees, October 10, 1887, Trinity United Methodist Church Archives). An extensive record of expenses, payments, and all aspects pertaining to the construction of the new church are compiled in these documents from the Trinity archives. The general contractor responsible for the superstructure was Hallack and Howard Lumber Company, a substantial Denver firm that worked with RSR on East High School (1882 and 1889) and many other buildings. As Trinity neared completion there was trouble with roof leakage which damaged the frescoing, but the contractors, too, can be considered patrons of the building project, as they carried much of the cost of construction. For a description of the cornerstone ceremonies, see *RMN*, September 6, 1887, pp. 2, 3.

19. Sara Bradford Landau, *Edward T. and William A. Potter: American Victorian Architects* (New York & London: Garland, 1979).

20. Beardsley states that the height of the spire is 181-1/2 feet; the drawing shows a measurement of 174 feet without the cross. As the *Rocky Mountain Christian Advocate* stated on December 27, 1888, "Looking up Eighteenth street, Tremont or Broadway, the newly completed Trinity Methodist Episcopal Church may be seen at the intersection of these streets, its tall, tapering spire of stone lifted high into the sky, a bold land mark from all parts of the city" (reprinted in Winne, *The Trail* 8 [April 1916], 20).

21. The foundation plan of March 1887 is signed "Roeschlaub and Hale," the latter a partner in the firm during 1886–87. The foundation walls of the tower are approximately eleven feet thick. Fig. 2–15 shows a belfry at level "C" which was never used as such.

22. RSR increased the proportion of spire to tower to 1:1 from his perspective rendering (compare cover to Fig. 2–6).

23. Recent attempts were made to duplicate this effect. Louvers to the side of the cross, in fact, allow little light to escape. Early eyewitnesses may have exaggerated the success of RSR's experiment.

24. William A. Coles, ed., *Architecture and Society: Selected Essays of Henry Van Brunt* (Cambridge, Mass.: Harvard University Press, 1969); James F. O'Gorman et al., *The Architecture of Frank Furness* (Philadelphia: Philadelphia Museum of Art, 1973).

25. See Michael W. Brooks, *John Ruskin and Victorian Architecture* (New Brunswick, N.J.: Rutgers University Press, 1987); Henry-Russell Hitchcock, "Ruskin and American Architecture, or Regeneration Long Delayed," in Sir John Summerson, ed., *Concerning Architecture* (London: Penquin/Allen Lane, 1968).

26. "The handsome iron grills in the entrance of the T. M. E. Church are worthy of notice. They are of Denver manufacture, having been made by Winter & Fitting" (*WABN* 1 [March 1889], 10). Gustave Winter and Jacob Fitting owned the Denver Iron Fence Co., which advertised as "wire workers, gun and locksmiths" (Denver City Directory, 1888).

27. See G. Naylor, *The Arts and Crafts Movement* (London: Studio Vista, 1971); "Aspects of the Arts and Crafts Movement in America" (symposium papers, Department of Art and Archaeology, Princeton University, November, 1972). RSR was able to use the best of materials. The finials on the main roof and towers were copper. His insistence on careful execution of detailing is evident from instructions on his drawings: "All Finials, Downspouts, etc. tinted red shall be made in the best manner of copper of various weights according to the character of the work....None of this work will be pointed [;] consequently it must be a neat and workman like job in every particular." Drawing 37 "Details of Galv. Iron and Copper work for Trinity M.E. Church Denver Colo" (see Fig. 2–17). The copper work and slating was executed by Joseph Walters. Another instruction demanding excellence in the finishing details of the roof reads: "Hip beads, crestings, terminals, etc.,—tinted red—shall be of first class terra cotta, well secured in place."

28. Brettell, *Historic Denver*, 115.

29. Ibid.

30. Sometimes labeled "kyune stone" on the drawings.

31. Roeschlaub-Fuller Collection, CHS. Richard Brettell in *Historic Denver* has interpreted RSR's undoubted "restlessness" and profuse detail as the dominant characteristic of Trinity. He believes that RSR retained a conservative Queen Anne mentality unredeemed by Richardsonian boldness. "For Roeschlaub, a building was put together from separately designed elements rather than conceived as a whole. Roeschlaub's eye moved everywhere" (118). Although true, the present author, rather, is impressed by RSR's control of the rugged rhyolite surface and bold massing, which Brettell has described so well in his perceptive analysis of Trinity: "The building has a grounded look...in spite of its dramatic tower.... The forms of the nave, exaggerated transept, corner towers, and outbuildings huddle together to form a single composition grouped massively around the defining corner spire" (115–16). "His massing schemes were often far more complex and subtle than Richardson's own" (121).

32. During Trinity's restoration in the 1980s the ground floor was modernized. It is now level with the entrance. Originally lowered 1-1/2 feet beneath Broadway, this unusual split-level organization resembled (in this feature and nothing else) the Murray Universalist Church (Attleboro, Massachusetts) by Gould and Angell, architects of Providence, Rhode Island, published in the *American Architect and Building News*, December 4, 1886, of which RSR possessed an illustration. In the plan of the lower level itself, directly forward from the main entrance was the large Sunday School room, which could be set up to accommodate 1,000 seats. At the east end of the room was a raised platform for the principal, or superintendent. In back of the platform were draperies which separated off parlors used as classrooms and containing the Sunday School library. At the back, or east, end was the kitchen. The music room was in the southeast angle of the building. Under the supervision of the congregation's music director, members of the choir could rehearse. The base of the tower at the northwest angle of the building contained a small infants' classroom. These small rooms honed out of a building's mass were typical of nineteenth-century architecture.

RSR loved tinkering, inventing practical solutions to an immediate functional problem. In this regard, the west end of the main room and the superintendent's platform on the east were enclosed with rolling partitions which subdivided the main space (Fig. 2–25). These partitions were nine feet high, with glass in the space between the top and the ceiling. They were made of white wood, varnished, and could be coiled into the casings overhead. When they were thrown up, the room could seat 1,400. So RSR's experience in manipulating borrowed light as architect for Denver's public schools is transferred to this Sunday School. Although minimally decorated, the entire ground floor was furnished in white pine, varnished and polished: paint would have been a falsification of the material, according to the pervasive Arts and Crafts aesthetic of the edifice. The floor was of hard pine. The room was lighted by handsome, stained-glass windows of delicate tints, which remain in place.

33. *Rocky Mountain Christian Advocate*, December 27, 1888, in Winne, *The Trail* 8 (April 1916): 22.

34. The First Universalist Church (North Attleboro, Massachusetts) by William Walker and Con, architects of Providence, Rhode Island, published in the *American Architect and Building News* (April 14, 1883), had auditorium seating in a fan-shaped plan but with four aisles. RSR also saved an illustration of the Beloit College Chapel (Beloit, Wisconsin, 1890) by Patton and Fisher, Chicago architects, which duplicated the Trinity arrangement.

35. *Rocky Mountain Christian Advocate*, December 27, 1888, in Winne, *The Trail* 8 (April 1916): 22.

36. Ibid.

37. This furniture "fully sustains their [Lamb's] reputations as having no superiors in their specialty" (ibid, 22).

38. David Hanks, "Louis J. Millet and The Art Institute of Chicago," *The Art Institute of Chicago Bulletin* (March/April 1973): 13–19. Healy and Millet's other interiors for Sullivan were McVicker's Theater, the Transportation Building of the World's Columbian Exposition, the Schiller Building and the banks at Owatonna (Minnesota) and Sidney (Ohio). They also carried out the Sullivanesque interior decoration of the Grand Hall of the St. Louis Union Station Terminal 1891–94 designed by Theodore Link. See Patricia M. Holmes, "The St. Louis Union Station," *The Bulletin* (Missouri Historical Society, July 1971): 248–58.

According to a contemporary source, *Industrial Chicago*, Healy and Millet, "designers and manufacturers of fine stained glass, and artistic frescoers and general decorators, are among the leaders in their department of the building interest, not only in Chicago but in the entire country." It continues: "George Louis Healy is a son of [a] portrait painter, and was born in Paris, France, [in] l856. Louis J. Millet, son of a composer and musician, and nephew of Aime Millet, the French sculptor, was born in New York in July 1855. They both entered the School of Fine Arts, Paris, in 1873, and in 1879 after completing their course as architects and decorators, they came to Chicago. Their work came into demand at once and it has embraced numerous first-class buildings of all kinds, among the more notable ones having been, besides the great Auditorium building, a number of elegant churches including Grace Episcopal church, Chicago, the residences of Potter Palmer and others of Chicago's millionaires, besides many other magnificent residences in other cities" (*Industrial Chicago*, vol. 2 [Chicago: Goodspeed Publishing Co., 1891], 707–8, as quoted in Hanks, "Louis J. Millet," 14). The firm's additional work mentioned was the Calumet and Union League clubs, the Metropolitan Opera House in St. Paul, Minnesota, "a fine theatre at Seattle," the Las Vegas, New Mexico, courthouse, and the Central Music Hall in Chicago.

39. Ed. Didron, "Le Vitrail depuis cent ans et l'Exposition de 1889," *Revue des Arts Décoratifs* 10 (1889–90): 145, 148, 152 (trans. from the French by Francine Haber). Five illustrations. Curiously enough, considering Louis Comfort Tiffany's great fame, "it was not [he] who introduced the new way of making stained-glass windows to Europe. It was his fellow artist and rival John La Farge, as well as the Chicago glass-making firm of Healy and Millet" (Herwin Schaefer, "Tiffany's Fame in Europe," *Art Bulletin* 44 [December 1962]: 311).

40. "This milky glass, pearly, of changing tones" was praised for the small dimensions of the pieces: again, direct use of material and color was considered true, which "augmented its moral value." "American glass is a superb material...deeply streaked and uneven, rumpled, spangled, mottled,...flecked with varied tones which sometimes make it iridescent like all the colors of a prism" (Didron, "Le Vitrail depuis cent ans," 148–52).

41. According to Schaefer, "Tiffany glass" in Europe usually meant this particular kind of stained-glass window, whether made by Tiffany himself or others, windows in which the design was achieved entirely by colored pieces of glass, a method in which painting had been abandoned ("Tiffany's Fame in Europe," 309). This may be the origin of the belief that Trinity's windows were designed by Tiffany. This technique of semi-opaque, rich color was, by pure serendipity, especially suited to modulate the bright intensity of Colorado light. RSR's wood framework for the windows is rather thick-set and sturdy; the concept, recalling Early English precedents, is one of jewels set into stone rather than disintegration of substance by light.

42. Louis J. Millet, "Interior Decoration: Its Development in America," part 1, *Inland Architect and Builder* 1 (February 1882): 3.

43. Millet, "Interior Decoration," part 2, *Inland Architect and Builder* 1 (March 1883): 17–18. Apropos of the unity in stained glass, "design and color, those two factors of decorative result, are so closely allied that the rules of one define the function of the other. The process of the mind in composing a polychromatic ornament is but one" (Millet, "Interior Decoration, part 3, *Inland Architect and Builder* 1 [May 1883]: 52).

44. Schaefer, "Tiffany's Fame in Europe," 312, 320–21. The purely ornamental patterns of Healy and Millet achieved a kind of translucent tapestry. Simplified and contained within the strong dark lines of the leading, they produced mosaic-like designs in glass similar in form and color to the post-Impressionist painters.

45. *Rocky Mountain Christian Advocate*, December 27, 1888, in Winne, *The Trail* 8 (April 1916), 23. "Denver was one of the earliest of America's cities to have electricity; Colorado Edison demonstrated incandescent lighting for sale in the summer of 1880. A competitor, with the Brush arc franchise, was formed in 1881, merged with Colorado Edison in 1883 to form the Denver Consolidated Electric Company, which in 1885 installed an arc lighting system claimed by [Jerome C.] Smiley to be the third or fourth street lighting system in the world. It might have been installed earlier but a wait was necessary until the gas lighting franchise was vacated" (Gary Long, "Roeschlaub, Architecture, and Technology," unpublished paper, University of California–Santa Barbara, January 1988, 22).

46. Noteworthy is the nearly instantaneous knowledge that RSR shared of this complex architectural device. The Chicago

Auditorium was designed in 1886 and executed in 1888–89. While the frescoers Healy and Millet as well as RSR could have perfected the more sophisticated final ornament, compared to the orthodox and banal neo-Gothic frieze surrounds for the electric bulbs shown on RSR's drawing, it would have been no more than the freedom accorded them by Sullivan himself. RSR drew in the lights and, as we have seen elsewhere in the building, created some intricate and original ornament very similar to the final version of the Trinity arch—in plaster, in wood, in stone—by August 3, 1887. This concurrence of ideas demonstrates that RSR at Trinity was no mere passive receiver of influences and sources of the Arts and Crafts movement but an equal participant and colleague in the formulation of American "modern Gothic" architecture and design. Just as the electric light of the cross atop the spire "shed down on the church like a benediction" (*The Trail*, 23), the proscenium arch created a halo reinterpreted for modern times.

47. It was not only the generous sum of his $30,000 donation that distinguished Trinity trustee Isaac E. Blake, a leading Colorado businessman and president of Continental Petroleum, as the patron of the organ, but the fact that he was a respected musician, variously the church's choir director and its tenor soloist. This gifted and knowledgeable man oversaw every aspect of its commission.

48. There are actually 114 seats for the chorus (anonymous commercial flyer published by Trinity Church or by the Roosevelt Organ Company entitled "July 1887. Roosevelt Organ, No. 380, now being built for Trinity Methodist Episcopal Church, Denver, Colo., U.S.A. Isaac E. Blake, Esq., Donor." For extensive information on the organ see also Howard Price (with Norman Lane), "The Roosevelt Organ," an unpublished report, 1972, Trinity United Methodist Church Archives. The flyer provides much technical information on the organ: the 1972 Trinity organ restoration, which overhauled the system from top to bottom and installed the present console at a cost of $60,000, tried to bring the organ back as near as possible to its original sound and appearance. Built by the celebrated Roosevelt firm of New York, the organ incorporated several recently invented mechanical features. The entire organ was supplied with "Roosevelt Patent Windchests" of their new so-called sliderless type. Valves were opened by combination of air, supplied by water engines, and electricity, according to Price, "this organ being among the first half dozen major organs in the world to have electropneumatic action throughout." Electric key action resulted in "a touch lighter than a piano." The adaption of the "swellbox" was thought extraordinary (all pipes being enclosed in boxes and capable of "expression" except the pedal organ and four of the great organ stops). The stop of thirty-two foot pipes was rare and noteworthy. RSR's job was to understand and accommodate the organ. The east end of RSR's tranverse section shows the "motor room," and above it the "bellows room."

49. According to Audsley, function was an opportunity for aesthetic invention. Accounts about how the new improvement in the workings of the organ could bear fruit in good design or, more emphatically, be the criteria of design, paralleled RSR's architectural principles. "Certain instruments erected by Roosevelt, of New York, in churches of other denominations, and which occupy commanding positions, are models of good internal arrangement. A noteworthy example obtains in the Organ in Trinity Methodist Episcopal Church, at Denver, Col.; which is most conveniently arranged, both for the free egress of sound from all its divisions and for easy access to all its parts. The pedal department may in some cases be relieved by mounting one or more of its small-scaled wood stops as external ornamental features, as has been done, on our suggestion, in the wings of the Organ in Trinity Church, at Denver, Col. We have spoken on the desirability of employing wood pipes as decorative features in our Chapter on the External Design of the Organ and the Decoration of the Organ" (George Ashdown Audsley, *The Art of Organ Building* [New York: Dodd, Mead & Co., 1905; New York: Dover Publications, Inc., 1963], 349, 354).

A great Romantic organ, Trinity's instrument was known for its expressive tone, just as RSR's modern Gothic architecture expressed the value of true sentiment directly presented. Having introduced the question of expression in connection with that division called the Great Organ in his chapter "The Church Organ," Audsley states: "Up to the present time no steps, so far as our knowledge extends, have been taken by English, French, or German builders, of the present organ-building epoch, to apply the swell-box, and consequently powers of expression, to the Great division of the Church Organ. It was left to the greatest of American organ builders to establish the new treatment of the Great Organ which we have advocated for a period of nearly forty years. By way of illustrating what the late Mr. Hilborne L. Roosevelt achieved in this important direction [we publish] the scheme of the Great division of the large Organ erected in Trinity Methodist Episcopal Church, Denver, Colorado (229). The scheme for the Swell-Organ "inclosed [*sic*] in a special swell-box [and] unquestionably imposing" of the Roosevelt Organ in Trinity Church is given as well. Although Audsley had some reservations as to whether the swell-organ's harmonic structure was equal to "so great a weight of unison tone," the Trinity organ was presented as a prime example for emulation (ibid., 233–36).

Audsley's problem was a difficult one. The position of the organ was extremely wide compared with its height. His design solved this by means of the broken line of the case and the graceful contour of the top of the pipes, all leading up to and framing the central feature. Color and materials were paramount: "The woodwork of the case," according to Peter Winne, "is a massive ash slightly stained so that the beautiful grain of the wood may be more accentuated; it extends in a graceful broken line across the room, and in the center is higher than at the side. Standing upon this are pipes. At either side is a group of slender wooden pipes made of Georgia pine and mahogany, in their natural colors. From these toward the center appear metal pipes in curved and straight lines. The main feature of the design is the central portion, which is flanked upon each side by towers of large metal pipes which extend to the highest point reached. Between these towers are two rows of pipes, one in front of the other, the outer one sloping downward and the inner one upward toward the middle. The decoration is characterized by the beauty of extreme simplicity. The bodies of the smaller pipes from a point a little above the mouth appear in the natural color of the metal zinc. The larger ones are silvered, making this a contrast of bright silver, with the effect of oxidized silver of the zinc. The lower part of each pipe is gilded and around them, dividing the gold from the silver, extends a band of red with ornament of black. The mouths are of polished metal ornamented with black. The inner pipes of the row of the center portion are gilded" (Winne, *The Trail* 8 [April 1916]: 23).

50. *Rocky Mountain Christian Advocate* in Winne, *The Trail* 8 (April 1916): 22–23.

51. *Denver Republican*, April 2, 1888, p. 2.

Or, "the building builds the builder" (*Rocky Mountain Christian Advocate*, in Winne, *The Trail* 8 [March 1916]: 19).

52. *Rocky Mountain Christian Advocate*, December 27, 1888, in Winne, *The Trail* 8 (March 1916): 17.

53. As church membership dwindled in the late 1960s and early 1970s, the trustees went to heroic lengths to provide minimum maintenance. Offers to sell the property and demolish the building for substantial sums were received. The executive committee negotiated with a major real estate company, setting conditions: the church would not be destroyed; an annex added in the 1920s could be demolished; replacement space would be provided; there would be a substantial endowment fund; and adequate parking would be available. There has been a tremendous resurgence in church activity under the present leadership and since restoration.

54. Manley Dayton and Eleanor R. Ormes, *The Book of Colorado Springs* (Colorado Springs: Denton Printing Co., 1933, 201). Only a small portion of the original building remains.

55. *Colorado Springs Gazette*, April 13, 1888, p. 1. Janis Falkenberg has discovered that the First Congregational Church on North Tejon and East St. Vrain in Colorado Springs has incorrectly been attributed to RSR. At the cornerstone laying, the architect was reported as Henry Rutgers Marshall of New York, represented locally by L. A. Pease (*Colorado Springs Gazette*, September 9, 1888, p. 1). However, the National Register of Historic Places inventory nomination form for the First Congregational Church of Manitou, Colorado (August 16, 1979), states: "Although the evidence is inconclusive, there is some thought that Robert A. [*sic*] Roeschlaub of Denver offered a design" but the report attributes the church to architects Angus Gillis and George W. Snider.

56. According to building permit 215 of February 8, 1907 (Western History Department, DPL), the projected cost of the building was $23,000 or about one eighth the price of Trinity Methodist Episcopal Church.

57. "Our Greeting: First Congregational Church and Parsonage," newspaper clipping, August 18, 1918 (clipping file, Western History Department, DPL). A similar Lombard exterior appeared at St. George's Church, Newburgh, New York, for which Frederick C. Withers, architect, New York, designed the tower in 1885. The church was illustrated in the *American Architect and Building News* (January 2, 1886). RSR possessed a copy.

58. All factual information on the First Congregational Church was provided by Rodd L. Wheaton of the National Park Service, who prepared a National Register nomination form for the church, and Pastor Charles Arehart and Assistant Minister Dan Mahoney, Metropolitan Community Church of the Rockies. The conclusions expressed here, however, are the author's own.

59. The pulpit platform has been modified; it ended in a straight edge just beyond the alcove. There was at least one more row of pews towards the apse. The arm rests of the wood pews have an elegant late Art Nouveau sweep. The building is now undergoing restoration, and the stained glass of the west window will be reinstalled. The apse originally housed a small pipe organ, which has been located and donated to the congregation.

60. Franklin Kidder, *Churches and Chapels* (New York: W. T. Comstock, 1895), 6, as cited in Brettell, *Historic Denver*, 140–41. Kidder had published a similar fan-shaped diagonally-set plan, but with a curved balcony, as "Design C" in *Churches and Chapels*. At the First Congregational, a low wing that directly abuts the sanctuary and contains a meeting room was added by Roeschlaub and Son in 1910 to the east. Like Kidder's Plan C, a vertical sliding screen wall can be opened to expand the sanctuary. This is a gigantic version of the movable screens RSR installed in Trinity's original Sunday School.

 Chapter Three: Schools

1. Andrew Gulliford, *America's Country Schools* (Washington, D.C.: The Preservation Press, 1984).

2. Frank Hall, *History of the State of Colorado* vol. 4 (Chicago: Blakely Printing Co., 1895), 39.

3. *RMN*, January 1, 1880, 22.

4. "The Architecture of Light: The Board Schools," in Mark Girouard, *Sweetness and Light: The "Queen Anne" Movement, 1860–1900* (Oxford: Clarendon Press, 1977).

5. *Denver Times*, September 20, 1879, p. 2.

6. *RMN*, April 14, 1883, p. 3. In spite of this visit by Bicknell, no article on Denver's schools appeared in the *New England Journal of Education* between April 1883

and June 1884. Sarah Otis published only an article in the *Boston Commonwealth* on the planned company town of Pullman near Chicago as a result of her trip west.

7. "His [RSR's] principal work of importance has been school-house architecture.... To such an extent is the reputation of these buildings known, that copies of them are called for from all parts of the country. In 18— the Bavarian Government, asked for copies of plans and photographs of three of the buildings; and the Educator General of Canada, published plans and views of seven of them in the Dominion Reports as examples of special merit" (*WABN* 1 [February 1890]: 3). Also in 1890, the *WABN* 2 (April 1890), 19, reported this item about RSR's High School: "Major Aaron Gove, superintendent of Schools, has received a letter from the Brooklyn, N.Y., School Board, in which the following appears: 'We are about to erect a new High School Building, and it is the desire of the committee to erect one that shall be a credit to the city. Your High School building has a reputation throughout the country, and we hope to get from you, if possible, prints showing the elevation and interior arrangement of your building.'"

8. Andrew Gulliford, *America's Country Schools* (Washington, D.C.: The Preservation Press, 1984), 39–40.

9. *Denver Times*, September 20, 1879, p. 2. And: "The common school is the safeguard of the community" (*RMN*, January 1, 1880, p. 22).

10. *RMN*, May 11, 1884, pp. 15–16.

11. Gary Long, "Roeschlaub, Architecture, and Technology" (unpublished paper, University of California–Santa Barbara, January 1988), 13. A learned lecturer of 1866 attributed nearly half the deaths in New York City to the presence of foul air. This concern also related to lighting. According to Long, a Mr. Emile Trelat, for instance, extolled the virtues of lighting schoolrooms from only one side. High windows on the north were considered best for students' eyes: "At regular intervals in the school day he would have the pupils sent into the playground, and the shutters [on the south side] and windows thrown wide open, flooding the room with sunshine and fresh air, sweeping away the gathered effluvia which a gentler aeration might not be able to dislodge, and filling the room with a new and sweet atmosphere into which the children can return from their bath of fresh air" (from the *American Architect and Building News* 8 [June 12,

1880]: 256 See also Gavin Townsend, "Victorian Systems of Heating and Ventilation," unpublished master's thesis, University of California, 1986, for an extensive bibliography on the subject.

12. "Builders of the late nineteenth century were...party to a wonderful explosion of engineering creativity answering social wants and needs for more healthful and more convenient habitat. The U.S. Patent Office granted 36,000 patents from 1790 to 1860, an overwhelming 440,000 from 1860 to 1890" (W. H. G. Armytage, *A Social History of Engineering*, 4th ed. [Boulder, Colorado: Westview Press, 1976], 179, quoted in Long, "Roeschlaub, Architecture, and Technology," 4–5). For example, the *American Architect and Building News* 8 (April and May 1880): 225–27, published a three-installment treatise on ventilation, a "lecture by Mr. Edward Philbrick, C.E., to M.I.T. students," which qualifies as textbook material.

13. District One annual report, 1875, 20.

14. "Mr. Roeschlaub, the architect, who furnished the design for the new public school house in Pueblo, has gone down in that city to receive bids for the work on the building" (*RMN*, February 13, 1876, p. 4). The building is illustrated in the *Pueblo Daily Chieftain*, February 27, 1889, p. 1

15. Lambert and Parker were the contractors for Longfellow School, which cost $31,068 (District One annual report, 1885, 34).

16. Ibid., 21.

17. All the classrooms have a raised teacher's platform, and all schools a recitation room, both standard features that remain constant throughout RSR's career as school architect. Students were taught the three "R's," for both recitation and elocution played prominent roles in the late nineteenth-century curriculum.

18. J. R. Millard was the contractor for the Broadway school at a bid of $21,389 (District One annual report, 1885, 21–22).

19. The cost for the Twenty-fourth Street School was $21,653, the contractor C. D. McPhee and Company (ibid., 23).

20. *RMN*, January 1, 1880, p. 3.

21. *Denver Times*, September 20, 1879, p. 2. The reporter was not the only person impressed with the Twenty-fourth Street School. In Leadville there was a "large and elegant building known as the Central school, completed in 1881. It is modeled after the Twenty-Fourth street school in

Denver" (Hall, *History of Colorado* 4:426).

22. These brackets seem close to the European "neo-grec" of Henri Labrouste and his disciples, a strange, one-time occurrence in RSR's work.

23. Gilpin cost $36,497; D. Coey was the contractor (*RMN*, June 4, 1881, p. 8).

24. Richard Brettell, *Historic Denver: The Architects and the Architecture, 1858–1893* (Denver: Historic Denver, Inc., 1973), 98.

25. Built by contractor Harvey and Washburn for $23,983 (*RMN*, May 28, 1884, p. 8).

26. For its time, Whittier was spacious in a practical sense: "This house has attracted more attention than any other one from the completeness of its interior arrangements. The heating, lighting, ventilation and adjustment of rooms, basement, etc., are a marvel of convenience and comfort. The cost of the entire establishment [$45,000] is as well a surprise to all who inspect it. It seats 650 pupils and has air space, floor space and light surface per pupil in excess of any other grammar school house" (District One annual report, 1885, 15). Part of the basement of Whittier was used for play rooms during bad weather, and as a lunch room.

27. Ibid., 40.

28. *RMN*, May 28, 1884, p. 15. The site in 1988 seems neither high nor commanding.

29. Ibid. Emerson cost $1,000 less than Longfellow, probably because more brick trim than stone was used.

30. "The Emerson School House in Denver," *Colorado School Journal* 1 (October 1885): n.p.

31. Brettell, *Historic Denver*, 100, describes these neo-Gothic and Renaissance features, but neo-Tudor seems a neater appellation.

32. The brick craftsmanship at Emerson is special: "In the original contract ordinary stock brick facing was provided for, but Mr. Benn Brewer, of the E. E. Hallack Manufacturing Company, the sub-contractor for the brick work—having taken a special interest in the building—faced it with Denver pressed brick, the whole making one of the finest jobs of brick work to be found in the city" ("The Emerson School House in Denver," *Colorado School Journal*).

33. Ibid.

34. Illustrated in Harriet Seibel, *A History of the Colorado Springs Schools* (Colorado

Springs: Century One Press, 1975), 40–41. Seibel gives the following description from the *Colorado Springs Gazette*, related when the school was dedicated in 1884: "Liller School was formally opened yesterday for inspection. It was visited by not less than 500 people. It is by far the most commodious structure of its kind in southern colorado, if not in the state, and the $20,000 expended could not have been devoted to a better purpose. It is a commodious four-room two-story building with a basement. It is of modern architecture, built of brick with sandstone trim. The main entrance is from the northwest corner leading into a broad and well-lighted hall extending diagonally across the building from the northwest to the southeast. On the southeast is also an entrance for pupils coming from that direction. Upon either side of the hall is a well-lighted and well-ventilated school room with a seating capacity of sixty pupils each. Both rooms are provided with separate cloak and hat rooms for boys and girls. A broad staircase leads from the lower floor to the upper floor. The ceilings in all of the rooms are high and the windows are large. A transom window above each door gives the best ventilation possible. The entire building is plastered in hard finish with the exception of the halls which are rough and blocked off to represent stone. They are wainscoated with Colorado pine. In the basement are three large well-furnished rooms for the janitor. Separate are the coal room, the wood room and the heating apparatus. The building is provided with water and gas throughout, although the fixtures for gas will be placed in only one room. The building fronts Wahsatch on the west and Cucharras on the south. A drinking fountain is in the front of each entrance. The building reflects much credit to Mr. Roeschlaub, the architect." Information provided by Janis Falkenberg.

35. The school was commissioned in May and completed by October 8, 1884. There was dissension in the town of Eaton, Colorado, as to what size the school should be: "Some maintained a building of two rooms would be adequate enough, while others, chief among whom was ex-Governor Eaton, stood firm in their demands for a larger building. The latter group overruled the first, and Architect Rosechlaub [sic] of Denver drew the plans" (Pauline Allison, *The History of Eaton, Colorado*, first published serially in the *Eaton Herald*, 1937–42, n.p., illustrated). The school was torn down in 1937.

36. *RMN*, June 16, 1882, p. 2.

37. *WABN* 1 (March 1889): 10. An illustration of RSR's rendering of the high school was published in this issue.

38. Brettell, *Historic Denver*, 100.

39. District One annual report, 1890, 39.

40. Aaron Gove hoped that with its construction, "every man and woman be invited [sic] to participate personally in the benefits of a grand free public library" (District One annual report, 1885, 40). A newspaper article assured that it "contains a variety of instructive and entertaining literature far above the average. Extensive reading rooms bring large numbers of visitors each day" (*Denver Times*, December 31, 1898, p. 13).

41. "The ground will be so graded as to leave the house on a terrace, which will be put into lawn. [T]he block will be surrounded with a neat stone coping and iron fence. Fountains, gas lamps, trees, etc., will, when the plan is carried out, be equal to if not eclipse our beautiful Court-house square" (*RMN*, May 11, 1884, p. 16, quoted verbatim in District One annual report, 1885, 39).

42. District One annual report, 1890, 33.

43. *Denver Republican*, January 1, 1888, p. 10. The final cost was higher: an unprecedented $325,000 (District One annual report, 1890, 39).

44. Brettell, *Historic Denver*, 100.

45. "The Emerson School House in Denver," *Colorado School Journal*.

46. Brettell, *Historic Denver*, 102.

47. Richardson, of course, placed two such *tourettes* at Sever Hall, Harvard, which was a reference point for collegiate architecture during this period, but to reinforce the severity and symmetry of the facade. The little tower at Hyde Park, in its placement and form, is close to J. P. Seddon's University College (Aberystwyth, Wales, 1864); the similarity is probably coincidental.

48. *WABN* 1 (March 1889): 10 and *WABN* 1 (October 1889): 110. Its opening was announced in the journal: "This will be one of the handsomest buildings in the city." The contract price was $71,000. The foundations were constructed by Messrs. Tooney and Baynes.

49. "[Corona] stands on high ground at the corner of Corona and Ninth avenues, overlooking the city and commanding an extensive view of mountain range and plain. The structure is built of brick, with red sandstone and terra cotta trimmings. Square towers on each corner fifteen feet square are capped with domes, and add much to the general appearance. The building proper is about 70 x 90 feet in dimension and two stories high. On each floor there are six large class-rooms, each capable of seating sixty pupils, and four recitation-rooms. The total seating capacity of the house is about 700. The building is well lighted, and the ventilation is as perfect as can be secured. A thirty-horse power boiler in the basement will heat the building by steam. The building is one of the most complete of its kind in the country" (*Denver Times*, September 8, 1890, p. 7).

50. "The section shows also the full development of Roeschlaub's structures, a combination of exterior bearing walls, interior wood framing with some cast iron columns, and wood trussed roofs, this with lattice membranes as well" (Long, "Roeschlaub, Architecture, and Technology," 20–21).

51. Ibid.

52. *RMN*, January 1, 1881, p. 11.

53. Long, "Roeschlaub, Architecture, and Technology," 15–21.

54. Ibid.

55. Ibid.

 Chapter Four: Commercial Buildings

1. Richard R. Brettell, *Historic Denver: The Architects and the Architecture, 1858–1893* (Denver: Historic Denver, Inc., 1973), 33.

2. Dependent as the Boston and Colorado Smelter was for its operation on railroad lines, which either penetrated the sheds or lay alongside them, this work is akin as a building type to the three depots for which RSR takes credit (see RSR office inventory of projects, Roeschlaub-Fuller Collection, CHS). The buildings listed on the inventory are a depot at Darley (May 11, 1889), the Sloan Lake Station (July 23, 1890), the Boulevard (Station) in North Denver, and a mysterious "Electric [Railway Station] at Manhattan Beach" (no dates for either).

3. See "Argo Smelting Works," *Grand Army Magazine* 1 (March 1883): 149.

4. David R. Hill, *Colorado Urbanization and Planning Context* (Denver: Office of Archaeology and Historic Preservation, Colorado Historical Society, 1984).

5. Georgetown Society, Inc., and the People for Silver Plume, *Guide to the George-town–Silver Plume Historic District* (Evergreen, Colo.: Cordillera Press, Inc., 1986), 7.

6. Long Hoeft Architects and Peter Snell, Architectural Museum Services, *Properties Plan* (Georgetown Society, Inc., August 1985) and Long Hoeft Architects, *Measured Drawings and Restoration Study of the Hamill Office and Carriage House* (Georgetown, Colo.: Georgetown Society, Inc., 1981). These studies provide the basis for the commentary on Hamill's properties in Georgetown. The Long Hoeft drawings have been recorded for the Historic American Buildings Survey (HABS) and are located in the Library of Congress.

7. See Chapter 5, "Public Buildings and Residences."

8. Long Hoeft Architects, *Measured Drawings and Restoration Study*.

9. Long Hoeft/Snell, *Properties Plan*, 42.

10. According to Long Hoeft Architects, "the quality of stonework at the building's base is mediocre and inconsistent. Three to five feet above the foundation, however, the stonework improves significantly suggesting that the workmen for this job were unfamiliar with building in granite, and that somehow the skilled work force was improved in the course of construction" (*Measured Drawings and Restoration Study*).

11. See Chapter 5, "Public Buildings and Residences." Long Hoeft Architects has discovered that the office stair leading from the second floor to the attic matches in all details the stair in the front central hall of the Hamill House, which was installed in 1880.

12. Long Hoeft Architects, *Measured Drawings and Restoration Study*.

13. The English architect Charles Locke Eastlake advanced his design principles in *Hints on Household Taste*, "first published in London in 1868, and then in an even more popular American edition of 1872. Eastlake decried the heavy bloated mid-century designs of furniture, providing designs of lighter pieces fashioned of straight wooden members, often somewhat mechanical in appearance, with scroll-sawn decoration and relatively delicate incised linear ornamental motifs. Eastlake's plea for the expression of the natural color and texture of materials and for form following function is a direct counterpart to what theorists and architects were attempting at this time, and, in fact, some architects and builders enlarged Eastlake's lathe-turned

spindles, straight flat structural members, and engraved ornament to true architectural scale and an Eastlake variant of domestic design was created" (Leland M. Roth, *A Concise History of American Architecture* [New York: Harper & Row, Icon Editions, 1979], 137–38).

14. Long Hoeft Architects, *Measured Drawings and Restoration Study.*

15. See Leon Krier, "Reconstruction of the European City," *Architectural Design* 54 (1984), and Rob Krier, *Urban Space* (New York: Rizzoli International Publications, Inc., 1979).

16. For example, Charles R. Hurd, for whom RSR built the Hurd and Cooper "business house" in 1875 at 371 Holladay Street (later 1517–19 Market), was among his first clients. A businessman of the early days, Hurd arrived in Denver in 1873, the same year as RSR. His line of goods came to determine the character of what is now lower downtown: "As a merchandise broker...[h]is specialties include canned goods, sugars, dried fruits, etc., and manufactured goods of various kinds peculiarly adapted to the Western trade" (*Denver Times*, November 11, 1902, sec. 2, p. 12). "Canned beef" illustrates an advertisement for "Chas. R. Hurd" in *RMN*, September 4, 1879, p. 5. RSR's correspondence (to Margaret Roeschlaub, September 1875, mentions a store for L. Barney: it may never have been built. Before RSR came to Denver this notice appeared: "L. Barney has begun work on a two-story brick building on Larimer street, which will contain two stores" (*RMN*, September 8, 1870, p. 4). RSR provided plans for the Sundham and Hoffman (or Huffman) carriage repository on Fifteenth and Wewatta streets in August 1879; the "substantial" brick building was completed by October at a cost of $4,800 (*RMN*, January 1, 1880, p. 4). William R. Whitehead was a physician of national stature; in 1877 he was elected president of the Denver Medical Association. "Dr. Whitehead has contributed his share to the improvement and growth of the city by erecting a handsome block on the corner of Fifteenth and Stout streets, containing three beautiful storerooms, equipped with all the modern conveniences, besides other buildings in different parts of the city" (W. B. Vickers, *History of the City of Denver, Arapahoe County, and Colorado* [Chicago: O. L. Baskin & Co., Historical Publishers, 1880], 630). This 1880 brick building, which cost $9,000 to build, was RSR's; G. W. Brown was the builder (*RMN*, January 1, 1880, p. 3).

One regrets the lack of visual material for the Alex Brandenburg Block (1880–81), as it was RSR's first known attempt at metal construction. The heating and ventilation systems were significant: "This building, situated on Larimer street between Sixteenth and Seventeenth streets, is three stories high, with basement. It has a frontage of 25 feet and a depth of 75 feet. The first story is 16 feet, the second story 14 feet, and the third story 13 feet. The ground floor comprises a store and staircase entrance to stories above. The superincumbent store front is carried upon a heavy triple girder of rolled wrought iron beams supported upon two heavy cast-iron pilasters....[It] is built of Fort Collins white and Morrison red sand stone, with rustic work in purple lava. The windows are glazed with best French plate glass. The second and third stories are divided into offices and dwelling rooms, with bathrooms and closets. The interior rooms are lighted by a large skylight. The apartments are provided with grates, and transoms for ventilation. The entire building is heated by steam with an apparatus from the well-known house of Hay & Prentice, of Chicago. Mr. Roeschlaub has but recently completed this building. It certainly is a credit to the street. Its cost was less than $16,000" (*RMN*, January 1, 1881, p. 11).

John J. Lichter, born in Germany in 1832, was a brewer in Pennsylvania, Kentucky, and Missouri. He came to Denver in 1876, where his business "increased to large proportions" (Frank Hall, *History of the State of Colorado*, vol. 4 [Chicago: Blakely Printing Co., 1895], 506). He conducted a successful malt house, designed by RSR in 1880–81 on Holladay (Market) and Twenty-third Street at a cost of $3,942 (*RMN*, January 1, 1881, p. 12). Also on Holladay was the addition RSR built for Edward B. Light, president of the Denver Manufacturing Company, a business noteworthy both for its employee cooperative structure and for proving that the tanning and manufacturing of quality leather goods could profitably be carried on in Colorado, in spite of high alkali in the water. Light's poor health led him to the congenial Denver climate in 1874. He prospered, first in West Denver, then at Larimer and Fourteenth streets. "In the spring of 1879, having added saddlery hardware to their business, they removed to their present storeroom on Holladay street, seeking more room for their rapidly growing business. Their capital stock was increased to $50,000. Although but a few months had elapsed, their quarters were found insufficient to accommodate their enormous business, and, in January, 1880, they increased their capital stock to $100,000, and doubled the capacity of their workship, tannery, saddletree and collar factory, and employed about one hundred hands. Their annual sales amount to over $200,000. Their store and factory occupy a floor-space of about 25,000 square feet" (Vickers, *History of Denver*, 50–57). The later is RSR's addition, which cost $600. Of RSR's warehouse, built for Bacon and Son in 1881, one knows only the cost of construction, $1,500.

The "Robertson Block" is listed on the architect's office inventory, with a date of 1887, in Colorado Springs. Janis Falkenberg has found that the 1890 Colorado Springs City Directory lists "Robertson & Co., jeweler, 113 E. Huerfano" and "Robertson & Dashwood, new & second hand goods, 20 E. Huerfano." The directories for 1892, 1896, 1898, and 1900 list "Robertson Block, NW cor. Tejon & Huerfano" and Robertson & Co. jewelers & opticians, 1235 Tejon." None can conclusively be attributed to RSR.

17. *RMN*, January 1, 1880, p. 4.

18. Brettell, *Historic Denver*, 15.

19. *Denver Times,* January 8, 1902, p. 11.

20. *RMN*, January 1, 1880, p. 4.

21. *Denver Times,* January 8, 1902, p. 11.

22. Sandra Dallas, *Cherry Creek Gothic* (Norman: University of Oklahoma Press, 1971), 142; see also CWA files, s.v. "Union Block," CHS.

23. Of a similar formula but with a triangular pediment was the Union National Bank (1883) at the corner of Eighth Avenue and Eighth Street in Greeley (now the Madison and Main Building), which RSR lists on his office inventory.

24. Brettell, *Historic Denver*, 115.

25. Ibid.

26. "Denver Illustrated," *The Grand Army Magazine* 1 (July 1883), 454.

27. Ibid., 449. The best detailed description of the Union Block appears with a good illustration of the Sixteenth Street elevation in the *Denver Republican*, January 1, 1883, p. 1. The third floor of "Gottesleben's Jewelry Palace" was fitted up into private apartments occupied by families; thus the block was a mixed-use complex with residential as well as office rentals. RSR's brother Henry, who brought his family to Denver several years after RSR, was the general bookkeeper of the Union Bank. In

late 1963 the block was torn down; its shopfronts had been opened up and "modernized," and the subtle relationship of the architecture to the street had been lost. See Marjorie Barrett, "A Block of History Is Being Erased," *RMN*, October 12, 1963, p. 37.

28. *Grand Army Magazine*, 449.

29. Ibid.

30. Ibid., 447–48.

31. *Denver Times*, March 11, 1902, p. 6. The Bancroft Block (1880), located on the southwest corner of Stout and Sixteenth streets, occupied four lots (1551–63 Stout and 800–806 Sixteenth). The site at one time marked the suburban home of Dr. F. J. Bancroft, a leading Denver physician. Later, on the increasingly profitable property, he built the four-story Bancroft Block at a cost of $3,500. C. T. Cochran and Company were the builders. "At the top of the boom he sold it to Mr. Bell, a Nebraska banker, for a fortune of about $200,000 and Mr. Bell turned it over a few weeks afterward to Mr. Holzman, the present owner, at a profit of $40,000. Those were the days for which the real estate men sigh. Perhaps they will come again" (*Times*, February 14, 1902, p. 5). Also on the Bancroft Block, see Jerome C. Smiley, *History of the City of Denver, with Outlines of the Earlier History of the Rocky Mountain Country* [Denver: Denver Times/Times-Sun Publishing Co., 1901], 955), who gives the date as 1881, and *RMN*, January 1, 1880, p. 3.

The owner of one RSR building was responsible for the destruction of another. S. L. Holzman owned RSR's 1891 Holzman-Appel Block at 808–16 Sixteenth Street next-door to the Bancroft. Holzman's original tenant, Salomon's Bazaar, was replaced by the Lewis and Son dry goods store. Holzman bought the Bancroft property in 1902, tore down the old block, and built a new enlargement of Lewis and Son as an addition to RSR's Holzman-Appel Block (see note 44 below).

32. *Denver Times*, March 27, 1899, p. 6. An illustration of the block in this article was the result of "remodeling and modernizing" which "changed the appearance of the entire place, both interior and exterior." RSR did the remodeling, according to his office inventory, which conforms to the 1899 date of this article.

33. Supplement to *The Great Divide* 2 (December 1889): 161–68. This article includes an illustration of RSR's first version of the Central Block.

34. Henry-Russell Hitchcock, *Architecture: Nineteenth and Twentieth Centuries*, 4th ed. (Harmondsworth [Middlesex], England and New York: Pelican History of Art, Penguin Books, Ltd., 1977), 339.

35. States William H. Jordy ("The Tall Buildings," in Wim de Wit, ed., *Louis Sullivan: The Function of Ornament* [New York and London: W. W. Norton & Co. with the Chicago Historical Society and the Saint Louis Art Museum, 1986], 67–68): "[T]he severe granite block of H. H. Richardson's Marshall Field Wholesale Store...came to have special meaning for Sullivan....Its base of low, segmental arched openings provides visual support to the tiers of semicircular arching above....Richardson closes the visual ascent of the stacked arches by the staccato horizontal rhythm of small rectangular windows in close-packed bursts of four, immediately beneath the heavy cornice which barely breaks the compact monumentality of the giant, rough-hewn box."

36. *Pueblo Daily Chieftain*, April 21, 1889, p. 12. The building is also illustrated in John Lethem, *Historical and Descriptive Review of Denver: Her Leading Business Houses and Enterprising Men* (Denver: Jno. Lethem, [1893]), 196.

37. *Pueblo Daily Chieftain*, April 21, 1889, p. 12. Even among notable Pueblo works, the Central Block was in a select subgroup of four or five of the "most imposing and costly of these buildings" (*Pueblo Daily Chieftain*, April 21, 1889, p. 12). This article mentions "Robert S. Roeschlaub, architect of Denver, has the work in charge." See *Pueblo Daily Chieftain*, January 1, 1890, p. 10, which refers to the great deal of iron work used in the Central Block "now being erected" at Main and Second streets. Indeed, at $185,000, it was the most expensive of the contemporary business blocks in Pueblo. To put this price into perspective, the building work completed in Pueblo during 1888–90 included forty-six structures intended for business purposes that cost $563,000, an average of $12,250 each. (The Union Depot was more extravagant at $450,000, the Grand Opera House, $400,000.) "The greater part of the money put into these improvements, is that of residents, but considerable of it is contributed by nonresidents;...the Thurlow-Hutton block [is funded] by a syndicate of Eastern capitalists" (ibid.).

38. A contemporary comment about the warm coloration of the Opera House applies to the Central Block. It exhibited, "like the other handsome edifices rising at Pueblo on every side, all those fine effects and 'tones' that have been impressed upon American architecture, by the Richardsons and other native masters of the building art" (Andrew Morrison, *The City of Pueblo and the State of Colorado* [St. Louis and Pueblo: Geo. W. Engelhardt & Co., 1890], 88).

39. From the *Pueblo Daily Chieftain* come several references to the appearance of the Chicago architects in Pueblo: June 30, 1888, p. 4; January 10, 1890, p. 6; August 22, 1890, p. 6; and September 21, 1890, p. 4. This chronology was compiled by Lloyd C. Engelbrecht and the late Ellen Micaud. For the definitive statement about the Pueblo Opera House "as a case study of trans-Mississippi urbanism in the nineteenth century," see Engelbrecht, "Adler and Sullivan's Pueblo Opera House: City Status for a New Town in the Rockies," *Art Bulletin* 69 (June 1985): 277–95. The Central Block is cited on page 293. The total cost for the opera house is given as $225,000.

40. Is it possible that there was a Colorado-Chicago axis, and not exclusively the reverse? Perhaps Sullivan thought over RSR's use of a deep-relief flourish of ornament as a finish for emphasis of the vertical structure of a tall building and incorporated it in his masterpieces of the 1890s. Sullivan had in the exteriors of his early work (such as the Rothschild Store, Chicago, 1881) used something of this organization but with flat, stylized decoration derived from such diverse sources as the Frenchman Victor Ruprich-Robert, the neo-Gothic Celtic books, and Owen Jones (see David Van Zanten, "Sullivan to 1890," in Wim, ed., *Louis Sullivan: The Function of Ornament*, 13–22). In the Auditorium Building Sullivan stayed away from external ornament almost completely while on the interior developing his repertoire of both tight linear motifs and floral designs that were as heavily modeled as RSR's capitals. RSR's are very Sullivanesque in style. Nevertheless, general critical opinion still holds true that although there were numerous midwestern and western buildings based on Sullivan's architecture, none, including RSR's, achieved Sullivan's high level of, and his distinctive personal signature in, ornamentation.

41. *Pueblo Daily Chieftain*, April 21, 1889, p. 12. This description of the Thurlow and Hutton Block justifies the contemporary judgment that the new five-story brick-and-stone business block at the intersection of Union Avenue and Main and Second streets would be "a fine structure,...as complete and imposing...as can be found in the state of Colorado, not excepting the fine blocks of Denver." The excavations for the building were well under way in April 1889. The surviving set of final drawings dates from September 3, 1889. The building was supposed to be ready for occupancy in November 1889 but probably was ready in early 1890.

The sheer size of the building was impressive. It had a frontage of 120 feet on Union Avenue and 140 feet on Second Street. An eight-foot cellar extended under the entire building. The foundation walls were of massive stone masonry. RSR's elevation of the foundations shows stepped stone footings which spread the building's load. In the basement plan, the cast-iron columns of the irregular grid set in concrete are indicated. The basement was paved with cement. It was divided into cellar rooms for the stores above and contained a room for the "modern" elevator machinery as well as the usual mechanical support for the heating and ventilation systems: boiler, pump room, coal vaults, etc.

The building was modern, too, in that it was well serviced by the latest mechanical devices. The ground floor was laid off into six stores, all with frontage to the street. They were of various plans, quite deep, some running back to the alley. RSR took great care with lighting: "All the alley fronts will be of iron and glass, insuring ample light. Three of the stores are also furnished with over head light at their centers"(ibid.). Indeed, the store fronts were completely transparent. They were of iron and polished plate glass with cut glass transoms and trimmings of heavy bronze. Each store was provided with freight elevators, the cellars amply lit by means of bulkheads and sidewalk lights. These "prismatic lights," as RSR refers to them on his drawings, were a typical feature of city streets before World War I. Little glass blocks set into concrete, they not only served as a light source but allowed the owner more storage area, as the basement could be carried out under the sidewalk beyond the property line. Here there is about a four-foot extension onto the pavement. RSR carries the prismatic lights into the entrances of the shops.

The Central Block's ceremonial entrance, not simply its mechanical services, distinguished it as grand architecture. We have mentioned that the main entrance to the upper floors was in the center of the building on Union Avenue through a wide stone archway. This led to a tiled third vestibule thirteen feet by twenty-four feet, complete with letter chute. Show windows of the stores on either side opened onto the vesibule, thus expanding the vista of the space. An oak stairway and the passenger elevator rose to the floors above. While "lifts" for the vertical transportation of people had been in general use since the New York high-rise offices of the early 1870s, it generated excitement in Pueblo: "The elevator will be of large size, handsome in design and will run at the rate of 400 feet per minute" (ibid.). A building of five stories introduced a great change in the rise of the Pueblo skyline: the building was high not so much because of the number of stories but because of the increase in story height (Hitchcock, *Nineteenth and Twentieth Century Architecture*, 335). It would have been possible for clients to climb stairs, but the elevator made the Central Block a more desirable business proposition. All this, "together with the general finish, will give the main entrance a most imposing effect" (*Pueblo Daily Chieftain* April 21, 1889, p. 12).

The second, third, and fourth floors, as RSR's original plans show (hereinafter RSR plans, CHS), were laid off into offices. RSR again demonstrates his concern for a well-lit building. These plans indicate a second-story skylight over ground level stores. The block, therefore, from the second through fifth stories was a very shallow U-shape; there was a mini-light court on the alley side, on axis with the main portal and main entrance. The alley wall is labeled a "firewall."

The rotunda, which occupied the center of the building, was a substantial forty-five by fifty-four feet; it extended to the roof where it was covered with an immense heavy glass skylight meant to afford both light and ventilation to the inside rooms surrounding it. Beginning on the tiled surface of the second floor, it was surrounded at each floor with a balcony six feet wide, railed with oak and brass panels. The offices were marked off in a variety of shapes and dimensions which could be used in numerous combinations as suites. RSR made a point of giving nearly each office room an independent entrance from the corridor or balconies. Wood paneling complemented the image of a well-serviced building: the rotunda and corridors were finished in oak, varnished and grained in all the office rooms: "The office fronts, opening on the rotunda and balconies, will be of plate glass making a most handsome effect from the corridors, while the office rooms will receive ample light" (ibid.). Each floor was provided with water closets and like conveniences. The aesthetic effect of the light-flooded rotunda augmented the prestige of RSR's building, in addition to being of obvious practicality.

The fifth floor may have been finished for offices like the others, "with restaurant accommodations, after the style of the Chicago restaurants" or designed to function as "lodge and hall rooms" (ibid.); there is some mention in later literature of a law library.

RSR's business block was fine architecture as good property speculation. Much space was rented before it was completed; to judge from several Pueblo directories of the early 1890s it was occupied to capacity. Its Colorado Springs developers, Thurlow and Hutton, "have a wide spread reputation as careful and conservative investors. They know what they are about and the demand for rooms in this building shows that their judgment in erecting this handsome block in Pueblo is not at fault" (ibid.).

RSR's work was up-to-date (though not radical) in its technologies and appreciated as such from the beginning: "The Central and Swift blocks are such as grace the business districts of the larger cities. They are heated by steam, have elevators and every modern convenience" (Morrison, *The City of Pueblo*, 86–91). And: "The [Central] building will be heated with steam thoughout and lighted with electricity. In short nothing will be left undone to make this a complete modern building in every particular" (*Pueblo Daily Chieftain*, April 21, 1889, p. 12).

42. Dunn and Myers, comp., *Pueblo, Colorado: Its Resources and Developments* (Pueblo: Daily Chieftain, 1891). Pamphlet C987.84/P964pa, Western History Department, DPL).

43. Hitchcock, *Architecture*, 338–46.

44. Thus RSR's rendering has four bays on Sixteenth Street, the surviving block seven. The original Salomon's Bazaar is the present 808 Sixteenth Street, with the property line at the alley. Building permit 379 (April 2, 1891), cites RSR as architect of block 130 on Lots 29–32. (All references to building permits are from microfilm records in the Western History Department at the Denver Public Library, hereafter cited, for example, as BP379 [4/2/91]). By 1896, while still owned by Holzman, the building was occupied by a tenant, A. T. Lewis and Son (Lewis and Barrow), and included a new 1902 expansion, now 800 Sixteenth on the corner of Stout. This corner was the site of the demolished Bancroft Building and Preis

Department Store. BP94 (2/1/13) refers to a minor 1913 renovation, a $2,000 alteration to the first-story storefront, the work of Roeschlaub and Son, architects. The builder was Charles Morcom, the owner no longer Holzman but A. T. Lewis and Son (which went bankrupt in 1933). Further renovations were made in the 1940s, as cited in the text. Our thanks to Barbara Norgren for locating the Holzman Block building permit applications. See also *Denver Republican*, January 1, 1892, p. 4, and *Denver Post*, November 26, 1902, p. 6, and note 31 above.

45. Today, appropriate to its open-floor planning, the building is being used as the School of Architecture and Planning by the University of Colorado–Denver. A passenger elevator shaft and reception area on the Lawrence Street and alley side is a later addition. RSR designed other industrial buildings in the lower downtown area between 1894 and 1902. The Hendrie and Bolthoff Warehouse that RSR constructed in June 1894 is most likely one of those still standing at 323–77 Inca Street, originally 333–81 Corbett. As opposed to Hover, the oldest are basic utilitarian buildings, so RSR's cannot be distinguished from the type.

William Church purchased what was the Cooper property at Arapahoe and Fifteenth streets through Bennett and Myers for $75,000. In 1901 the *Times* reported that "Mr. Church intends to erect a business block on the site" (*Denver Times*, March 14, 1901, p. 7). The building permit citing RSR as architect for the Church Estate store dates from 1905.

There is a connection with the Elephant Corral, Denver's oldest livestock exchange, inn, and once-notorious gaming house. The Elephant Corral was bought by John Thames in 1888. In 1902 he rebuilt it and erected a warehouse (BP552, 4/18/02) The permit cites RSR as the architect, the contractor as Walter Sharp, and the owner as the J. F. Williams Store (listed as the I. L. Williams store in RSR's office inventory). RSR's work at 1444 Wazee, the third version on the site, built around a courtyard, was for a two-and-a-half-story, brick-and-stone building, 50 by 115 feet, which cost $7,000 (see also M. Riordan, "Elephant Corral, Historic Denver Trading Post, Never Once Sold a Jumbo," *The Westerner* [June 1941]: 12–13, 28). The building was completely remodeled in 1981.

46. Had the Meyer Building been realized in this version, it would have been one of Sullivan's handsomest but one of his more

conservative solutions for commercial buildings: "[T]he Meyer Store...stay[s] with the articulated cube" (Jordy, "The Tall Buildings," in de Wit, ed., *Louis Sullivan: The Function of Ornament*, 90). The corner piers become very evident. Jordy describes a parallel conservatism in the lower stages of the Fraternity Temple tower by Sullivan: "insistently framed and stacked, the fields of pier-and-spandrel openings take on a somewhat panelled effect as isolated elevational screens....[T]he cornice is lifted away from the field of piers below, so as to enframe it, immure it, within the wall. The cornice floats above the range of piers as another discrete compositional element....[A]ll sense of skeletal construction is lost....The pier-and-spandrel rationale as...generating impulse...gives way to the sheer wall plane traditionally punched with openings for standard sash windows" (ibid.). And this comment on the Meyer Store project is even more pertinent to Hover: "The gridded pier-and-spandrel wall becomes a range of five-story stacks of paired windows, each strongly framed as panels....[B]ands of ornament edge the panels, like picture frames, in a crinkle of light and shadow. Similarly, the loggia-like run of the windows under the cornice (which again floats as an isolated entity on the plane of the wall), and the long void for the show windows subdivided by columns, close the elevations top and bottom in a panelled effect. So the entire building appears as an interplay of wall and openings organized as frame and panels" (ibid., 91).

The Hover Block's cornice is heavier and even more isolated, the windows tripartite rather than paired, and the Meyer project is a more sophisticated work, but there is a curious affinity as well as an inversion: Sullivan's scheme, though of skyscraper construction, comes close to articulating a traditional masonry wall. RSR's facade is load-bearing but uses Sullivan's aesthetic to give traditional construction a new clarity.

47. RSR was required to reuse a great deal of the salvaged old metal shelving and walkways. He fit the old and new together perfectly. He and his draftsmen were annoyed with the finicky task, as any architect might be. Along with prosaic indications on the original drawings for RSR's building, such as "old shelving" and "old table" is "old stuff used and refitted" (RSR plans, CHS). Details were left to RSR's assistants, as the presentation is not up to his standard.

48. A specific example of this heavy con-

struction is demonstrated in RSR's drawing 13, "Elevation of steel beams supporting floor joists." The floors have mammoth steel I-beams which measure 12 inches by 20 inches and weigh 65 pounds per foot, so each beam weighs about 1,000 pounds throughout. As is typical in "mill buildings," joists are laid at right angles to the beams. Atypical, however, is the size of these great wood joists (called *purlins*), each about 10 inches wide, which were dropped into and are supported by the oversized bracketing. Each floor then had a wood deck put on and poured concrete slab to finish it off. So the span between each purlin was only about 3 feet 2 inches. This span is extremely narrow and was one device which allowed the building to carry such heavy loads. This system gave the floors tremendous strength.

49. The third-floor plan shows some typical old H-shaped plates. Several are of a very uncommon double-Z section.

50. In the solid walls of the first and third floors are "bearing stones"; on the second floor are steel "bearing plates." Bearing plates are commonly used today to spread out the load so as not to crush the outer walls.

51. RSR drew a "birch mantel in office" for Hover, a fireplace of the same simple brick detailing and harmonious rectangular proportions as the exterior spandrels. Some wood wainscoting of a generic character survives on the first floor as a remnant of these white-collar functions.

52. He labeled one cubicle on the first floor plan "new cigar room—pared with stock press brick, herringbone on 2" sand and resin papered ceiling of Oregon pine then felt 1-1/2" strips and gallery floor of 1-1/4" maple" (see also National Register of Historic Places inventory form for W. A. Hover Drug Company Building/Bromley Building compiled by Leslie Ullman, February 24, 1987 [Office of Archaeology and Historic Preservation, Colorado Historical Society]).

Chapter Five: Public Buildings and Residences

1. Ellen Micaud, "Alone on the Prairie: Old Main on Colorado Campuses," *Colorado Heritage* 1983, Issue 4: 2–17.

2. University of Denver catalog, 1906–7 and *University Bulletin* 7 (University of Denver, July 25, 1906). Illustrations: "A Corner of the Law Library" (p. 158), "North End Infirmary" (n.p.), "Freshman Laboratory" (p. 180), and "Lecture Room" (pp. 185, 200).

RSR modified the building in 1900. (Special Collections, University of Denver).

3. Smiley, *History of Denver*, 758–61. See also *WABN* 3 (May 1891): 36: "The greatest progress—that is, the largest amount of money being expended—is in South Denver and vicinity. Like the other suburbs, a number of residences are being built. In addition to this, the Denver University buildings are gradually assuming mammoth proportion." The eighty acres was donated by Denver's "potato king," Rufus Clark. Iliff Hall is usually attributed to Denver architect Frank E. Edbrooke, but Micaud ("Alone on the Prairie," 13) attributes it to the Albany, New York, firm of Fuller and Wheeler.

4. Micaud, "Alone on the Prairie," 2.

5. For a detailed description of the activities housed in University Hall, see *RMN*, October 18, 1891, p. 3.

6. Richard Brettell, *Historic Denver: The Architects and the Architecture, 1858–1893* (Denver: Historic Denver, Inc., 1973), 174.

7. Micaud, "Alone on the Prairie," 13. Also: "The system of heating adopted is that of hot air, as used in the Massachusetts Institute of Technology....The boilers are in a separate building several hundred feet distant, and the hot air is sent by Sturdevant blowers" (*RMN*, October 18, 1891, p. 3).

8. *WABN* 2 (April 1890): 19–20. This small observatory was intended for student use.

9. Claire I. Moyer, *Silver Domes: A Directory of the Observatories of the World* (Denver: Big Mountain Press, 1955), 129–32, and Marjorie Barrett, "Chamberlin Observatory Awaits Throng," *RMN*, September 7, 1987, p. 70. See also Don Etter, *University Park: Four Walking Tours* (Denver: Graphic Impressions, 1974). According to the *WABN* of August 1890 (p. 87), the superstructure of the Chamberlin Observatory was let to E. F. Hallack Lumber and Manufacturing Company.

10. Brettell, *Historic Denver*, 174.

11. Moyer, *Silver Domes*, 129–32, and Barrett, "Chamberlin Observatory Awaits Throng," 70. The principal rooms in the large observatory were the dome room, transit room, library, computing room, director's office, clock room, janitor's quarters, sleeping room, photographic room, and store room. Besides the main telescope, the subsidiary instruments were a four-inch steel meridian circle, a standard mean-time clock, a standard sidereal clock, chronometers, three chronographs, a sextant, and two solar transits. The telescope

was suited for photographic and spectroscopic work as well as visual observations.

12. The installation of an observatory near the School of Theology was a thoughtful gesture in a university under Methodist sponsorship. Chamberlin was favorably compared to the patron of the Girard College in Philadelphia (1833–47), who, it seems, included an anticlerical proviso along with his posthumous donation. The Girard College complex was one of the most influential works of Greek Revival architecture in America, a style that embodied rational humanism: "How much nobler the Chamberlin Observatory of the Denver University will shine on the scrolls of science in the ages to come, crowned with the aurora of a Christian's belief, than will the Girard Orphan Asylum, clouded by the shadow of infidelity and a dead man's dictum that prevents the entrance of the highest type of humanity—the Christian Minister—inside its gates" (*Magazine of Western History* 10 [June 1889]: 147–48).

13. *The White City* (Chicago: White City Art Co., 1894), engravings in the Roeschlaub-Fuller Collection, CHS.

14. University of California, *Prospectus for the Phoebe Hearst Architectural Plan of the University of California* (San Francisco: n.p., 1897), in Joan Draper, "John Galen Howard and the Beaux-Arts Movement in the United States" (unpublished M.A. thesis, University of California, 1972), 53–69.

15. RSR to Henry A. Buchtel, June 22, 1907 (Special Collections, University of Denver, s.v. "Robert S. Roeschlaub: Chapel, Science Hall, Carnegie Library").

16. Roeschlaub and Son designed a neoclassical Science Hall in harmony with the Carnegie Library. Illustrations of RSR's building were published in 1907 as the new Science Hall (brochure, Subject Collection, Colorado Historical Society, s.v. "Denver University"). As a series of letters to the University trustees makes clear, the firm was convinced it had received the commission. On a suggestion of Andrew Carnegie's secretary, New York architects Whitfield and (Beverly S.) King were appointed in March 1908 by the trustees as architects of the Science Hall. According to the *Records of the Executive Committee of the Colorado Seminary, Book G* of June 1907, the New York firm "had large experience in planning similar buildings in different parts of the country." In private the affair was acrimonious and embarrassing to RSR, who was to "superintend the erec-

tion of the building." By May 31, 1911, two university-affiliated men, Drs. Engle and Nyswander, "worked out a tentative floor plan for the new building" and went to New York "to complete the details with the architect," according to an article in the *Clarion*, the university's newspaper. An intermediary project for the Science Hall published in the University of Denver *Catalog* of 1911–12 shows a neo-Palladian block with a central pediment, portico, and pilasters, a revamping of RSR's basic design. The building as constructed is entirely different, a Mediterranean villa but with none of the irregularity or charm usually associated with that style. The ground-breaking ceremony for the Science Hall took place on Taft Day in 1913 during a visit by the president of the United States to DU. A photograph in the 1915 student yearbook, *Kynewisbok*, shows the Gymnasium, the Buchtel Chapel (a work which took as its model the Spanish missions of California), and the completed Science Hall. The barracks-like Science Hall and the ornate Chapel were meant to relate because of their towers and southern European stylistic derivation (Leslie Ullman researched the material on RSR in DU's Special Collections and determined the attributions of the Science Hall and the Denver and Gross College of Medicine).

17. Ellen C. Micaud, memo to Carnegie Hall fact-finding committee, March 5, 1985 (with March 14 update) about proposed demolition of Carnegie Hall (Western History Department, DPL, clippings file, s.v. "Colleges and Universities: Colorado: Denver University Buildings").

18. Ibid.

19. Ibid.

20. RSR to Board of Trustees, Denver and Gross College of Medicine, August 9, 1907 (Special Collections, University of Denver, s.v. "Robert S. Roeschlaub, Chapel, Science Hall, Carnegie Library").

21. "Bids are now being taken on the Normal School building, to be erected at Greeley....At present the east wing only will be erected" (*WABN* 1 [October 1889]: 107).

22. John Dugan, *Greeley and Weld County: A Pictorial History* (Norfolk, Va.: Donning Co., 1986), 67.

23. Micaud, "Alone on the Prairie," 14.

24. Ibid.

25. "As early as April, 1903, the building committee was authorized to get plans and specifications for a library building, but not until December 27, 1905, were instructions definitely given to [RSR] to prepare complete drawings." On June 6, 1906, a motion was made that "the plans be developed for a building to cost not more than $45,000." The contract was awarded to Bate and Elliott for $47,476 (Albert F. Carter and Elizabeth Hays Kendel, *Forty Years of Colorado State Teachers College, Formerly the State Normal School of Colorado, 1890–1930* [Greeley: Colorado State Teachers College, 1930], 80). This information was provided by Martha Ewald, a Colorado Historical Society volunteer.

26. *RMN*, March 5, 1878, p. 4. The opera house has had structural problems. Perhaps because of RSR's relative inexperience, he allowed the building to be built over an old mine flume. This contributed to weaknesses in its masonry, especially the back wall, which has recently been reinforced with heavy steel beams (see Glenn Griffin, "Putting the Opera House in Order," *Denver Post*, July 15, 1982, p. 9).

27. Ibid.

28. Brettell, *Historic Denver*, 96.

29. "Mr. Roeschlaub...has given the building his personal supervision, and it having been carefully and slowly erected, has given him an opportunity to see that each detail of his plans was carefully carried out. Mullen and Sartori had the contract of the mason work and McFarlane & Co. of the woodwork. The standing of these firms with this community is a sufficient guarantee that the work is well done and material carefully selected. The building is heated by hot air pipes from two furnaces, which were furnished and placed by Bacon & Son, of Denver. The size of the building is 55 x 115 feet. The dress circle and parquette will seat about 500 persons. The gallery will seat about 250 persons.

A *News* reporter was shown over the completed edifice yesterday. Mr. Roeschlaub, who was present, also furnished every facility for gathering information of the work done and money expended, which now amounts to about $23,000 [the opera company has a capital stock of $50,000]. There is not a bad seat anywhere. The orchestra is placed a little below the level of the front seats, so that the "big fiddle" and its engineer do not loom up above everything else in the building, as in our (alleged) Denver [Tabor] opera house. The interior is well heated and lighted. The great stage is fully equipped with handsome new scenery and there are four elegant dressing rooms, besides all the space necessary for the multitudinous "properties" of the profession. Taken all in all it is a theater of which any city might be proud, and is as far superior to anything Denver has or ever had that no comparison need be instituted" (*RMN*, March 5, 1878, p. 4).

The ceiling was restored in the 1930s by mural painter Allen True. Some of the black-and-white marble tile from the first story of RSR's demolished East Denver High School was installed in the opera house during its 1932 renovation. The author thanks Edward D. White, Jr., for his comments on the opera house.

30. This was designed and executed by Moseman, who seems from his work at Central City to have been thoroughly familiar with the lush furnishings of the recently completed Paris Opera (1861–74), of which this is a country version. As commented at the time, "there is not much 'gingerbread' about the wood work of the interior, which is 'neat not gaudy,' but the frescoing is fine, very fine, as elegant in its line as anything in the country" (*RMN*, March 5, 1878, p. 4).

31. Ibid.

32. Ibid.

33. Thomas J. Noel and Barbara S. Norgren, *Denver: The City Beautiful and Its Architects, 1893–1941* (Denver: Historic Denver, Inc., 1987), 112–13.

34. *RMN*, September 22, 1912, sec. 4, p. 8. A contract was signed on June 28, 1912, with contractor M. J. Kenney and the Denver Master Builders Association for $90,900. The figures of the frieze were executed by W. H. Millins Company of Salem, Ohio, manufacturers of art and architectural sheet metal work and statuary (pamphlet, Roeschlaub-Fuller Collection, Colorado Historical Society).

35. Orientalism was a strong current in contemporary post-Impressionist art and Arts and Crafts architecture, but this is RSR's only acknowledgment of it.

36. Long Hoeft Architects and Peter Snell, Architectural Museum Services, *Properties Plan* (Georgetown Society, Inc., August 1985), 81.

37. Gary Long, "Roeschlaub, Architecture, and Technology" (unpublished paper, University of California–Santa Barbara, 1988), 10.

38. Ibid., 12. Long continues: "[T]he operable sash ventilators which can be seen at the top of the conservatory were produced by Lord and Burnham, makers of greenhouses and conservatories since 1856. Lord and Burnham was an exhibitor at the 1876 centennial exhibition at Philadelphia which Hamill had attended: perhaps that was his stimulus for including a conservatory in his expansion. The floor of the conservatory is made up of gapped boards of walnut and oak, alternating, open to the basement below. Basement air is thus heated in the conservatory and directed to the library and dining room through large doors, or, in warmer weather, dumped through the overhead ventilating sash. Many plants plus a fountain add moisture to dry winter air. The conservatory is an extraordinary treasure integrating function, technology, and culture. With cast iron and glass on the outside and a wealth of walnut paneling on the inside, this is an elegant nineteenth century artifact."

Kathleen Hoeft and Peter Snell have discovered the pattern book from which the balusters (#1200) and newel (#1302) of the back stairs of the Hamill House were ordered. From the same catalog came the baluster of the back stair of the Hamill Office (#1304). The latter is the same as the newel post of the front hall stair at the William Church House in Georgetown. This is further evidence that the Church House is also a work by RSR, who lists it in his office inventory of buildings. See *Late Victorian Architectural Details: An Abridged Facsimile...* (New York: American Life Foundation Study Institute, 1978).

39. Eric C. Stoehr, *Bonanza Victorian: Architecture and Society in Colorado Mining Towns* (Albuquerque: University of New Mexico Press, 1975), 45–46.

40. Sarah J. Pearce and Merrill A. Wilson, *A Guide to Colorado Architecture* (Denver: Colorado Historical Society, 1983), 36. See also "Foursquare (Denver Square)" in Noel and Norgren, *Denver: The City Beautiful*, 43–48.

Bibliography

Armytage, W. H. G. *A Social History of Engineering*. 4th ed. Boulder, Colo.: Westview Press, 1976.

Athearn, Robert. *The Coloradans*. Albuquerque: University of New Mexico Press, 1976.

Audsley, George Ashdown. *The Art of Organ Building*. Vol. 1. New York: Dodd, Mead & Co., 1905.

Baker, Paul R. *Richard Morris Hunt*. Cambridge, Mass.: MIT Press, 1980.

Barrett, Marjorie. "Chamberlin Observatory Awaits Throng." *Rocky Mountain News*, September 7, 1987.

Beardsley, Isaac Haight. *Echoes from Peak and Plain; or, Tales of Life, War, Travel, and Colorado Methodism*. Cincinnati: Curts & Jennings; New York: Eaton & Mains, 1898.

Bird, Isabella. *A Lady's Life in the Rocky Mountains*. Norman: University of Oklahoma Press, 1960.

Brenneman, Bill. *Miracle on Cherry Creek: An Informal History of the Birth and Re-birth of a Neighborhood*. Denver: World Press, Inc., 1973.

Brettell, Richard R. *Historic Denver: The Architects and the Architecture, 1858–1893*. Denver: Historic Denver, Inc., 1973.

Brooklyn Museum. *The American Renaissance, 1876–1917*. With essays by Richard Guy Wilson, Dianne H. Pilgrim, and Richard N. Murray. New York, 1979.

Brooks, Michael W. *John Ruskin and Victorian Architecture*. New Brunswick, N.J.: Rutgers University Press, 1987.

Brunvand, Judith. "Frederick Albert Hale, Architect." *Utah Historical Quarterly* 54 (Winter 1986): 5–30.

Central Presbyterian Church: Pioneers through the Years. Denver Public Library, Western History Department.

The City of Denver: Its Resources and Their Development. Denver: Denver Times, [1891]. Colorado Historical Society.

Committee for the Preservation of Architectural Records. *Directory of Historic American Architectural Firms*. Washington, D.C.: American Institute of Architects Foundation and Committee for the Preservation of Architectural Records, 1979.

Condit, Carl W. *The Chicago School of Architecture: A History of Commercial and Public Buildings in the Chicago Area, 1875–1925*. Chicago: University of Chicago Press, 1964.

Dallas, Sandra. *Cherry Creek Gothic*. Norman: University of Oklahoma Press, 1971.

Denver District One annual reports, 1875–1900.

"Denver Illustrated," *The Grand Army Magazine* 1 (July 1883): 431–55.

Denver Post, November 1902, June 1941, July 1982.

Denver Republican, January 1883–January 1892.

Denver Times, September 1879–November 1902.

Denver Tribune-Republican, December 1884.

Didron, Ed. "Le Vitrail depuis cent ans et l'Exposition de 1889." *Revue des Arts Decoratifs* 10 (1889–90): 148–52.

Dorsett, Lyle. *The Queen City: A History of Denver*. Boulder, Colo.: Pruett Publishing Co., 1977.

Downing, Andrew Jackson. *The Architecture of Country Houses*. New York: D. Appleton & Co., 1850. Reprint. Dover Publications, 1969.

Draper, Joan. "John Galen Howard and the Beaux-Arts Movement in the United States." Unpublished master's thesis, University of California, 1972.

Drexler, Arthur, ed. *The Architecture of the École des Beaux-Arts*. New York: Museum of Modern Art. Cambridge, Mass.: distributed by MIT Press, 1977.

Dugan, John. *Greeley and Weld County*. Norfolk, Virginia: The Donning Co., 1986.

Dunn and Myers, comps. *Pueblo, Colorado: Its Resources and Developments*. Denver Public Library, Western History Department.

Dyos, H. J. and M. Wolff, eds. *The Victorian City: Image and Reality*. 2 vols. London and Boston: Routledge & Kegan Paul, 1973.

East High School (Denver). *East, 1875–1950: Past and Present*. Denver: privately printed, [c. 1951].

Eastlake, C. L. *A History of the Gothic Revival in England* (1872). Reprint. Watkins Glen, N.Y.: American Life Foundation, 1975.

"Emerson School House." *Colorado School Journal* 1 (October 1885): n.p.

Engelbrecht, Lloyd C. "Adler and Sullivan's Pueblo Opera House: City Status for a New Town in the Rockies." *Art Bulletin* 69 (June 1985): 277–95.

Etter, Don. *University Park, Denver: Four Walking Tours*. Denver: Graphic Impressions, 1974.

Fell, James E. *Ores to Metals: The Rocky Mountain Smelter Industry*. Lincoln and London: University of Nebraska Press, 1979.

Fuller, Kenneth R. "Background History of AIA Colorado." *Field Report* (AIA newsletter), 1985.

Gebhard, David, and Deborah Nevins. *Two Hundred Years of American Architectural Drawings*. New York: Whitney Library of Design, 1977.

Genosky, Rev. Landry, O.F.M., ed. *People's History of Quincy and Adams County, Illinois*. Quincy: Jost & Kiefer Printing Co., [1973].

Georgetown Society, Inc., and the People for Silver Plume. *Guide to the Georgetown—Silver Plume Historic District*. Evergreen, Colo.: Cordillera Press, 1986.

Girouard, Mark. *Sweetness and Light: The "Queen Anne" Movement, 1860–1900*. Oxford: Clarendon Press, 1977.

Gottdiener, M., and Alexandros Ph. Lagopoulos. *The City and the Sign: An Introduction to Urban Semiotics*. New York: Columbia University Press, 1986.

Gove, Aaron. Correspondence. Denver Public Library, Western History Department.

Gowans, Alan. *The Comfortable House: North American Suburban Architecture, 1890–1930*. Cambridge, Mass.: MIT Press, 1986.

Gulliford, Andrew. *America's Country Schools*. Washington, D.C.: The Preservation Press, 1984.

Haase, Carl L. "Gothic, Colorado: City of Silver Wires." *The Colorado Magazine* 51 (Fall 1974): 294–316.

Hale, Frederick. Scrapbooks. Utah Historical Society, Salt Lake City, Utah.

Hall, Frank. *History of the State of Colorado*. 4 vols. Chicago: Blakely Printing Co., 1895.

Hamlin, Talbot F. *The American Spirit in Architecture*. New Haven: Yale University Press, 1926.

Handlin, David P. *The American Home: Architecture and Society, 1815–1915*. Boston: Little, Brown & Co., 1979.

Handschin, Robert. Letter to Carl Landrum, August 3, 1983 (copy in possession of Kenneth R. Fuller).

Hanks, David. "Louis J. Millet and the Art Institute of Chicago." *The Art Institute of Chicago Bulletin* (March-April, 1973): 13–19.

Hersey, George L. *High Victorian Gothic: A Study in Associationism*. Baltimore: Johns Hopkins University Press, 1972.

Hicks, Dave. *Littleton: From the Beginning*. Denver: Egan Printing/A-T-P Publishing Co., 1975.

Hill, David R. *Colorado Urbanization and Planning Context*. Office of Archaeology and Historic Preservation, Colorado Historical Society, Denver.

Hines, Thomas S. *Burnham of Chicago: Architect and Planner*. New York: Oxford University Press, 1974.

History of Adams County, Illinois...containing...Portraits of Early Settlers and Prominent Men. Chicago: Murray, Williamson & Phelps, 1879.

Hitchcock, Henry-Russell. *American Architectural Books: A List of Books, Portfolios, and Pamphlets on Architecture and Related Subjects Published in America before 1895*. New York: Da Capo, 1975.

———. "Ruskin and American Architecture, or Regeneration Long Delayed," in *Concerning Architecture*. Sir John Summerson, ed. London: Penguin/Allen Lane, 1968.

———. *Architecture: Nineteenth and Twentieth Centuries*. 4th ed. Harmondsworth (Middlesex) England and New York: Pelican History of Art, Penguin Books, Ltd., 1977.

———. *American Architectural Books: A List of Books, Portfolios, and Pamphlets on Architecture and Related Subjects Published in America before 1895, 1946, 1962*. Rev. ed. New York: Da Capo, 1976.

———. *The Architecture of H. H. Richardson and His Times*. 2d ed., rev. Cambridge, Mass.: 1936.

Hoeft, Kathleen and Peter Snell. *Pioneer Greek Revival Log House*. Denver: Long Hoeft Architects, 1981.

Holborn, Hajo. *A History of Modern Germany, 1840–1945*. New York: Alfred A. Knopf, 1969.

Holmes, M. Patricia. "The St. Louis Union Station." *The Bulletin* (Missouri Historical Society, July 1971): 248–58.

Johnson, Charlie H. *The Central City Opera House: A 100 Year History*. Colorado Springs: Little London Press, 1980.

Jordy, William H. *American Buildings and Their Architects*. Vol. 3. *Progressive and Academic Ideals at the Turn of the Twentieth Century*. Garden City, N.Y.: Doubleday, 1972.

Kidder, Franklin. *Churches and Chapels*. New York: W. T. Comstock, 1895.

Kidney, Walter C. *The Architecture of Choice: Eclecticism in America, 1880–1930*. New York, 1974.

Kimball, S. Fiske. *American Architecture*. Indianapolis and New York: The Bobbs-Merrill Co, 1928.

Kostof, Spiro, ed. *The Architect: Chapters in the History of the Profession*. New York: Oxford University Press, 1977.

———. *America by Design*. New York: Oxford University Press, 1987.

Krier, Rob. *Elements of Architecture*. London: Architectural Design Publications; New York: St. Martin's Press, 1983.

———. *On Architecture*. London: Academy Editions; New York: St. Martin's Press, 1982.

———. *Urban Space*. New York: Rizzoli International Publications, 1979.

Landau, Sara Bradford. *Edward T. and William A. Potter: American Victorian Architects*. New York: Garland, 1979.

Landrum, Carl. "Jewish Congregation Formed in 1856." *Quincy Herald-Whig*, September 25, 1983.

———. "That Building at Sixth and Maine." *Quincy Herald-Whig*, November 3, 1968.

———. "When Pranksters Had Their Day." *Quincy Herald-Whig*, January 11, 1981.

Lobato, Rudolph B. *An Architectural and Historical Building Survey, Inventory, and Evaluation: Littleton, Colorado*. Littleton: Littleton Area Historical Museum, 1972.

Long, Gary. "Roeschlaub, Architecture, and Technology." University of California—Santa Barbara, January 1, 1988 (Colorado Historical Society collection).

Long Hoeft Architects, *Measured Drawings and Restoration Study of the Hamill Office and Carriage House*. Georgetown, Colo.: Georgetown Society, Inc., 1981

Long Hoeft Architects and Peter Snell, Architectural Museum Services. *Properties Plan*. Georgetown, Colo.: Georgetown Society, Inc., 1985.

Longstreth, Richard W. "Academic Eclecticism in American Architecture." *Winterthur Portfolio* 17 (Spring 1982): 55–82.

Lynch, Kevin. *The Image of the City*. Cambridge, Mass.: MIT Press, 1965.

Martinson, Tom. *A Guide to the Architecture of Minnesota*. Minneapolis: University of Minnesota Press, 1977.

Micaud, Ellen C. "Alone on the Prairie." *Colorado Heritage* 1983, Issue 4 (Fall 1983): 2–17.

———. Memo to Carnegie Hall Factfinding Committee, University of Denver, March 5, 1985. Western History Collection, Denver Public Library.

Millet, Louis J. "Interior Decoration." Parts 1–3. *Inland Architect and Builder* 1 (February, March, May 1883): 3; 17–18; 52.

Morris, Langdon. *Denver Landmarks*. Denver: Charles W. Cleworth, 1979.

Morrison, Andrew. *The City of Pueblo and the State of Colorado*. St. Louis: Engelhardt & Co., 1890.

Morrison, Hugh. *Louis Sullivan: Prophet of Modern Architecture*. 1935. Reprint, New York: W. W. Norton, 1962.

Moyer, Claire I. *Silver Domes: A Directory of the Observatories of the World*. Denver: Big Mountain Press, 1955.

Noel, Thomas J. and Barbara S. Norgren. *Denver: The City Beautiful and Its Architects, 1893–1941*. Denver: Historic Denver, Inc., 1987.

O'Gorman, James F., and George E. Thomas. *The Architecture of Frank Furness*. Philadelphia: Philadelphia Museum of Art, 1973.

Oakley, Allen. Letters to Kenneth R. Fuller, 1983–88 (in the possession of Kenneth R. Fuller).

"Old and New Colorado." *Grand Army Magazine* 1 (March 1883): 142–48.

Ormes, Manly Dayton and Eleanor R. *The Book of Colorado Springs*. Colorado Springs: D. Denton Printing Co., 1933.

Pearce, Sarah J. and Merrill A. Wilson. *A Guide to Colorado Architecture*. Denver: Colorado Historical Society, 1983.

Platt, Frederick. *America's Gilded Age: Its Architecture and Decoration*. South Brunswick, N.J.: A. S Barnes, 1976.

Price, Howard with Norman Lane. "The Roosevelt Organ." Unpublished report, Trinity United Methodist Church, Denver.

Pueblo Daily Chieftain, April 1889–January 1890.

Quincy Herald-Whig, November 1968–September 1983.

Reps, J. W. *Cities of the American West: A History of Frontier Urban Planning*. Princeton, N.J.: Princeton University Press, 1979.

Riordan, M. "Elephant Corral, Historic Denver Trading Post, Never Once Sold a Jumbo." *The Westerner* (June 1941): 12–13, 28.

Rocky Mountain News, September 1870–January 1892, October 1963, September 1987.

Roeschlaub, Robert S. "The Pioneers' Trail." *Sons of Colorado* 1 (May 1907): 33–36.

———. "Three Questions...from Robert S. Roeschlaub, Architect," *Western Architect and Building News* 1 (February 1890): 180–81.

———. "War Reminiscences: A Sixty Days' Race with Hood's Army." *The Great Divide*, July 1894: 170–71.

———. Letter to Board of Trustees, Gross College of Medicine, August 9, 1907. Special Collections, University of Denver.

———. *Personal, Military, and Civil History*. Soldiers and Sailors Historical and Benevolent Society, 1908 (Colorado Historical Society collection).

Roosevelt Organ No. 380." Commercial flyer. Trinity United Methodist Church, Denver.

Roth, Leland. *American Buildings: Source Documents in American Architecture and Planning*. New York: Harper & Row, 1983.

———. *A Concise History of American Architecture*. New York: Harper & Row, Icon Editions, 1979.

———. *McKim, Mead and White: Architects*. New York: Harper & Row, 1983.

Saylor, Henry H. *The A.I.A.'s First Hundred Years*. Washington, D.C.: Octagon, 1957.

Schaefer, Herwin. "Tiffany's Fame in Europe." *Art Bulletin* 44 (December 1962): 309–28.

Scully, Vincent. *American Architecture and Urbanism*. New York: Praeger, 1969.

———. *The Shingle Style*. New Haven, 1955. Rev. ed. Yale University Press, 1971.

Seibel, Harriet. *A History of the Colorado Springs Schools*. Colorado Springs: Century One Press, 1975.

Smiley, Jerome C., ed. *History of Denver, with Outlines of the Earlier History of the Rocky Mountain Country*. Denver: Denver Times/Times-Sun Publishing Co., 1901.

Stanton, Phoebe. *The Gothic Revival and American Church Architecture*. Baltimore: Johns Hopkins University Press, 1968.

Stoehr, C. Eric. *Bonanza Victorian: Architecture and Society in Colorado Mining Towns*. Albuquerque: University of New Mexico Press, 1975.

Stone, Wilbur Fisk. *History of Colorado*. Chicago: S. J. Clarke Publishing Co., 1918.

Tallmadge, Thomas E. *Architecture in Old Chicago*. Chicago: University of Chicago Press, 1941.

Teetor, Henry Dudley. "Architecture in Denver: Captain Robert S. Roeschlaub." *Magazine of Western History* 13 (December 1890): 176–77.

———. "The Chamberlin Observatory, Denver." *Magazine of Western History* 10 (June 1889): 147–48.

———. "A Chapter of Denver's History: H. B. Chamberlin's Visit in Search of Health and What Came of It." *Magazine of Western History* 10 (June 1889): 148–52.

The Littleton Gazette, June 1889.

Townsend, Gavin. "Victorian Systems of Heating and Ventilation." Unpublished master's thesis, University of California, 1986.

Trinity United Methodist Church, Denver. Minutes, Board of Trustees of Lawrence St. M. E. Church, January 1–September 28, 1891.

Turner, Paul Venable. *Campus: An American Planning Tradition*. Cambridge, Mass.: MIT Press, 1984.

Ullman, Leslie. Nomination form for W. A. Hover Drug Company Building (Bromley Building), National Register of Historic Places. Office of Archaeology and Historic Preservation, Colorado Historical Society, 1987.

University of California. *Prospectus for the Phoebe Hearst Architectural Plan of the University of California*. San Francisco: n.p., 1897.

University of Denver. *University Bulletin* 7 (July 25, 1906).

Van Brunt, Henry. *Architecture and Society: Selected Essays of Henry Van Brunt*. William Coles, ed. Cambridge, Mass.: Harvard University Press, 1969.

Van Rensselaer, Mariana Griswold. *Henry Hobson Richardson and His Works*. New York: Houghton Mifflin & Co., 1888. Reprint. New York: Dover, 1969.

Vickers, W. B. *History of the City of Denver, Arapahoe County, and Colorado*. Chicago: O. L. Baskin & Co., 1880.

WPA Guide to 1930s Colorado. Intro. by Thomas J. Noel. Lawrence: University Press of Kansas, 1987.

Wheaton, Rodd. Nomination form for First Congregational Church, National Register of Historic Places. Office of Archaeology and Historic Preservation, Colorado Historical Society, 1987.

Whiffen, Marcus, and Frederick Koeper. *American Architecture, 1607–1976*. Cambridge, Mass.: MIT Press, 1981.

The White City. Chicago: White City Art Co., 1894. Colorado Historical Society, Denver.

Wilcox, David F. *Quincy and Adams County: History and Representative Men*. Vol. 1. Chicago and New York: Lewis Publishing Co., 1919.

Williams, Alice Roeschlaub. Biographical account of Robert S. Roeschlaub. Colorado Historical Society.

Wilson, Richard Guy. "American Architecture and the Search for a National Style in the 1870's," *Nineteenth Century* 3 (Autumn 1977): 74–80.

Winne, Peter. "Events in the History of Trinity M. E. Church." *The Trail* (February 1915 through April 1916).

Wit, Wim de, ed. *Louis Sullivan: The Function of Ornament*. New York and London: W. W. Norton & Co. with the Chicago Historical Society and the Saint Louis Art Museum, 1986.

Chronological
List of
Buildings

1875

Broadway School
Denver: Broadway between 13th and
    14th
No longer standing

Central Presbyterian Church
Denver: 18th and Champa
No longer standing

Hurd & Cooper Business
Denver: 371 Holladay

E. B. Light Residence

1876

Centennial School
Pueblo
No longer standing

John B. Church Residence
Georgetown, Colorado: Rose and
    Tenth
Standing

1879

Chever Block
Denver: Larimer and 17th Street
No longer standing

William A. Hamill Residence
Georgetown: 305 Argentine
Standing

Boston & Colorado Smelter
North Denver (Argo)
No longer standing

Central City Opera House
Central City, Colorado
Standing

**William A. Hamill Office and Carriage
    House**
Georgetown: 305 Argentine
Standing

King Block
Denver: Lawrence between 16th and
    17th
No longer standing

Twenty-fourth Street School
Denver: Twenty-fourth and Market
No longer standing

1880

Mrs. V. D. Armstrong Residence
Denver: Broadway

Bancroft Block
Denver: Stout and 16th Street
No longer standing

E. J. Binford Residence
Denver: [329 Wasoola]

Mrs. E. J. Bluford Residence
Denver

Denver County Hospital Addition
Denver: West 6th Ave and Cherokee
Possibly standing

Ebert School
Denver: Logan and 22d Street
No longer standing

A. C. Fenster Residence
Denver: South 15th Street

Capt. W. P. Gray Residence
Denver: [331 Glenarm]

John R. Hanna Residence
Denver: 14th and Glenarm

F. A. Keener Residence
Denver: Curtis Street

Lake City School
Lake City, Colorado
No longer standing

W. C. Lathrop Brick Livery Stable
Denver: 18th between Larimer and
    Lawrence
No longer standing

Frank McGuire Residence
Denver: Welton between 14th and 15th

Nesmith Store Block
Denver: 15th Street

Thomas M. Patterson Carriage House
Denver: 17th and Welton

Mrs. M. S. Roeschlaub Residence
Quincy, Illinois

Robert S. Roeschlaub Residence
Denver: Colfax and Delaware
No longer standing

E. W. Rollins Residence
Denver: Corner 13th and Stout
No longer standing

Sundham & Hoffman Brick Repository
Denver: 15th and Wewatta

Joseph A. Thatcher Residence
Denver: Glenarm and 13th

Thomas J. Troy Residence
Denver

W. D. Todd Residence
Denver: Delaware near Colfax
No longer standing

Leopold B. Weil Residence
Denver: [601 Stout]

Dr. R. W. Whitehead Block
Denver: Stout and 15th

Benjamin W. Wisebart Residence
Denver: [595 Arapahoe]

1880-81

C. A. Avery Mining & Smelting
Gothic City, Colorado

Bacon & Son Warehouse
Denver

Bacon Cottage
Denver: South 15th Street

Isaac T. Beck Residence
Denver: 1432 Grant Avenue
No longer standing

Brandenburg Block
Denver: Lawrence between 16th and
    17th
No longer standing

Canon City (Washington) School
Canon City
No longer standing

Centennial High School
Pueblo
No longer standing

**Denver Manufacturing Company
    Tannery**
Denver

Theodore W. Herr Residence
Denver: Lawrence between 23d and
    24th

Nathaniel P. Hill Residence (interior)
Denver: 14th and Welton

J. Lichter Malt House
Denver: Holladay and 23d Street

Col. William Moore Residence
Idaho Springs, Colorado

A. J. Sampson Residence
Denver: South 14th Street

Maj. J. W. Stanton Residence
Pueblo

Wolfe Hall Addition
Denver: Champa between 16th and
    17th

1881

Callaway Brothers Store
Denver: 409–11 Lawrence Street

F. J. B. Crane Double Residence
Denver: 1518 Champa

East Denver High School
First wing
Denver: 19th and 20th, Stout and
    California
No longer standing

Benjamin H. Eaton Residence
Greeley

Gilpin School
Denver: 29th between Stout and
    California
No longer standing

Times Building
Denver: 1547–51 Lawrence
No longer standing

Union Block
Denver: 16th and Arapahoe
No longer standing

1882

Barth Block
Denver: 1210 16th Street
No longer standing

Longfellow School
Denver: 13th and Welton
No longer standing

J. S. Raynolds Residence
Las Vegas, New Mexico

1883

Hinsdale School
Pueblo
No longer standing

Thomas M. Patterson Residence
Denver: 17th and Welton

Whittier School
Denver: Marion between 24th and 25th
No longer standing

1884

Emerson School
Denver: 14th and Ogden
Standing

1885

Delgany School
Denver: 21st and Delgany
No longer standing

1887

First Presbyterian Church
Colorado Springs: Nevada and Bijou
Mostly destroyed

Hyde Park (Wyatt) School
Denver: 3620 Franklin
Standing

St. Peter's Church and Rectory
Pueblo Projects

1888

Peter Gottesleben Residence
Denver: 1901 Sherman
No longer standing

Haish Manual Training School
Denver: 14th and Arapahoe
No longer standing

Trinity Methodist Episcopal Church
Denver: 18th and Broadway
Standing

1889

Mrs. George Ady Terrace
Denver: 1332–38 Tremont
Standing

Arlington Terrace
Denver: Broadway and 10th
No longer standing

**Central Block
(Thurlow & Hutton Building)**
Pueblo: Union and 12th
No longer standing

Corona (Dora Moore) School
Denver: 846 Corona Street
Standing

Mrs. C. A. Deane Residence
Denver: 1353 Delaware
No longer standing

**Executive Building
Colorado School of Mines**
Golden, Colorado
No longer standing

Hays & McGilvery
Denver: 14th and Bannock
No longer standing

E. B. Hendrie Residence
Denver: Alta between 9th and 10th

W. A. Hover Residence
Denver: Delaware between Colfax and
    14th
No longer standing

Mrs. Elizabeth Price Residence
Denver: 2952 Champa
Standing

Michael Spangler Residence
975 Pennsylvania
No longer standing

William Toovey & Barnes
Denver: 16th between Clarkson and
    Washington

1889–90

Chamberlin Observatory
Denver: University Park
Standing

Frank Church Terrace
Denver: 13th and California

John B. Church Residence
Denver: 900 Pennsylvania
No longer standing

Cranford Hall (State Normal School)
Greeley: University of Northern
    Colorado
No longer standing

Depot at Darley

Luke Dumphy Residence
Denver: Champa between 12th and
    13th streets
No longer standing

1890

Bell Terrace
Denver: 14th and Bannock
No longer standing

Benn Brewer Terrace
Denver: 16th between Clarkson and
    Washington

Susan C. Brown Residence
Denver: 1411 Delaware
No longer standing

State School for the Deaf and Blind
Colorado Springs: Institute and Kiowa
No longer standing

Colorado Soap Works
Denver: 15th between Delgany and
    Wewatta

E. C. Dewey Residence
Denver: Stout between 16th and 17th
No longer standing

E. C. Dewey Store
Denver: 1625 Stout Street

East Denver High School
Main building
Denver: 19th and 20th, Stout and
    California
No longer standing

A. J. Fowler Residence
Denver: 2401 Gaylord
Standing

Free Kindergarten School
Denver: Delgany between 20th and
    21st
No longer standing

William F. Geddis Residence
Denver: Williams between 17th and
    18th

H. J. Kruse Duplex
Denver: Corner 25th and Stout
Standing

E. B. Light Terrace
Denver: Colfax between Downing and
    Marion
No longer standing

William B. Palmer Residence
Denver: 1712 Grant
No longer standing

A. C. Phelps Residence
Denver: 1231 Grant
No longer standing

Science Building
University of Denver
Denver: University Park
Project

D. D. Seerie Residence
Denver: 1763 Williams
Standing

Sloan's Lake Depot
Denver: Sheridan Boulevard and
    Emerald

M. L. Smith Duplex
Denver: 30th and Marion
Standing

C. G. Symes Residence
Denver: 16th between Champa and
 Stout
No longer standing

Tucker and Scholtz Store
Denver: 16th and Stout

University Hall, University of Denver
Denver: University Park
Standing

Valverde School
Denver

Charles M. Williams Store
Durango

Wyman School
Denver: 17th and Williams
No longer standing

1891

G. G. Anderson Apartment House
Denver: 1505 1/2 Grant
No longer standing

Gilpin Residence (remodeling)
Denver: South 14th Street

Golden High School
Golden
No longer standing

**Salomon's Bazaar
(Holzman and Appel Store)**
Denver: 16th between Champa and
 Stout
Enlarged in 1902
Standing

H. A. Howe Residence
Denver: 2201 Fillmore Street
Standing

Lincoln County Jail
Hugo, Colorado
No longer standing

Rev. Clarenden M. Sanders Residence
Denver: 1257 Corona
Standing

1892

A. A. Blow Residence
Denver: 722 Clarkson Street
Standing

Columbine School
Denver: Columbine between 28th and
 29th
No longer standing

A. Z. Salomon Residence
Denver: 964 Logan

F. F. Sayre Residence
Denver: Williams between 18th and
 19th
No longer standing

M. D. Van Horn Residence
Denver: 27 West 3d Avenue

1893

Manual Training High School
Denver: Corner Franklin and 27th
No longer standing

1894

Cheyenne County Jail
Cheyenne Wells, Colorado
Standing

Engineering Hall
Golden: Colorado School of Mines
Standing

1898

Lafayette (Maria Mitchell) School
Denver: Corner Lafayette and 32d
No longer standing

1899

Clayton (Stevens) School
Denver: 1140 Columbine
Standing

1900

W. J. Wykins
Denver: California between 15th and
 16th

1901

Hover Wholesale Drug Warehouse
Denver: Lawrence and 14th Street
Standing

Mary C. Michael Duplex
Denver: 1463–65 Delaware
No longer standing

1902

I. F. Williams Store
Denver: Wazee between 14th and 15th
 streets
Standing

1903

Dr. F. P. Gengenbach Office Residence
Denver: 1434 Glenarm
No longer standing

J. K. Marsh Residence
Denver: 4205 Irving
Standing

1904

C. Brown Duplex
Denver: 14th and Delaware
No longer standing

1905

Academy of Medicine
University of Denver
Denver: Glenarm between 14th and
 15th

Central High School
Pueblo
Standing

William Church Store
Denver: 15th between Arapahoe and
 Lawrence
No longer standing

1906

Carnegie Library
Denver: University of Denver
Standing

University of Denver campus plan

1907

Carter Library, State Normal School
Greeley: University of Northern
 Colorado
No longer standing

First Congregational Church
Denver: 10th and Clarkson
Standing

Dispensary Building
Denver: University of Denver
Arapahoe between 13th and 14th

1911

Greeley High School
Greeley, Colorado

1912

Isis Theater
Denver: 1716–26 Curtis Street
No longer standing

Index

NOTE: Page references to photographs in the text are given in italic type in the index.